THE POLITICAL AND MILITARY LAWS OF WAR
Swedish Studies in International Relations 9

SWEDISH STUDIES IN INTERNATIONAL RELATIONS is a series published by the Swedish Institute of International Affairs. It comprises reports on research carried out at the Institute or otherwise published under its auspices. The Institute, a non-profit organisation, is a centre for information and research on international relations. The views put forth in its publications do not necessarily represent those of the Institute itself.

1   Kjell Goldmann, *International Norms and War Between States: Three Studies in International Politics*, Stockholm: Läromedelsförlagen, 1971.

2   Katarina Brodin, *Finlands utrikespolitiska doktrin: En innehållsanalys av Paasikivis och Kekkonens uttalanden aren 1944-1968*, Stockholm: Läromedelsförlagen, 1971.

3   Daniel Tarschys, *Beyond the State: The Future Polity in Classical and Soviet Marxism*, Stockholm: Läromedelsförlagen, 1972.

4   Kjell Goldmann, *Tension and Detente in Bipolar Europe*, Stockholm: Esselte Studium, 1974.

5   Harold Hamrin, *Between Bolshevism and Revisionism: The Italian Communist Party 1944-1947*, Stockholm: Esselte Studium, 1975.

6   Thomas G. Hart, *The Cognitive World of Swedish Security Elites*, Stockholm: Esselte Studium, 1976.

7   Gunnar Sjöstedt, *The External Role of the European Community*. Farnborough, Hants: Saxon House, 1977.

8   Julian Lider, *On the nature of war*, Farnborough, Hants: Saxon House, 1977.

9   Julian Lider, *The Political and Military Laws of War: An Analysis of Marxist-Leninist Concepts*, Farnborough, Hants: Saxon House, 1979.

The Political and Military Laws of War

An Analysis of Marxist-Leninist Concepts

JULIAN LIDER

SAXON HOUSE

British Library Cataloguing in Publication Data

    Lider, J.
    The Political and Military Laws of War
    (Swedish Studies in International Relations, 9)
    1. War and Socialism
    I. Title   II. Theories
    355.02'01   HX 545

ISBN 0 566 00231 0

Published by Saxon House
Teakfield Limited,
Westmead, Farnborough, Hants., England

ISBN 0 566 00231 0

Typeset by Inforum Ltd., Portsmouth
Printed in Great Britain by Biddles Ltd., Guildford, Surrey

Contents

Acknowledgements

Thanks go in the first place to Donald Lavery, my friend and colleague at the Swedish Institute of International Affairs, who by his invaluable comments, criticism and consultation helped me clarify many ideas and the general structure of this study.

My gratitude should also be expressed to my other colleagues at the Institute who directed my attention to various aspects of the subject that I had overlooked in my original draft.

I am indebted to Anne-Marie Bratt, Sonja Johnson and Elsa Lindberg who patiently gathered material for my research, much of which is difficult to obtain in the West.

To Janka

1 Introduction

The aim of every science dealing with man in society is to proceed from a description of the past and empirical observation of the present to the ascertainment of the immediate causes of particular events and processes; then follow even more advanced theoretical stages, with the discovery of causal regularities in the occurrence and course of events. The attainment of such theoretical accounts of human activities will not only make it possible to understand them more completely, to explain why something that occurred in the past was in fact to be expected, but also to predict events, to encourage desirable and to prevent harmful outcomes. If it is desirable to eliminate war, a scientific inquiry into the nature of war is necessary. While this is the common ground for both Soviet and Western research on the theory of war, there are also some essential conceptual differences.

The Marxist-Leninist philosophy of science posits that to gain knowledge of the world, society and human activities one has to discover the laws that govern them. That such laws exist is one of the main pillars of this philosophy. Laws imply the repetition of events, phenomena and processes under recurring conditions, the repeatability of their features and of ties and relationships between them and other events, phenomena and processes. Without such recurrence and repeatability, in a world consisting of innumerable unique things and phenomena, no science explaining and predicting events could emerge. Science is about laws, and the laws of science reflect objectively existing laws.

Thus the theory of war should lead to the discovery of the complex of laws of war: this insistent postulate that the search for explanation involves search for laws seems to be the distinctive feature of the Soviet study of war. [1]

The theory of war is several thousand years old, but no single scientific explanation of it has been found very satisfactory; in particular, no theory has had predictive value. There has always been controversy as to what an adequate explanation of war should entail — whether it is possible to give such an explanation at all; and doubts have been expressed as to whether a scientific explanation must be phrased in terms of laws.

The present age, with its extremely rapid social and technological changes, does not favour the construction of general theories, encompassing the whole past, present and future of social activity. On the contrary, in Western science past experience is often questioned, traditional theories are rejected but no new theoretical system is agreed on. Even the concepts and definitions that for ages have served as scientific tools are challenged, and new concepts are sought that better correspond to the new reality.

War is a case in point. Under the new conditions of the restructured world and

1

revolutionary development of military technology, radical changes have occurred in the way internal and international conflicts are being resolved. Many in the West suggest that the boundaries between war and peace are becomming unclear; traditional kinds of war seem unlikely while new kinds occur more frequently. Thus they have begun to doubt the adequacy of the traditionally accepted conception of war as a key to understanding the conflicts of our times and to call for a reappraisal. New terms have been coined to capture the essence of the variety of armed violence, of using new forms of military power and using military power in new forms. All agree that it is difficult to agree on the meaning of war as a general concept.

Obviously, under such conditions, it is even more difficult to agree on whether certain laws of war do exist - and if they do - how to capture their elusive essence in scientific formulae. Nor is there a common view concerning the nature of the law-like generalisations about war, even if they could be made: whether they should express universal and uniform ties and regularities in the form of covering laws, or only some probabilistic correlation of events, phenomena, and objects of war. Whether they should be sought, and could be cognised by empirical observation and inductive generalisation of the findings, or whether they can be grasped by logical analysis, and reflective understanding, or, finally, whether a composite technique of cognition should be applied. Answers vary from one intellectual tradition to another, from one school of thought to another and from writer to writer.

What is now urgent, according to many scholars, is to work out the principles of an effective national strategy for managing crises and preventing war, and on the outbreak of war, for conducting it rationally. This would make it possible to diminish the losses, to achieve a quick victory, or to bring about an early termination of hostilities. In particular, the concern should be to decide how different factors facilitate or impede decisions to go to war, and to escalate military operations. An argument about the existence - or non-existence - of laws of war would lead nowhere, it is maintained. The fate of war - its outbreak, course and outcome - depends chiefly on what we think and do about it, and not on its hypothetical laws. Even if such a pattern of thought is far from prevalent and some studies aim at putting war in a general conceptual framework, it may well characterise the trend in the Western study of war.

Soviet theoreticians, on the other hand, maintain that they have arrived at the explanation of war, i.e. created a system of concepts and categories concerning war as a whole and armed struggle as its main component part, and of scientific propositions and hypotheses on war, which has culminated in a system of laws. These reflect the objective laws of war and thus express the motivating forces, the tendencies and the inner dynamics of war, and explain its occurrence, course and outcome.

To Soviet science, the revolutionary changes in the socio-political and techno-material picture of the world not only do not necessitate a re-examination of all scientific developments hitherto, but on the contrary confirm all the primary

2

principles of Marxism-Leninism, and, in particular its theory of war. Neither the diminishing instrumentality of war, nor the changing forms in which wars have been fought invalidate the basic tenets of the Marxist-Leninist concept of war and there is no reason for redefining any part of it. Changes in the world have made it obvious that class struggle on both the domestic and international scales is the motivating force of historical development, and when the struggle can no longer be kept within peaceful bounds, war becomes its main instrument. In a world where all forms of class struggle and policy intertwine, the notion of war is more than ever internally coherent and it covers all forms of such social action.

According to Soviet scholars, this allows for more rather than fewer generalisations,[2] in the search for laws and for the creation of a unified military theory.[3] Very recently they have increased their effort to complete a system of scientific laws of war: it includes a constant accretion of new laws reflecting the newly-discovered objective laws of war. In particular, Soviet scholars state that just now is the time to complete the theory of the genesis of war, i.e. to show in more detail why and how it occurs in accordance with the laws of social development, and the sharpening contradictions giving rise to its outbreak. In the Soviet view, because of the radical changes and the extraordinarily rapid development of science and technology it is necessary to make the theory of war a genuine science in order finally to subordinate war to rational thinking, and to prevent its outbreak.

This study involves an examination of the Soviet concept of laws governing the genesis and conduct of war. Since the notion of a social causal law is probably an unfamiliar one to most Western readers, a very brief indication of what is meant by it in Marxism-Leninism may facilitate an understanding of the main topic of this study.

Laws are the determining ties between phenomena, and as such, are assumed to exist in reality. In this sense, laws are 'objective', for their existence is independent of man's knowledge of them. To the extent that we do in fact have knowledge of reality, laws must also be included in that knowledge; but these laws are obviously not the same as the objective laws themselves, only a reflection of them. The laws as we know them are called 'scientific laws' to distinguish them from 'objective laws', which are independent of our knowledge.

One of the central problems in the Western philosophy of science is the relation between knowledge and reality. While ontology deals with the nature of reality, epistemology is concerned with such problems as how we can be sure that our knowledge corresponds to reality. In terms of this distinction, 'objective law' is an ontological concept, while scientific law is an epistemological one. Is it necessary to commit oneself to the ontological assumption that laws exist to be able to make true statements about relations between phenomena, either in terms of laws or other epistemological expressions of determination? And if not necessary, is it desirable to do so, since our ontological commitments foreclose what we can consider to be true knowledge? Since these are controversial issues on which few social scientists probably have any definite opinion, most find it

3

wise to make as few ontological commitments as possible. Moreover, most also avoid using the term 'law' altogether since it suggests a type of determination too strong for the explanation of social behaviour.

While recognising these problems, Soviet scholars are less troubled by them. Since Marxism-Leninism is considered to be a true science, it can be taken for granted that a Marxist-Leninist law of science properly reflects some underlying objective law. Because of this general assumption Soviet scholars, when discussing the laws of war, do not seem to devote much attention to the distinction between the ontological and epistemological senses in which the term law is used; when laws are defined as the features, ties, and relationships of war what is often implied is both that the objective laws of war are these features, ties, and relationships, and that the scientific formulae presented by Soviet scholars as laws reflect and express them properly. These formulae are therefore at times used interchangeably to mean both the objective *and* the scientific laws.

The aim of this study is neither to answer the question whether laws of war objectively exist or not, nor whether the Soviet statements about these objective laws properly reflect and express the features, ties, and relationships of war. The two principal aims are:

1 To organise the views representing the Soviet concept of laws of war and its development; to assess what character has been attributed to these laws, and whether the particular groups of laws can actually be classified within this general concept. I have tried to present these problems as an ontological and epistemological unity, in correspondence to Soviet theory.

2 To describe and assess Soviet attempts to construct a system of scientific laws, as a reflection of the objective laws discovered; this system has only begun to take shape.

Although the construction of a comprehensive system of scientific laws of war has been considered one of the primary scientific tasks, nowhere in Soviet literature has such a system been fully presented.[4] Thus, to fulfil the aims of this study, I have had not only to present in an organised fashion the Soviet conceptual framework concerning the laws of war - to put together from many more or less consistent expositions a coherent account of the nature of these laws and of their philosophical roots - but also to suggest what the Soviet system of laws might look like on the basis of various, often fragmentary presentations dispersed in Soviet studies.

I have based my investigation on what I believe to be all the non-classified material on the subject published in the Soviet Union — viz. studies in international relations and in the philosophy of war; studies recommended as texts for military education and training; political and military periodicals, such as 'Kommunist', 'Mezhdunarodnaya Zhizn', 'Mirovaya Ekonomika i Mezhdunarodnye Otnosheniya', 'Voprosy Filosofii', 'Voenno-Istoricheskii Zhurnal', 'Kommunist Vooruzhennykh Sil' and others; books edited by 'Izd. "Mezhdunarodnye Otnosheniya"', 'Nauka', 'Gospolitizdat', and 'Voenizdat'; the latter are given the greatest attention.

4

given the greatest attention.

The views I have analysed may thus be considered to express Soviet doctrine on the subject. The investigation begins with the concept of laws of war and of the system of laws; — the general laws of war, then the laws of armed struggle — and closes with a comment on both the concept of laws and the construction of the system. In the Appendix Soviet criticism of Western ideas is reviewed.

I hope that regardless of whether the so-called scientific explanation of war by Soviet scholars can be accepted as such by others, or whether the Soviet scientific laws are laws by Western standards, the presentation and analysis of their work and ideas can give some insight into Soviet military theory as regards its content and its methodology. My expectation is based on the fact that Soviet scholars have attempted to present the main propositions of their military science, doctrine and policy in the form of scientific laws, i.e. the main ideas on the sources, nature and dynamics of war and the techniques of preparing and waging it.

Notes

[1] Historical experience demonstrates that wars, like other social phenomena, do not proceed spontaneously, but according to laws ('Istoriya voin i voennogo iskusstva', 1970, p. 7). 'Successful leadership in the development of social phenomena, and consequently also of war, first of all assumes a thorough understanding and skillful use of those laws which govern the development of these phenomena ... It is well known that war is governed by a system of laws' (Zemskov 1972, p.15).

As Soviet scholars always stress, the history of science and technology is the history of the discovery of laws of nature (Grigorenko et al., 1959, p.36). 'There is no science without laws' (O sovetskoi voennoi nauke, 1964, p.70). The revolution in military affairs is said to further increase the importance of a deep and comprehensive knowledge of laws and regularities of war which permits predictions of the character of possible future wars (M. Kozlov, 'Vazhnyi faktor mogushchestva Vooruzhennykh Sil', *Krasnaya Zvezda*, April 21, 1976).

Zavyalov writes that the discovery of the nature of war and its laws is the primary task of military science ('Die Dialektik des Krieges und die Militärdoktrin', transl. in Militärwesen, 1976:1); cf. Gareyev, 1976. The study of the character of wars, laws of war, and methods of its conduct are presented as the content of military science ('Voennaya nauka', in Sovetskaya Voennaya Entsiklopediya, Vol. 2, pp.208ff.). Cf. note 3 to this chapter. Galkin proposes the following as the three main directions of research in military theory: (1) the nature of war and the laws of military activities; (2) laws of war; (3) the character of the future war, the theory of preparation for it and its conduct (1975, pp.7-8). Cf. Metodologiya voennogo poznaniya, 1977.

[2] In particular, the concern of Soviet scholars has been for a comprehensive

definition of war, the interpretation of its component parts, its stable and changing elements, its tripartite structure, etc.; then, for the definition of armed struggle and examination of its systemic structure, and also its relation to war as a whole; for the reflection of the so-called twin-categories in war; for the main categories of war, such as the type of war, class character of war, strategy, operational art, tactics, offence, defence, etc. Comp. Grudinin, 1971; Filosofskoe nasledie V.I. Lenina i problemy sovremennoi voiny, 1972 (quoted in the following as 'Filosofskoe nasledie'); Nauchno-tekhnicheskii progress i revolutsiya v voennom dele, 1973 (quoted in the following as 'Nauchno-tekhnicheskii progress'); Tyushkevich, 1975.

[3] Many Soviet scholars point out that the primary criterion according to which the scope of the particular sciences is determined, and distinguished from that of other sciences, is the complex of laws and regularities which they deal with. (Gareyev, 1977; Gast, Müller, 1977; W. Kieck, 'Die Marxistisch-Leninistische Philosophie als Grundlage für die Klassifikation der Militärwissenschaft', *Militärwesen*, 1976:4; 'Über die sowjetische Militärwissenschaft' / Übersetzung aus der sowjetischen Militärpresse/, *Militärwesen*, 1978:1).

Such an approach has been reflected in many definitions of military science, some of which are here quoted: 'Military science is a system of knowledge about the laws of armed struggle and the methods of preparing for it and engaging in it.' (Istoriya voin i voennogo 'iskusstva' Voenizdat, Moscow 1970, p.5). 'Soviet military science is a system of knowledge about the character and laws of armed struggle, about the military preparation of the country and armed forces to rebuff agression, and about the methods of waging war' (Grechko, 1975, ch.10).

'Scientific laws provide the basic means for the scientific explanation of the methods of waging and comprehensively sustaining armed struggle, of the armed forces development, and the training and education of personnel. The cognition and application of the laws of armed struggle, of the armed forces development, of the command and control of armed forces, the training and education of personnel, and the relationship between armed struggle and economic, political, and ideological factors is one of the important tasks of our military science' (Zavizion, Kirshin, 1972, p.10).

'Soviet military science is a unified system of knowledge of the laws of armed struggle, the nature and peculiarities of modern wars, and the methods and forms of waging them . . .' (Milovidov, 1973). The ideas and developments proposed by military science are based on a profound investigation of the essence and natural laws of war phenomena (Kulikov, 1973).

[4] In the article on laws of war in the military encyclopaedia ('Zakony i obychai voiny', Sovetskaya Voennaya Entsiklopediya, Vol. 3, pp.375-8) only a set of five laws, concerning the dependence of war, and its course and outcome on various external factors is presented (the definition concerns the internal ties of war). There follow some remarks concerning the differences between laws of war as a whole and laws of fighting proper at different levels, without any presentation of the latter, and with a comment that, because of the complex and con-

tradictory character of armed struggle and of war as a whole, cognition of the laws is difficult. Finally, it is stated that there also exist other laws determining the direct outcome of war (one of them is presented). No premises or criteria for the division of the set of laws into groups, and the less into categories of laws are provided. The whole is far from being a systematic review of the problem, and even further from a presentation of a system of laws. In some other publications sets of groups of laws have been presented which can serve as a point of departure for a system, if they will be worked out on the basis of agreed criteria (e.g. Popov, 1964, Zakharov, 1967, Marxism-Leninism on War and Army, 1972).

Part 1

The Concept

2 Laws of war: the concept

In the Soviet view, war, although a complex and internally contradictory phenomenon, full of accidental and fortuitous events and immensely affected by subjective factors, is governed by objective laws. These laws cover the whole process
of the origin, development and termination of war;[1] accordingly, the main
task of science is to cognise them. War, in its origins, depends on the objective
socio-political development of particular societies and of the international system as a whole; its aims are determined by the interests of classes, states, and
nations; its material basis, the military might of warring sides, is determined by
their socio-economic system and level of economic development.

The way military operations are conducted - military art - depends on the
material basis; consequently, so also does the course and outcome of war. Thus
war depends wholly on material conditions, and it proceeds, like all social phenomena and processes, according to the laws of dialectics. The laws which govern
its origin and course reflect more general laws covering the whole gamut of
social development, which, in the final analysis, is also rooted in the material conditions of social life. These assumptions underlie the Soviet concept of the laws
of war.[2]

Definition and characteristics of the laws

The definition

It is maintained that between the objects, phenomena and processes of war, as
well as between war and other social phenomena, there exist objective essential
ties and relationships which necessarily recur in each war. These recurrent ties
and relationships are called in Soviet theory the laws of war.[3] For instance, the
Soviet Military Encyclopaedia defines the laws of war as 'internal essential necessary ties between the phenomena of war conditioning its character and role in
the historical process, and its origin, course and outcome'. These laws constitute
'an objective reality existing independently of human consciousness and will'.[4]

To some Western scholars the very idea of an objectively operating social law
may appear strange, and for various reasons. It seems, however, that if they do
not accept both the ontological principle of the existence of laws and the epistem-
ological-analytical status of the Soviet law-like statements about the ties and
relationships of war, they can view them as basic Soviet theses concerning the
nature and dynamics of war and its links with other social phenomena, and
assess from that angle their validity and utility as scientific tools.

Soviet theory of the laws of war concentrates on the causal ties and relationships of war, although it also considers other connections.[5] Conceptually, these laws are deeply anchored in the Marxist-Leninist philosophy, with its causal-deterministic interpretation of society and the world. The general assumption underlying all Soviet science is that all things, phenomena and processes are conditioned causally (the universal law, or principle, of causation). The universal validity of this law is said to underlie the whole process of making war: its origin, course and outcome.[6]

In presenting the laws of war as a manifestation of the universal law of causation, Soviet theorists repeat the idea which is the core of Marxist-Leninist philosophy - that is, the objective character of causal links, the really occurring and recurring ties between material (really existing) things and phenomena, which are not mere intellectual fabrications whose correspondence to reality cannot be verified.

The Soviet theory of war focuses on those laws which concern the causal influence of external factors on war, its origin, course and outcome. How war, in turn, influences those factors is not the primary concern of military theory, although recently a little more attention has been paid to the social consequences of war. Among the many kinds of internal relationships in war, the causal ones are also pinpointed, since they are said to explain the essence and main trend of the dynamics of war.

Thus the essential recurring ties and relationships which are termed laws are in fact confined to the causal ones, although this is not reflected in the definition of the law of war in Soviet science. Occasionally, Soviet scholars mention other kinds - laws of interdependence, structure, function - but they remind the reader that, in the final analysis, causal laws underlie all other kinds of law, since any structural, functional and other similar ties and relationships have their recurring causes.

Here, perhaps, it can be asked what does the term 'essential' mean in the Soviet concept of the law of war. Soviet scholars would answer that, while there are innumerable connections between objects, phenomena, and processes, only some of them are to be regarded as laws, namely the most important ones, those which characterise the essence,[7] or decisively affect the determining characteristics or qualitative definiteness of the object (phenomenon, process) and its development, and at the same time recur in each case, characterising each singular object in question (or each instance of the phenomenon or process). Policy, for instance, decisively affects the whole character of each war, its role in social development, the main features of its strategy, its course and outcome; its impact is a law. By contrast, weather may affect the course of particular military operations; however, its effects are different in different cases, its impact is only occasionally important and rarely decisive. It should be regarded as a factor to some degree influencing the course of fighting and the individual picture, but not the main development. Such an impact cannot be called law.

Naturally, the definition of 'essential' as 'expressing the essence', or 'most important', is very vague, and some may consider it tautological. Moreover, one can be tempted to describe as law *any* feature or relationship which for any reason has seemed to be important. Instead of saying 'this is very important' one states 'this is a law'. However, Soviet scholars consider that the difference between factors decisively influencing war and those of much less importance is big enough to permit the discovery of objective laws.

Place of the laws

Before beginning a more detailed discussion of the main features of the laws of war, it may be appropriate to speculate on the place of these laws in the general hierarchy of laws in Soviet science. No formal hierarchy has ever been described and it will be here only suggested or rather hypothesised from the established hierarchy of disciplines in Soviet science.

The Marxist-Leninist theory is considered the most general and all-encompassing discipline and the one that underlies all others. Then come particular disciplines and among them sociology which is the application of Marxism-Leninism to the analysis of society.[8] The theory of war follows as the application not only of sociology but also of political economy and the theory of the socialist revolution to the analysis of this special kind of social activity.[9] The theory of armed struggle deals with the main component of war. Finally come the theories of the particular components of warfare.

Accordingly, the laws can be arranged hierarchically as follows:

1 Laws of dialectical materialism concerning all phenomena and processes in the world
2 Laws of historical materialism which constitute the application of the above laws to social life
3 Laws of war as a kind of social action according to the laws of dialectical and historical materialism [10]
4 Laws of armed struggle as the main component of war
5 Laws covering particular phenomena and processes of armed struggle.

Social laws

Since laws of war are considered to be social laws, concerning an important field of social activity, the difference between social laws and laws of nature is often the subject of discussion in studies on military theory. There is, indeed, much repetition of similar presentations in philosophical, sociological and other literature. Soviet scholars consider that while laws of nature exist independently of human activity, and operated before man appeared, social laws do not exist apart from such activity; they arise in its course and through it. They are at the same time a product and a prerequisite of social action. While laws of nature determine mutual relations between objects, social laws relate both to social objects and subjects (people). Thereby the subjective factor is introduced into the mechanism of the action of laws (see below).[11]

Laws of science

Scientists try to cognise the objective laws and to formulate the so-called laws of science (or scientific laws), which are presented by Soviet theory as mental models of the objective laws of nature and society - i.e. their reflection in the human mind. They are expressions of what people think about reality (e.g. about war).[12] The reflection is never absolutely exact, perfect and adequate, but with the development of science it comes closer to the objective reality. Besides one does not aim at a complete equation, which is impossible, but at the most adequate reflection possible of the most essential features of, and ties between, things, phenomena and processes. Such a task seems to be fully possible according to Soviet researchers.[13] This work, however, can be accomplished only by socialist science, which, by using the right methodology, can penetrate to the essence of objective laws.

To conclude this section, we should mention the emphasis which Soviet researchers place on the study and discovery of laws of war. This is presented as one of the main objectives of military theory. Essentially, this theory should consist of:

1 Verified knowledge of the phenomena and processes of war.
2 The methodological apparatus: definitions, categories, and concepts.
3 Scientific laws expressing the objective laws.
4 Propositions and theories based on both the empirical material and the objective laws discovered.

In the discussion concerning the concept of laws of war, four problems seem to be in focus: their objective character and its relationship with the subjective factor in war; their inevitable manifestation and its interaction with fortuity; their probabilistic (or probabilistic-statistical) character as compared with the so-called dynamic one; and their historical (i.e. changeable) content.

Interdependence of objective and subjective elements in war

Soviet scholars posit that laws of war, being objective, operate regardless of whether men know them and wish them to operate.[14] They cannot be annulled, repealed, or otherwise abolished, nor can they be neglected in our plans and actions. The political and military leadership of any warring country (or other political unit at war) and of its armed forces must take into account the decisive impact of several factors on the strategy of war. This impact is expressed in several laws which will be discussed later.[15]

In particular, the military leadership must plan and conduct war in correspondence with:

1 The political aims of war and the corresponding military goals
2 The military power of the country concerned - in particular, the state, level and quantity of technique, armament, and equipment at disposal, and also the number of military personnel available
3 The correlation of the country's power to that of the enemy.[16]

The key question

From the emphasis on the objective character of laws of war it could be concluded that Soviet writers leave very little scope for conscious human activity. However, Soviet scholars devote much time and effort to emphasising the role of what they call the subjective factor.

This problem is presented as that of the relation between the objective and subjective aspects of the conduct of war, and its reflection in the action of the objective laws of war and in the outcome of this action.[17] It may take the form of a set of questions: do the conditions generating wars inevitably lead to them? If not, what role is played by governments, and the political leaderships of states, nations, and classes in the political interplay preceding war? Do the conditions under which war is waged, combined with the objective character of the laws of war, predetermine human action - for instance, the war leaders' and commanders' decisions? Does the course of fighting unfold with inevitable force?

But before turning to these questions, mention should be made of the Soviet interpretation of the relation between the objective and subjective in all social activity. In this view, men can act successfully only if their actions take into account the impact of the laws governing the given kind of action, the way in which human activity determines how the operation of the laws is utilised, and what room is left for its impact. Each law imposes certain demands, some conditions which must be fulfilled for its action, and only by reckoning with these demands can the desired results be obtained. The unintended violation of the demands of a given law, or a conscious action against it (if one wants to counteract its influence) may give results opposite to those which should follow.[18] In other words, human behaviour decides to a great extent how much scope has been granted for the action of the objective laws, and thus, although it is not absolutely voluntary, it influences the outcome of the action of the laws and the course of events. More concrete examples concerning war will be discussed in the next section.

In this study, expressions such as 'the action of a law' or 'a law operates' are used. Here there is a difference from the ordinary use and interpretation of the term 'action', since laws are not 'actors' in the ordinary sense.[19] In Soviet usage, laws are considered regularly recurring relationships between phenomena (things, processes) or characteristics of them, but they do not exist as separate things or phenomena.[20] Accordingly, in this study the expression in question should mean that events proceed according to laws, or lawfully; they are determined by other events in accordance with objective laws.

The objective and subjective in war

What is meant, however, by the words 'objective' and 'subjective' when Soviet scholars discuss war, and in particular armed struggle?[21] The objective side of war is presented as including:

(a) the character of the socio-political systems of the warring sides;
(b) the international and internal situation, with emphasis on contradictions and conflicts of interests;
(c) the size of the population and its moral-political condition;
(d) the level of technology, science and the economy;
(e) the territorial-geographical conditions;
(f) laws of society, including laws of war;
(g) the level of military art;
(h) the size and quality of the armed forces, including their armament and training.

Since some of the above mentioned components of the objective factor are relative magnitudes, which have to be assessed in relation to the corresponding components on the enemy side, the objective factor may also be presented as the correlation of the entire economic, moral-political and military potentials of the warring parties in conjunction with the political and military international situation.

The thoughts, emotions and actions of the protagonists in war constitute the subjective factor. They exert influence over the genesis, conduct and outcome of war. Assessments of the situation by the leaders and governments, their thoughts and emotions have a direct bearing on the decision for war and the thoughts and emotions of the population and the armies contribute to such a decision. The direction of war by the political and military leadership, the thoughts, emotions, decisions and actions of commanders and the knowledge, skill and morale of the armed forces contribute to victory or to defeat.[22]

It seems, however, that in practice the above conceptual distinction between the objective and subjective in war is not clear, and they overlap in some respects.

It is hardly possible to reduce human actions to a single category - that of the subjective. One may ask: Is political activity which changes the material environment subjective? Is killing subjective? The main argument for calling the actions of the political and military leaders, of the commanders and soldiers subjective is that the feelings, abilities, assessments, decisions of the protagonists in war, which are subjective, constitute the necessary prerequisites and component parts of their actions. But they are only one part: they are inseparably connected with the action, with creating facts and changing the material conditions. It seems that the objective and subjective components of these actions can hardly be separated from one another. The assumptions that circumstances are purely objective can also be questioned. The politico-military situation, the potentialities of science and technology, conflicts of interests - these reflect relations between human beings having thoughts, feelings and spiritual and moral qualities. The view that human actions, including the established patterns of human behaviour, are not fully voluntary since they are ultimately determined by objective conditions and objective laws (see Chap. 4 p.78 'On the premises of laws'), only confirm the premise that the objective is hardly separable from the subjective.

I have assumed that the Soviet argument is fully consistent. In fact, it is not. In the Soviet presentation of the distinction between the two categories, the critical element, the action of armed forces, is not precisely pinned down but is assigned sometimes to the objective category, sometimes to the subjective category, or to both.

In theory, the actions of armed forces are subjective, and they constitute the main element in the subjective factor when its influence on the course of fighting is considered. 'The conscious, creative, purposeful, expedient activity of soldiers, officers, and generals'[23] (Savkin, 1972), 'the behaviour of the soldiers and units in the struggle'[24] (Tyushkevich, 1975) are presented as subjective. Tyushkevich writes that, in general, 'the warring class, parties and armed forces are subjective' (sic); elsewhere he says however, that the process of armed struggle, i.e. the actions of belligerent forces, is material and therefore objective.[25]

Moreover, Soviet researchers sometimes point out that what for one side is subjective may, for the opposing side, be objective. For each warring side, the enemy with all his objective and subjective components is an objective reality.

The problem is further complicated by the possibility that subjective elements in one phenomenon or process may become objective elements in another. The crisis of governing-class policy and the growth of the class-consciousness among the exploited masses of the people, and consequently the growth of their political awareness and activities, which are essentially subjective phenomena, may become a component of the revolutionary situation i.e. of the objective conditions generating revolutionary uprising and civil war.[26]

The interaction

But what about the interaction of the objective and subjective in war? This seems to be the crucial point in the discussion of this theme, since it reveals the categories in their concrete manifestation and dynamics. The Soviet view, very roughly, is that the objective situation, including objective laws of war, determines the general tendency and dynamics of policy in war and armed struggle, inter alia, by affecting the thoughts and actions of groups and individuals. However, subjects who act according to the situation and the objective laws, by changing the situation and creating individual conditions for the action of laws, thereby affect the course and outcome of the war as well.

Two illustrations of this idea are often presented. One concerns the outbreak of war. The contradictions between classes, states or nations rooted, in our times, in the existence and policy of imperialism, lead to war, in the sense that they create the possibility of its outbreak. In fact, however, war can arise only from concrete action by political leaders, which will depend on their assessment of the situation, the escalation of emotions, the development of a crisis in relations between the protagonists and the choice of war as the means of resolving the contradictions.[27]

A revolution might bring the contradictions to a head and lead to the attainment of such political goals as the destruction of an outdated socio-economic and political system. Such a change will certainly result if the violent action is taken at the proper moment, when the crisis has ripened and people are ready to act; in other words, when the objective conditions are appropriately combined with the subjective factor and both are in accord with the laws of social development. The decision taken by the leadership of the Bolsheviks to start the revolutionary uprising is a well-known historical example. In the Soviet view, the development of internal contradictions in Russia, accelerated by the world war, had to lead to a revolution, but its timing and unleashing was decided by Lenin and others, according to their assessment of the contemporary situation.

Moreover, the variant of the revolutionary uprising, the manner of carrying out the revolution was also individual and a matter of choice. The leadership of the revolutionary forces decided to smash the old state apparatus - in particular, to disband the old army and police, to destroy the economic conditions necessary for the very existence of the exploiting class and to make a complete end of it. Such revolutionary violence applied inevitably led to civil war.

Revolutions in the east European countries, which were carried out more than a quarter of a century later, were an outcome of quite different conditions, and were achieved by quite different decisions, which varied even from country to country. Thus the implementation of the general law concerning the genesis of revolutionary wars, as generated by the growth of internal class contradictions, and presented by Soviet researchers as acting with the force of necessity, has always been effected through different kinds of human actions which gave them in each case an individual character.

The other illustration concerns a typical situation on the battlefield. The commander's decisions and actions arise from the concrete operational-tactical situation, which, however, can be subjected to various more or less correct interpretations and assessments, and his actions too may be more or less effective. His knowledge of the laws of war is also a variable in the decision process: the better he knows the laws of armed struggle, the better his chances of taking the right decision and winning. Moreover, he can change the situation - for instance, the correlation of forces participating in battle - by concentrating his own troops or destroying part of the enemy ones. The commander can act in accordance with the law of dependence of the course and outcome of military action on the concentration of forces on the direction of the main strike (see below) i.e. the direction assessed or even chosen by him as the main one. By such action he will 'force' the law to work for him at the place and time he chooses.

And on the contrary, if he takes a wrong decision and does not create favourable conditions, the law acts against him, since the enemy has a favourable proportion of forces on the main direction. Moreover, since in each situation many laws operate and may affect the course of fighting, the commander, through his decisions, determines which combination of laws can best be utilised[28] and which combination of conditions will be most favourable.

It follows that a person's choice of the most favourable conditions and transformation of them by his own actions are his main forms of creative and rational exploitation of the objective factor. He will probably choose some typical course of action in the given situation, since it is based on objective laws of war and principles of military art,[29] which are said to be reflected in regulations and instructions and well known to him. However, he can shape an individual picture of the combat, according to his assessment of the situation, his abilities as a commander, and so on. Without his decision and action, events will not proceed according to the respective laws. In other words, the very recurrence of similar courses of action is lawful, although these actions will be different in details. And although the interaction of the objective and subjective factors in war seems to be one of unequal partners, since the objective one is the primary and ultimately determining one, the subjective factor is far from being passive. On the contrary, without its contribution the possibility of a favourable outcome of events cannot be transformed into reality.[30]

Note that the boundaries between the objective and subjective are not fixed once and for all, because the outcome of the action of the subject becomes a component part of the new objective situation. Such reasoning may also be applied to the conduct of war in general. Given the same objective content of the political and military aims, the concrete plan of action may take various forms. It depends on the theory and methodology, including the assumptions about laws of the incipient war, the subjective characteristics of the leaders, the amount of attention paid to all other factors affecting the given situation.[31] Decisions on how to initiate and continue hostilities, when implemented, become a component part of the objective setting in which war is waged.

The above train of thought makes a mixed impression. It reveals difficulties in the attempt to combine two leading principles of Marxist-Leninist philosophy. One of these is the determining influence of objective laws and situations i.e. the *inevitable* course of events. The other is the heavy impact of the subjective factor i.e. of the choice by the political leader or commander regarding which laws of social development and genesis of war are acquiring decisive importance in the given politico-military situation, or which laws are to be exploited on the battlefield, and how to exploit and change the conditions.

As to the latter, the argument put forward by some Soviet scholars that the choice is limited to the manner of action and its impact confined to individual events - to the individual version of the inevitable general course of events - is unconvincing, since the manner of action may also determine the outcome, victory or defeat, in the action in question. Perhaps only the final outcome of war as a whole can be determined by the general situation in particular by the overall correlation of forces, which is quite consistent with law and logic.

At the same time, the presentation of objective and subjective interaction, the insistence on the simultaneous determining importance of both, reveals the determination of Soviet researchers to defend their philosophical position against charges of fatalistic determinism which prejudges human activity, and of the neglect of determinism by an over-estimation of free will. With regard to the military picture of war it also reveals Soviet preoccupation with the practical needs of war and preparation for it: the commander ought to be convinced both of the primary importance of orders and manuals which are said to reflect the objective laws of war and principles of military art (see below), and of the great importance of his own actions, of his own abilities to accomplish the tasks imposed on him by the orders. These abilities of the commander on the one hand include a knowledge of war (of its laws, principles, organisation, etc.) and on the other his will and readiness to exploit it creatively. In other words, he must be convinced of both the primary importance of objective laws, conditions and orders and of the great importance of his subjective activity.

Necessity and fortuitousness

The second problem in focus is the relation between the elements of necessity and fortuitousness in the action of the laws of war - how to combine the tenet of laws which establishes the inevitable recurrence of events under the same circumstances with the individual and various in each case picture of these events. What is the role of fortuitousness, if any?

General review

The various interpretations and comments on this problem[32] may be reviewed as follows. In general, it is stated that the occurrence of each phenomenon or process (event) is under determined conditions and in principle inevitable and its essence is always the same. In this sense, the occurrence of the phenomenon and its essence are 'necessary' and constitute its recurring aspects, common to all phenomena of this class. However, its manifestation and evolution, with all attendant details, is individual, unique and fortuitous. The phenomenon (or process) has to occur and proceed in a determined way because it is generated and conditioned by the whole previous evolution. However, each individual case of the phenomenon, even if similar in essence to other phenomena of this kind, cannot fail to differ in the complex or combination of all elements and aspects. Thus it is in each case and in many details unique, and in this sense fortuitous. This individual picture must be to some extent different from other phenomena of the kind since in each case there is a non-repetitive combination of time and place and the phenomenon is directly generated by a complex of various unique factors and events, many of them external to the main course of development, and also by many internal accidental factors, and circumstances, such as the character, views and feelings of the participating personalities.[33]

The words accidental and fortuitous are relative. Each event, phenomenon or process is a necessary outcome in its own causal chain and accidental only in relation to some other causal chain, which in our context may be regarded as the main chain and reference system.

The outbreak of a war is a case in point. On the one hand, it is generated by deep contradictions of interest between social groups and on the other by many concrete individual events and circumstances, political, economic, psychological and other, in a unique combination of time and place, often only distantly related to the development of the main contradictions i.e. to the main causal chain and reference system in the genesis of war.

The pretext for unleashing war in individual instances, the timing and the form it takes at the start, the accompanying diplomatic activity, may be accidental in relation to the deeper causes of war. Similar combinations of different factors may be pointed out in regard to the course of any war. In principle, it is determined by the correlation of forces, by the material and spiritual resources of the warring parties, but it is also full of fortuitous events, generated by the clash of two opposing forces: each side aims at the purposefulness, the most effective organisation of its own activity according to the laws of war, and attempts thereby at the same time to thwart and crush the analogous activity of the enemy.

The complex and peculiar character of armed struggle increases the influence of the fortuitous factors. Each element of war - battles and other operations - is a highly organised activity involving the cooperation of various component parts of armed forces and combination of fire and movement according to the laws of fighting and organisational prescriptions. However, every soldier has his individual psyche, experience, knowledge, physical abilities, and fulfils his tasks in an individual way. Consequently, while laws of war as well as the objective conditions, the place of the given action in the war in general and one campaign in particular, determine the main tendency and development of this action, and are expressed in the repetitive elements of the action, common to all actions of this class, it cannot fail to deviate in many details - indeed in its whole form - from any predicted standard picture.[34]

Finally, the differentiated picture of the manifestation of laws in different situations is even more complicated by the fact that each military event is simultaneously affected by many laws and by their aggregate action. Various laws of war interact, some of them may coincide, but particular laws may operate in opposition to one another. The complex character and extreme diversity of the simultaneous manifestation of different laws i.e. of simultaneous 'necessities', favour the workings of chance. In other words, while the action of the particular laws is necessary, and taken separately causes effects common to all actions of that kind, the aggregate outcome of their combined action may be fortuitous.[35]

In the Soviet view, the interaction of necessity and fortuitousness can be explained in terms of what Marxist philosophy calls 'twin categories' - closely connected categories with an apparent contrary essence. The train of thought is here, in a simplified form, as follows. Each phenomenon, process or event is a unity of necessity and fortuitousness. It is necessary in its main tendency, in the recurring elements which are identical in the whole class of such phenomena; this is because it proceeds according to laws, and is a link in the main causal chain. It is, however, at the same time fortuitous because it constitutes a unique combination of repetitive elements with non-repetitive single, individual, ones which are links in secondary causal chains. On the other hand, necessity is realised through the mass of single, individual happenings, phenomena, events and processes which are non-repetitive as wholes but which have a similar main tendency and some similar elements and the cumulation of which realises the main tendency, the necessity. To give a simple example, every soldier acts in an individual unique way - but all the soldiers' individual actions which have a common main tendency and common elements, produce a cumulative effect in the accomplishment of a given military task.

Three modifications

In recent studies, three modifications of the traditional views may be noted. Firstly, the scope of the concept of fortuitous events has seemingly been broadened to include factors which cause one side to use its forces ineffectively. For instance, each successful action of the enemy who always aims at disorganising the actions of Soviet troops should be regarded as a contingency, some say. His surprise attack may paralyse the actions planned by the Soviet forces and force them to act *ad hoc* i.e. fortuitously in relation to the plan of the whole battle or campaign.

Unsuccessful actions resulting from other circumstances are also called contingencies by some scholars: they include e.g. failures arising from lack of knowledge of laws, insufficient training, or faulty assessment of the situation, which cause deviations from the planned and predicted, 'lawful' course of events.[36]

Secondly, the effect of the intervention of contingencies has been presented as more far-reaching than was previously asserted. Some scholars have begun to contend that contingencies may affect not only the picture of events but even change the main tendency of military operations. They may affect the choice of one course of action among several alternatives, and may also affect its evolution and outcome. This brings accidental factors into the complex of factors which influence not only some secondary features but also the main course of armed struggle.[37] Such a contention contradicts, however, the definitional presentation of fortuity, as related to the form of the phenomena (events, processes) and to their external, at times secondary, features and not to their essence.[38]

Finally, mention should be made of the inclusion, in some recent publications, of contingencies in the list of the principal causes of war, and the attribution to them of much more influence on the outbreak of war than ever before. This modification also seems to contradict the very concept of fortuity and logically the concept of necessary determination which is considered essential to the explanation of the causes of war.

The tendency, and the doubts

It can be suggested that the above interpretations, comments and modifications reveal one common tendency: to enhance the role of the fortuitous aspects of armed struggle. Moreover, they become hardly discernible from the necessary inherent aspects; some Soviet scholars write that fortuity is a component part of necessity: the internal contingencies stemming from individual actions are a part of necessity since the general course of events is a sum of these individual actions, and the 'statistical' (i.e. recurring) contingencies are included in the 'necessary' general picture just as such recurring events.

The attempts to present enemy actions as generating fortuity in fighting, or - one of the recent novelties - one's own ineffective actions as caused by fortuitous weaknesses in one's own preparations, in the personalities of the commanders and the like, act in the same direction: they introduce fortuity as one aspect of the necessary course of events.

Although the emphasis on this tendency is presented by Soviet theoreticians as nothing new (since it is only a manifestation of the action of twin-categories), there seem to be good reasons why the fortuitous aspect of war and, in particular, of military operations, has recently been given so much attention. Some reasons for this may be suggested. Firstly, Soviet scholars may wish to give a theoretical explanation for the fact that deviations from a regular, adequate, course of events that fully corresponds to all the laws, occur very frequently.

Especially irritating for the orthodox theoreticians are the cases where people's armies (which, according to all theoretical assumptions, always fight for a just cause and thereby necessarily win) suffer temporary or even final defeats: this may contradict the law which states that just aims *determine* victory. The presentation of contingencies as 'law-like' may perhaps explain all such deviations.

However, quite different reasons may also be suggested. Just because there are so many deviations from a law-like course of events, and because at the same time the basic assumption that war, like all other social phenomena is governed by objective laws must be salvaged and confirmed, the theoretical justification of the occurrence of various kinds of counteractions, interferences, and thereby contingencies, has been assigned this task. The thesis on the existence of laws can be salvaged by the reasoning that even if the events do not proceed according to laws, the latter are not thereby invalidated. The laws always act, but the effect of their action may be paralysed either by the action of other laws, or by a conscious counteractivity by commanders or by fortuitous events presented as a component and necessary part of reality.

One further (and practical) reason can be hypothesised. It is supposedly necessary to convince the commanding personnel of armed forces that, in spite of the sharp increase in unexpected shifts in the fortunes of war, often generated by fortuitous events, these shifts can and should be neutralised, in other words, counteracted. That fortuitous factors and events cannot be allowed to prevail over the lawful, necessary and manageable action is the essence of this reasoning.[39]

These hypothetical reasons, however, do not change my impression that, in view of the extreme focus on the lawfulness of war, the unwonted emphasis on fortuity and the recent effort to conceptualise it, and perhaps in some way justify it, is artifical. This impression is strengthened by the fact that some arguments seem inconclusive. Let us consider the contention that actions of the enemy - hardly predictable from our perspective - must be included in the set of factors that generate fortuity in our action. Since armed struggle is a two-sided process, such enemy actions can hardly be called unpredictable and fortuitous *per se*. If the enemy attacks by surprise, it is a surprise for us, and fortuitous for us, but it is part of his war-plan, prepared and accomplished according to his interpretation and exploitation of the laws of war, in accordance with his assessment of the objective situation, and in this sense it is a law-like and necessary action. If laws are presented as valid for both sides, the contingencies must also be of the same nature, otherwise they cannot complement the lawful necessity. The contention that one's own ineffective actions can be termed contingencies because one did not expect them does not stand the test of logic. If the same actions brought success to the enemy, they might constitute a part of his planned counteraction, they were perhaps included in his long range war-plan, and for all these reasons they can be called necessary from his point of view.

This reflects the main peculiarity of armed struggle as a two-sided activity. It has not only two systems of reference, two main causal chains, one for each belligerent side, but also one common for both sides, resulting from their interaction. This is the main tendency of warfare. The actions of each side may be regarded as fortuitous only in relation to the actions of the enemy, to the chain of causes and effects at which he aims, but they can hardly be regarded as accidental in relation not only to one's own course of action, but also to the resultant course of fighting.

Whatever the reasons, with the introduction of fortuitous yet necessary factors the general picture of the actions of laws has become very complex. Laws operate through the actions of people - thousands and millions of different personalities - through the interaction of different, sometimes opposing tendencies, through innumerable and diverse chance happenings, in a complex and rapidly changing mutual interaction. To try to explain particular events by a simultaneous action of laws and of necessary contingencies is a very complex endeavour.[40]

24

The character of laws: dynamic or probabilistic?

In the traditional research (as well as the present non-Soviet one) social laws have often been discussed in terms of dichotomous typologies: causal or teleological, logical or empirical, absolute (universal) or probabilistic, and the like.

In Soviet military theory, the focus, as mentioned above, is on the causal laws. The discussion of their classification, according to the method of their discovery or manner of testing, has been given very little attention (see Chap. 7). The only distinction made concerns the degree in which various events are determined by laws; this has been presented as the difference between the so-called dynamic or probabilistic (or statistical, or probabilistic-statistical) character of particular laws of war.

Three views

The concept of a 'dynamic law' has been more described than defined. It 'expresses the nature of regular processes', 'determines each singular event', and 'fixes the behaviour of individual bodies'.[41] It is said clearly and precisely to express the causal ties between phenomena or between the successive states of an object. The effect of the action of dynamic laws is always the same; under the same conditions the same causes produce the same effects. Such a concept comes close to the traditional or contemporary Western concept of the deterministic law which expresses uniform ties between phenomena (called also a universal law or 'covering law').

Probabilistic or statistical laws are described in two principal ways. In the first, the point of departure is the individual action (behaviour). The regular repetition of a multitude of individual actions by members of a group means the manifestation of a regularity in its behaviour as a whole. At the same time, the behaviour of an individual can be predicted only with some probability. This is the reason why such regularities are regarded as 'probabilistic'. In a simplified form, probabilistic-statistical laws stating such regularities are presented as expressing irregular chaotic processes which determine the actions of groups but not of individuals.

Taking another approach, an event or process in which men and weapons are used on a massive scale, may be regarded as the object subordinated to a law. The manifold repetition of certain actions, relationships and other features under approximately identical conditions is regarded as expressing a law. Also here we are witnessing some kind of probability. Although the main course of the recurring events is similar, no singular event is an exact repetition of some model form since each instance depends on several different and changing conditions.[42]

The two approaches mentioned above can perhaps be brought closer together: different individual behaviour results in different group behaviour as regards details, although it does not change the main current of events, which is

25

governed by laws. There is disagreement as to which of these two kinds of laws prevails in war and particularly in armed struggle. The various positions may be summarised as follows.

The first view is that the principal general laws of war and laws of armed struggle - such as the law of correlation of forces, the law of the interaction of branches of armed forces (see below) - are of a dynamic nature expressing their uniform recurring ties and dependencies. However, in principle phenomena and processes of war ought to be regarded as subjected to the simultaneous influence of both dynamic and probabilistic-statistical laws.[43] Such mixed and combined influence may be explained by the fact that in war two kinds of processes occur simultaneously, interact and intertwine. Processes regulated by the political leadership of the military organisation, and by the managerial activities of commanders, are considered to be determined in a uniform fashion, i.e. subordinated to dynamic laws. Processes which are engendered by the violent actions and counteractions of warring protagonists, by disrupting attacks - which are affected by accidental factors and events and deviations from norms (e.g. caused by the individual character of commanders and soldiers) - are governed by probabilistic-statistical laws. Since war is a mixture of both processes, it is simultaneously subject to both types of laws.

In a variant of this approach,[44] no definite choice of the prevailing character of law has been made. Laws of war and especially laws of armed struggle 'do not belong to the kind of dynamic laws' but they 'cannot be relegated to statistical laws'. War, and in particular armed struggle, is simultaneously an orderly *and* a chaotic process. Each side aims at purposefulness, regularity and organisation in the action of its own troops and at disturbing order and organisation in the action of the enemy. The inter-relationship of these two opposing tendencies - to introduce order and to disrupt it - results in various combinations of the action and influence of laws.[45]

Taking a quite different approach,[46] war, in its nature and spirit, is said to be closely linked with the probabilistic-statistical laws. The fact that war is fought by masses of people whose action is affected by a multitude of factors, and that it is a two-sided process in which each side counteracts and tries to neutralise the actions of its opponent makes any uniform course of events impossible. Particular events and phenomena oscillate around an ideal picture but are never identical with it. Only some techno-physical processes which are secondary component parts of military actions are wholly subject to dynamic laws. These laws can therefore be regarded as constituting only one tendency in the process of realisation of the probabilistic-statistical laws. Views asserting the dynamic character of laws of war are characterised by these scholars as one-sided and as a remnant of an outmoded method which selected one causal relationship from many, absolutised it and left out of account all other relationships as secondary and accidental and not affecting the course of warfare.

The three above-mentioned views can hardly be found clearly and unambiguously formulated and consistently applied. Some scholars after presenting one view, add comments and qualifications which change their former position. Others, having expressed a certain view, express a quite different view in a later study. For instance, Prof. Gen. Tyushkevich, as a co-author of the semi-official textbook 'Marxism-Leninism on War and Army' (1972) asserts that laws of armed struggle can be relegated neither to the dynamic nor to the statistical kind, but in 'Filosofiya i voennaya teoriya' (1975) he argues at length that war is wholly subject to probabilistic-statistical laws.

Law-tendencies

In recent publications, some scholars argue that laws of war should be treated as a special kind of law, i.e. as law-tendencies. Perhaps this is one of the results of the discussion about the dynamic or probabilistic-statistical character of these laws. 'Law-tendencies'[47] (also called 'medium-laws', intermediate laws, or mass-laws) are similar to probabilistic-statistical laws. They constitute a tendency characterising many phenomena during a considerable period of time and allow us to predict with some probability not only individual events but also the main course of the whole process.[48] In an extreme interpretation, law-tendencies are considered to indicate the objective logic of events and their main direction, without presenting the given dependence in a more precise way.

These laws can be described as the most extreme kind of 'qualitative' laws[49] because they express the qualitative essence of the phenomena and reveal the general tendencies of their change and development without even roughly-assessed (much less measured) features and details of this change.

Laws of the dependence of the course and outcome of war on moral conditions, laws of the dependence of military art on men and armaments, or the dependence of the character of war and the methods used in it on the political aims, may here be mentioned. However, other laws of war (perhaps most of them) mentioned by Soviet scholars also can be named qualitative. Only some regularities can be quantitatively assessed, such as the probability of a typical action by a given unit in definite circumstances, or the prediction of the effects of such an action - for instance, the destruction of part of the enemy's equipment. The interpretation of laws of war as law-tendencies may constitute a significant modification in the traditional position. The consequences will be discussed later (Chap.4).

Comment on the probability

To conclude this section, one difference between Marxist-Leninist and Western science in the very concept of a social law may be noted. In the prevailing Western view, no regularity in social behaviour determines future action. Some say that social and, in particular, political behaviour depends on the one hand on conditions (and regularities, if they exist) which to some extent constrain freedom of the decision on how to act, and on the other hand on motives and goals which express the ability of men to choose how they will act. If the former are predictable, the latter are not.

In the Soviet concept, a law which expresses a necessary regularity - a recurrence of ties, relationships and processes - thereby includes a probable human action which will follow this law. In other words, if a law exists, men will probably act according to it, whether or not they are aware of its existence. As we see, Soviet theory allows for a qualification expressed by the word 'probably', which significantly diminishes the above-mentioned difference with regard to other approaches. Men will act according to a given law, if other laws do not interfere, and if other causal chains of events do not disturb the given action. Their individual motives and goals also may be affected by many different factors, so the choice of the way of action is not fatalistically predetermined by the given law. Their action is a result of the action of the given law and of other laws, and of a complex of conditions. There is a great probability that the influence of the given law, if it concerns the essence of the phenomenon, process, or field of activity, their main features will be the determining one, but probability is not identical with cast-iron inevitability. Thus, to Soviet scholars, in principle social laws are probabilistic laws. This problem will be discussed below.

The probabilistic nature of human action as a component of the action of the objective laws can but strengthen the assumption that a distinction should be observed between the *existence* of an objective law, its manifestation in the form of objective external and internal ties and relationships and its *concrete impact* on events. This may vary depending not only on the action of other laws, the individual characteristics of human activity which cannot be uniform in all details, and the occurrence of fortuitous events, but also on the above-mentioned possibility - however small it may be - that men will not act according to the laws.

To sum up, the probabilistic character of the concrete impact of the objective laws is due to the fact that they manifest themselves in human activity that is necessarily individual.

Laws are historical

In describing the main characteristics of laws of war Soviet scholars also emphasise their historical character, which in this interpretation means their changeability. Laws of war are not considered to be invariably valid through space and time. On the contrary they change together with the changes in the conditions under which wars occur and with the conditions of fighting. Such changes are especially evident when new socio-economic formations emerge, but they may also occur within one and the same formation if the types of war characteristic of the epoch change, and with them the means and methods of warfare.[50] The change may be significant: some laws may become secondary, others may even disappear.

While laws of nature are eternal (for instance, the laws of preservation and transformation of matter and energy), or very long-lived, laws of war as social laws are of different durability. Some may be valid in all class societies, or even as long as wars occur, others are comparatively short-lived, operating only during particular historical periods, and giving way to other laws when they become obsolete.[51]

The objective laws may naturally change in various ways. The main variants of change are as follows:

1 The most extreme manifestation of the historical character of these laws is constituted by the disappearance of the phenomenon with which the law is concerned. In this case, the change in the law simply means its disappearance. For instance, laws operating in national-liberation wars will cease to exist when such wars disappear.

2 The second kind of change occurs when the main relationship or tie which constitutes the law changes. Then the content of the law changes in a radical way. For instance, a change in relationship between the offensive and defence means that the corresponding law has radically changed or, rather, has been replaced by another law embodying the changed relationship or tie.

3 The manifestation or application of the law changes. For instance, according to one law the outcome of a battle is decided by a strike. For many centuries, this meant a strike with side-arms, but nowadays it means a nuclear strike.

4 The conditions under which a law is valid have changed. For example, some laws formerly valid for all wars nowadays apply only to conventional wars.

The change in the scientific laws which reflect the cognition of these changes in objective laws should be strictly corresponding. However, the changes in formulae are not always an adequate reflection of the objective laws. Soviet scholars rarely announce that certain laws have disappeared or radically changed. They are seemingly reluctant to liquidate propositions which were for a long time regarded as stable truths.

With regard to the other two kinds of changes, the scholars usually try to preserve the wording (or to change it very slightly), while changing or modifying the interpretation of the given formula. For instance, the changing application of a law is at times presented as a shift from one level of fighting to another. So the change in the application of the law of the determining influence exerted by forces and weapons on the means and methods used in armed struggle is described as the shift from the tactical through the operational-strategic, to the strategic level of fighting. Forces and weapons had a direct effect on the tactical level during World War I (e.g. the defences could be simultaneously neutralised only to a depth of 7-10 kilometres), they began to have a direct effect on an operational-strategic scale during World War II (operations became more dynamic and capable of deeper penetration and a number of simultaneous and consecutive strikes could defeat the enemy's principal groupings), and in a future war the effect of this law may be manifested on a strategic scale within a very short period.

Another shift in emphasis may be illustrated by the changed interpretation of the law of the determining influence of the economic and other potentialities (or of correlation of forces, see below) on the course and outcome of war. The radical change introduced by nuclear weapons into modern warfare is reflected in the wording of a corresponding scientific law in the shift of emphasis from the forces which influence warfare during its whole course, to those forces and means (or their correlation) which are available at the beginning of the nuclear war.[52]

Even the change in the above-mentioned law concerning the decisive importance of the strike for the outcome of a battle has often been reflected only in the interpretation. The general wording of the law has been preserved - victory can be achieved only by a strike (or offensive action) - while the explanation and description of the law focuses on the nuclear strike.

The above example illustrates the Soviet assertion that while laws of war will *remain valid* in a future nuclear war, the mechanism of their manifestation and action will be *specific*. The preservation of the formulae of the respective scientific laws while their interpretation is undergoing change, is a general tendency.

(To digress, the theoretical problem of the changeability of the objective laws is apparently to be distinguished from another, more practical point: laws, although stable in their principal content, operate and are exploited variously in different situations. The combination of concrete conditions and circumstances under which a specific military operation is carried out is always in some sense unique and requires a specific application of the laws and of principles based on them (see Chap.6). Thus while the exploitation of the objective laws and principles may take different forms, they themselves may remain unchanged and valid.)

As we see, Soviet researchers are reluctant to change formulae which for a long time have been regarded as scientific truths and achievements, but they emphasise that the objective laws are changeable. We may speculate a little on the reasons for such emphasis. Two explanations are conceivable here. One is connected with the very concept of law in Soviet military studies. The objective laws of war are firmly anchored in the material basis of society. The respective scientific laws are not logical constructions reflecting basic immutable ties between immutable social processes and phenomena, but reflections of real ties between real phenomena rooted in the changing material basis of society and its contradictions. All kinds of the objective laws of war - including laws of the development of military art and so-called internal laws of armed struggle (see below) - depend more or less directly on material conditions in particular, on the kind of economic system and level of production. Thus, *when the material basis changes, laws change too.*

This could perhaps explain the fact that, in the Soviet expositions, various kinds of laws seem to change variously: the more direct the dependence of the given law on its material basis the greater its changeability. Thus laws of armed struggle directly dependent on the development of armament change most rapidly.

The other suggestion resembles that raised when considering the increased emphasis on fortuity in the explanation of the nature of laws. Soviet scholars may have observed that it is difficult to apply the traditionally presented laws to all contemporary types of war and particularly to a possible future nuclear war. If the idea of the objective laws governing war is to be salvaged, laws have to be presented as changeable.

It should be noted that the approach to the changeability of the objective laws of war also depends on exta-scientific factors. For instance, the emphasis on the unchanging content of these laws was common in the first post-war years, when the Soviet Union was only at the beginning of its nuclear rearmament programme. An over-emphasis in the contrary direction - i.e. on the importance of missiles as completely changing the conditions under which the laws operate and their utilisation (for instance the primary importance of surprise and 'forces in being') was characteristic of the early 1960s, when Khrushchev used the Soviet superiority in these weapons as a political instrument. Such examples can be multiplied.

To digress, some Western scholars speak of the high mutability of social laws and regularities,[53] and at times present them as quickly decaying and any system of scientific generalisations based on them as being in a state of constant flux.[54] Others describe the regularities discovered in social relations, including politics, as 'soft' ones, meaning that they do not determine the occurrence and outcome of events with cast-iron necessity.[55] It is implied that both the above variants of characteristics turn the statements about social laws and regularities into pseudo-laws, which also may mean the negation of the very existence of objective social laws and regularities. The generalisations in social sciences are here distinguished in principle from proper laws - both objective and scientific - in the physical sciences. With such an approach, one cannot treat the events and phenomena of war as natural events leading to the same explanatory logic as is found in 'hard' sciences.

In contradistinction Soviet scholars take the following position on these problems:

1 The changeability of objective laws is not to be interpreted as high mutability. The main social laws, including laws of war, change only with radical, revolutionary social and techno-military changes.

2 The so-called free activity of men also depends on laws and conditions. Only the knowledge of laws and conditions allows men to act rationally, to choose the best way of acting, and to discover value-optimising solutions.

3 The probabilistic character of events does not change the status of objective laws since deviations from the normal course of events are caused by other laws and secondary causal chains of events.

4 To sum up, the historical character of laws is evidence of their being an aspect of reality. They change together with reality because they constitute the essence of it.

General tendencies

While much has been written in the Soviet Union on the laws of war, the main tendencies of change in the whole approach to the character of these laws has not been discussed. Thus a few suggestions will be presented here.

Many Soviet scholars, makers of military theory, appear to assume that laws of war must be treated as a separate body of laws, constituting an inherent component part of military theory as a separate discipline of science. Their treatment of the subject implies that they have abandoned the view held by many theorists from the first post-revolutionary period up to the 1950s that laws of social development, so-called laws of historical materialism, can be directly applied to military affairs and treated as the laws of war. The traditional view is also presented, for instance, in studies which classify laws of the origin of war or even all general laws of war with the laws of historical materialism.

One specific feature of laws of war, as distinct from other social laws, and accepted only since the late fifties, is that they operate in the action of all armies. Although Soviet theory maintained for a long time that there existed separate laws of war for the socialist states and armies, and for the so-called capitalist states and armies (even as there were separate economic laws for the two kinds of societies), this assertion has recently been withdrawn.

The orthodox assumption was presented in three versions. In the first, some laws were considered to be valid only in relation to the socialist armies, for instance the law which held that the party which waged a just war must inevitably win, since according to Soviet theory only socialist armies wage just wars. In the second variant, some laws could be cognised only by the socialist armies, since only Marxist-Leninist philosophy and methodology made it possible.

In the third version, only the socialist armies were regarded as able to apply and exploit certain laws. For instance, the laws of the determining influence of so-called permanently operating factors (i.e. the strength of the rear, high morale of the army, etc.) on victory in war were considered as acting only on behalf of the socialist armies, because only the socialist system ensured their exploitation. The bourgeois science and the politico-military leadership of the capitalist countries were said to deny the very existence of certain laws because they knew that they could not exploit them. Remnants of the above approach can be found even in recent studies. It is now held, however, that no separate laws for different kinds of states and armies exist. While the economic development of different socio-economic formations or systems are subject to different laws, war which is a two-sided process does not. The belligerents do not act identically, because they aim at different goals, and possess different resources, but they have to take account of the same objective laws.

(The discussion of this problem began with a well-known article, written in 1953, by Gen. N. Talenskii,[55] who stated that there existed objective laws identical for all armies. After eight years, the authors of 'Voennaya strategiya' decided to repeat his assertion and to emphasise that 'the laws of strategy are

objective, and apply inexorably and in the same degree to all belligerents').[56]
The view that the mechanism of the laws of war is automatic is gradually being abandoned. Traditionally, these laws were supposed to prejudge the final outcome of war, and even the main course of it. The modifications in the Soviet position on this problem can perhaps be summarised as follows

(a) The dependence of war on economic, political and ideological factors is now presented as being not direct but maintained through many intermediate factors, actions and stages. The superiority over the enemy in the 'factors' does not directly determine the course of fighting but must be knowingly and efficiently exploited.

(b) The importance of the subjective side of war and in particular armed struggle has been emphasised (see àbove). The effective interaction of the subjective and objective is even more important in war than in other activities. According to Soviet teaching, laws of social development unequivocally determine only the final result of the development: socialism will triumph sooner or later in spite of temporary defeats and delays. However, this is not true of every war. Previously, Soviet military theorists automatically applied such reasoning to wars in general, and to wars fought by the Soviet Union in particular, and were very reluctant to change this approach. Even discussions of possible deviations of individual events from a standard ideal course of war, have related such 'contingencies' to the course of fighting and not to its final outcome.
As we have seen only very recently it has been admitted (and it is yet rarely mentioned) that even the party fighting for a just cause may be defeated, because war is a clash of opposing wills, solved in a definite and limited time, and its outcome depends on how the parties are able to act according to the aggregate of laws. The outcome is not predetermined by the laws but depends on the effectiveness of human action.

(c) As another aspect of this modification, the importance of all conscious disorganising influences - i.e. of the actions of the enemy - on the course and outcome of war has been increasingly emphasised.

(d) The effect of the different contingencies (one of them being the above-mentioned actions of the enemy) has been pointed out.

(e) As a corollary, the so-called dynamic laws which traditionally dominated the theory of war, have gradually been replaced by the statistical-probabilistic laws, law-tendencies and the like.

(f) Following the above change and extending it, some scholars have begun to relate the probabilistic character of the laws of war not only to the course of military events but also to their final outcome. One interpretation of the probabilistic law is that while the details of individual events and processes vary, their essential features and general course are similar to analogous processes in similar circumstances (cf. the discussion on fortuity and on dynamic versus statistical laws). Although the course of warfare, for instance, is characterised by a multitude of individual events, its main tendency can be predicted. However, the alternative version of this law namely, that even the final outcome of warfare cannot be prejudged, because of many subjective and accidental factors which can change it, seems to have gained increasing attention.[57]

(g) It has increasingly been emphasised that any social action - and especially war - is subject to the simultaneous action and influence of many laws. In some wordings and interpretations the probabilistic laws of war have become aggregate laws which do not bear a single-value nature, but express a complex of many causal ties.

Interrelated with all the above tendencies is that to replace absolute magnitudes in the formulae on some laws by relative ones. This results logically from relating the laws to both opposing sides, and from treating the material conditions as creating the possibility of victory but not prejudging it, since the victor is he who better exploits the conditions. This tendency can be best exemplified by the fact that 'correlation of forces' has replaced 'factors' in the formulae on laws which deal with the dependence of the course and outcome of war on external variables.

Summing up, there is a marked tendency for Soviet theory (1) to develop a system of laws of war, to extend its scope and (2) to modify the explanation of the mechanism of the laws by multiplying factors which limit the power of their action which was previously regarded as determining the course of events in a uniform way. Why, one may ask, are these opposing tendencies presented together? To this question one answer may be given: the two tendencies are only allegedly in opposition. It is true that, in orthodox Soviet military theory, laws were presented as the highest and ultimate arbiters of the outcome of war and they spoke in the name of history. They operated the mechanism of war and always acted in favour of the Soviet armed forces which were always fighting just and progressive wars and thus conforming with the laws of dialectical and historical materialism. They confirmed belief in victory.

The emphasis on the larger role of all other factors influencing the course and outcome of war - circumstances, actions of both sides, contingencies - and the modified view of laws as probabilistic-statistical, or law-tendencies, may seem to weaken the special role of laws. However, as mentioned in the discussion of the role of contingencies, it 'salvages' the laws and re-affirms the main assumption that laws act objectively, independently of human will and independently of whether the action of a particular law actually prevails and determines the course of events.

Even if the course and outcome of war contradicts some expectations, and if it does not correspond to the laws that assert the victory of the just and progressive, it can always be explained by the simultaneous action of many laws, circumstances, actions and contingencies. Although the explanation is thereby complicated, the idea of laws governing war and armed struggle is salvaged.[58]

The modifications have been necessary, since the complex socio-political picture of the world and the new conditions of fighting virtually compelled a reassessment of the theory. Once more it must be stressed that such reassessments represent no more than a tendency that is far from full realisation.

The process of transformation of Soviet theory is specific: it is a mixture of several techniques some of which can only briefly be mentioned here since their analysis goes beyond the scope of this study. (a) Qualifications are added to the traditional assumptions which are sometimes tantamount to a contradiction. (b) New contentions are added with the comment that they are applicable under conditions different from the usual ones. (c) Certain details are changed which make it possible to change the whole interpretation significantly. (d) The whole interpretation is changed while the formula remains unchanged. (e) Contentions which do not constitute a consistent whole are put together.

To sum up, the orthodox answer to the question of how to appraise laws has proven resilient, in spite of the problems it has raised. Repeated attempts have been made to build up a system of laws that would cover all phenomena of war.

The working formula (equation) of war

It might first be appropriate to propose a working formula (or equation) of war, which would comprise the main factors affecting its incidence, course and outcome. This would have to be merely preliminary, as additional factors will emerge from the analysis of the Soviet system of laws.

Since Soviet scholars assert the causal character of laws of war, the working formula can be conceived as follows:

> The incidence, course and outcome of war (E) follows logically from the occurrence of human actions (A) under the determining circumstances, or conditions (C), according to objective laws (L).

The determining circumstances, or conditions, are represented in war by the components of the politico-military situation (before the war and during it) and other aforementioned factors. The activities of the political forces which decide on war and control its conduct and of the military units which carry on the fighting, constitute actions A. The laws L are naturally laws of war.

Notes

[1] In Soviet study, apart from the term 'law' (zakon), an almost synonymous term 'regularity' (zakonomernost) is often applied: 'Soviet military science is a system of knowledge about the regularities of armed struggle' (A. Strokov, I. Maryganov, 'Ob osnovakh sovetskoi voennoi nauki', *Propagandist i Agitator*, 1954:2, p.43). 'The thesis of the permanent acting factors . . . is of decisive import-

ance for the understanding of regularities of the contemporary armed struggle' (V. Zubarev, 'Lenin i voennaya nauka'; *P.i A.*, 1955:13); '. . . the objective regularities of armed struggle are the subject of Soviet military science' (S. Kozlov, 'O nekotorykh voprosakh sovetskoi voennoi nauki', *P.i A.*, 1957:2, p.26); 'military science reflects the objective regularities of armed struggle' (A. Bagreev, 'Sovetskaya voennaya nauka i ee preimuschchestva burzhuaznoi voennoi naukoi', *P.i A.*, 1957:3). They have often been used interchangeably: for instance, see V. Fedorov, 'Dialekticheskii materializm i sovetskaya voennaya nauka', *P.i A.*, 1955:8; Krupnov, 1963, examines four groups of regularities of war, calling them interchangeably regularities and laws; some scholars observe that the terms 'zakon' and 'zakonomernost' express relationships of the same order and are therefore often used interchangeably (Prokop'ev, 1964, p.198).

At the same time, it is pointed out that Lenin interpreted the term 'zakonomernost' as accordance with law, subordination to a law (Popov, 1964, p.39). The existence of a regularity indicates that in the given kind of events a law operates and governs their course. Thus, while a law expresses a necessary relation between phenomena, regularity shows only that the course of events is not accidental, that it proceeds according to laws (Prokop'ev, 1965, p.198; Popov, 1964, pp.39-41); law is primary, regularity constitutes its manifestation (Filosofskaya Entsiklopediya, Izd. Sovetskaya Entsiklopediya, Vol. II, p.149); law expresses one tie between phenomena, while regularity means subordination of the given process to one or many laws (Tyushkevich, 1962, pp.8-9). Tyushkevich also writes that 'regularity' is used to indicate that the class of phenomena in question evolves according to laws. In a later study, the same scholar put forward a compromise proposal. He contends that the category of law is in principle (v osnovnom) identical with the category of regularity, and the two are used interchangeably but at the same time there exists a distinction between them: law points out a concrete necessary tie between phenomena, while regularity means only that these phenomena are subject to laws. In other words, law expresses one type of tie, while regularity encompasses all laws in this realm of reality. Thus law and regularity are at the same time identical and different. Cf. Voina i armiya, 1977, p.144.

In the English translations, or in analyses of Soviet views, 'zakon' is usually translated as 'law', or sometimes as 'rule governing the . . .' (For instance, in the translation of Voennaya Strategiya in the Rand Corporation edition), and 'zakonomernost' as 'regularity'; the latter, however, is also sometimes translated as 'rule governing the . . .' - for instance, in The Nuclear Revolution in Soviet Military Affairs, 1968, or in the translation of Voennaya Strategiya in the Stanford Research Institute edition, 1971. And in the above-mentioned translation in the Rand Corporation edition, 'zakonomernost' is translated as 'law' or 'general rule governing the . . .' on the same page, 89.

Finally, the translators of Nauchno-Tekhnicheskii Progress i Revolutsiya v Voennom Dele interpreted 'zakonomernost' as 'pattern'; e.g. Scientific-Technical Progress and The Revolution in Military Affairs, U.S. Governments Printing Office, Washington, 1974, p.133, a.o. In this study, the term 'law' will be the usual one, and the term 'regularity' will be used only when the difference between the two should be pointed out; in such a case regularity would mean the manifestation of a law.

[2] Fedorov, 1955 (comp. note 1), p.15; Prokop'ev, 1965, p.198; Wörterbuch der marxistisch-leninistischen Soziologie, Westdeutscher Verlag, Wolfgang Eichhorn et. al., eds., 2A, Opladen, pp.162-8; Grigorenko, et al., Metodika Voenno-Nauchnogo Issledovaniya, Voenizdat, Moscow 1959, pp.34-35; Metodologicheskie problemy voennoi teorii i praktiki, 1969, Chap. XIV (quoted in the following as 'Metodologicheskie problemy'); Marxism-Leninism on War and Army, Chap. VIII:3; Filosofskoe nasledie, Chap. II; Savkin, 1972, Chap. 2; V. Morozov, 'The Laws of War and Military Art', *Soviet Military Review*, 1974:11; Popov, 1964, pp.38-39; Y. Rybkin, 'Zakony Vooruzhennoi bor'by', *Kommunist Vooruzhenn Sil*, 1965:7; Zakharov, 1967; Metodologiya voenno-nauchnogo poznaniya, 1977. Voina i armiya, pp.144-145.

[3] Osnovy marksistskoi filosofii, 1959, Chap. VI.2; Metodologicheskie problemy. p.319; Zakharov, 1967, p.46. Lenin has frequently been quoted: 'The law is the relationship . . . The relationship of their nature (of the phenomena-JL) or between their nature' (Dela, v. 29, p.138).

[4] 'Zakony i obychai voiny', in: Sovetskaya Voennaya Entsiklopediya, 1977, Vol. 3, p.375. Cf. 'Ob'ektivnye zakony voiny', in: Slovar osnovnykh voennykh terminov, Voenizdat, Moscow 1965.

[5] The definition of laws of war includes, apparently, not only necessary and recurring causal ties and relationships, but also structural laws expressing the coexistence of the components of the phenomenon or process, and ties between them; functional laws concerning functions of the phenomenon or process which constitute its determining characteristics and the functional interrelation between its parts; laws of interdependence between phenomena and processes must also be taken into account. One variant of these laws concerns attributes and features of phenomena and processes which express their necessary and recurring internal and external ties and relationships i.e. the qualitative definiteness of such phenomena and processes. Causal laws are said to underlie in the final analysis, all these (and perhaps other conceivable) kinds of laws since the very coexistence of things, phenomena and processes, and all recurring and necessary structural or functional ties and relationships connected with them have their recurring and necessary causes.

[6] The principle of determinism constitutes 'the main basis of the scientific world outlook and scientific methodology. This principle affects the direction and character of the theoretical analysis, determines its methodological orientation, the basic theoretical premises and resolution of concrete scientific problems' (Tyushkevich, 1975, p.7).

[7] 'Law is the essential in the movement of phenomena. Law and essence are of the same degree' (Osnovy marksistskoi filosofii, 1959, Chap. VI.2). Savkin writes that the concept of a law and the concept of essence are close, related and

of the same order, but they are not identical concepts. Law is narrower than essence and does not reflect all its various features and peculiarities (1972, p.54). All quotations after the English translation 'The Basic Principles of Operational Art and Tactics' (The US Air Force, US Gov. Printing Office 1974 0 - 532 - 028).

[8] Sociological laws are also divided into general sociological laws covering the whole social development and laws valid in particular socio-economic formations (formatsii). The law of the determining role of the method of production in social life or the law of the correspondence of productive relations to the level and character of the means of production are examples of the former (Grudinin, 1971, p.6).

[9] In some presentations, however, the Marxist-Leninist political economics and so-called scientific communism (theory of revolution) complement the general sociological (or socio-political) theory of war. The former is considered to include, for instance, the study of the economic roots of war, the sources of contemporary militarism, the ways of increasing the military power of the Soviet Union, etc. The latter is said to include the relationship between war and revolution, the military organisation of the fighting proletariat, problems of the defence of socialist states, and the like (Dmitriev, 1975, pp.11-12).

[10] Laws of war are based on 'more general social laws, determining the development of society as a whole, laws of the genesis, development and functioning of the socio-economic formations discovered by Marxist-Leninist science' ('Zakony i obychai voiny', loc. cit., p.375).

[11] To emphasise the similarity of the essence of laws of nature and of laws of war in their social nature, some scholars call the latter 'natural laws'. For instance, Lototsky, 1973, discusses several 'objective natural laws' of war and, in particular, of the development of military art. (After the translation in *Strategic Review*, Spring 1974).

[12] 'Laws of science are a more or less correct reflection of the objective laws of nature and of society in human consciousness' (M. Popov, 1964, 'Problema zakonomernosti vooruzhennoi borby v istorii burzhuaznoi voennoi nauki').

The basic theses of the 'theory of reflection', as Marxism-Leninism often calls its theory of cognition, are as follows: (1) The whole process of cognition is based on the reflection of the objective reality in the human mind; (2) our feelings, conceptions and notions are the subjective reflections of the things and processes that really exist, independently of human consciousness. (Metodologickeskie problemy, Chap. 1; Grudinin, 1971, Chap. V.5, esp. pp.175-6). 'As a reflection of the objective logic of modern warfare, Soviet military science includes a system of laws of military science as one of its most important aspects' (Filosofskoe nasledie, p.137). Lenin is quoted: 'The laws of the external world constitute the foundations of purposeful human activity.'

[13] The fact that social laws concern human activity has one additional and very important consequence: according to Soviet theory, since social laws - and in particular the laws of social struggle - touch on the vital interests of the strug-

gling classes, each of the latter tries to hinder the discovery and use of those laws, the action of which contradicts its interests. In other words, in contradistinction to the laws of nature, the cognition of social laws (not to mention their exploitation) is accomplished in the process of class struggle and, naturally, cannot proceed smoothly and quietly (Osnovy marksistskoi filosofii, 1959, Chap. VI 1,2.). Cf. Grudinin, 1971, Chap. VII; Savkin, 1972, p.63, Tyushkevich, 1975, Chap. I; Schaff, 1950, Chap. II.3. ('Dialektyka a prawo przyczynowosci').

[14] Krupnov, 1963, esp. 'Ob'ektivnye zakony i poznatelnaya deyatelnost ludei v voine', pp.93-99; Popov, 1964, Chap. 4, 1966, and 1968; Metodologicheskie problemy, Part I, Chap. VII, and Part 4; Grudinin, 1967, and his 1971, Chap. VII.2; Morozov, 1974.

[15] 'History knows no few cases when political and military leaders tried to plan and wage wars leaving all these objective connections out of account. But as a result, they only suffered defeat' (Morozov, 1974, p.2).

[16] Marxism-Leninism on War and Army, p.311; Morozov, ibidem; Savkin, p.115; Tyushkevich, 1975, p.217. Additional factors also influence the conduct of war: distances, space, territory, the geographical situation, temporal conditions, climatic and meteorological conditions, and the like.

[17] This problem is considered so important that some scholars define military science as the science of the relation between the objective and subjective sides in war (Popov, 1968; cf. Morozov, Tyushkevich, 1967).

[18] Savkin writes: 'Sometimes the opinion is expressed that it is generally impossible to violate the demands of objective laws of nature and society. This assertion contradicts numerous facts. If the demands of laws were impossible to violate, this would mean that any activity is carried on in accordance with laws and must be successful for this reason' (1972, p.62).

[19] Soviet scholars, however, occasionally present laws as actors or acting forces. An outstanding theorist writes: 'The discovery that laws of social progress are just the motive forces (dvizhushchie sily) which realise the historical process, was comprehensively discussed in the works of the classics of Marxism-Leninism' (Tyushkevich, 1975, p.216).

[20] Tyushkevich also states that laws are always united (sliten) with phenomena, which implies that they exist only as features of the phenomena or relations between them (p.218).

[21] Popov, 1964, p.113, 1966, p.12; Metodologicheskie problemy, pp.166-167.

[22] Popov, 1964, pp.110-113; Grudinin, 1971, p.226; Tyushkevich, 1975.

[23] Savkin, 1972.

[24] Tyushkevich, 1975.

[25] Certain contentions of this kind are not in full correspondence with Marxist-Leninist philosophical ideas. Military scholars emphasise that 'objective' is more than 'material' (Tyushkevich, 1975, p.259) perhaps because they emphasise the objective character of laws; in the classical Marxism, however, 'objective' and 'material' are closely linked, since all that exists independently of

the cognising subject is both material and objective. According to this interpretation, actions by armed forces are also both material and objective.

[26] Grudinin, 1971, p.225.

[27] Grudinin contends that while objective factors which generate war create a possibility of its occurrence, subjective factors cause direct preparation for it and unleashing it (ibid. p.224). Thus the interaction of objective and subjective transforms possibility into reality.

[28] Popov, 1964, observes that the right expression is 'to use laws', and not 'to apply laws'; one cannot 'apply' laws, since these are inherent in the processes themselves.

[29] Morozov, 1974, p.3. He observes that human activity in war is not arbitrary because of three features of war: (1) the political aims of war which are determined by concrete material interests, (2) the military power of a country and its correlation with the power of other countries, which are likewise definite quantities, and (3) the forms and methods of armed combat, the organisation and equipment of armed forces which, in the final analysis depend on economic conditions.

[30] Grudinin, 1971, p.227. In one presentation, three levels of such cognising and acting in accord with laws are described. The first level is the adaption to the working of law, acting in accordance with it, utilising it in one's favour. The second, higher, level consists of limiting the operation of the laws which may unfavourably influence one's own actions, and in choosing, from the many possibilities which arise in the course of fighting, the most advantageous. This can be regarded, in a way, as the mastering of laws. On the highest level, the armed forces dominate the laws. They not only make the most rational use of the given situation, but change it to their advantage, to pursue their aims. They intensify the operation of laws which are 'working' for them, and limit, or even reduce to a minimum, the operation of laws which could 'work' for the enemy. (Zamorsky, 1975, p.36.) More generally, the utilisation of laws is said to follow two main lines. Firstly the commander (or military leader) makes sure that his planned actions will correspond to the requirements of the situation i.e. to the laws and the given conditions. Secondly, he tries to change that situation, to force the laws to operate in his favour.

[31] Comp. Tyushkevich, 1975, pp.261-262.

[32] Marksizm-leninizm o voine i armii, 1968, pp.361-362; Tyushkevich,1962, pp.96-7; I Grudinin, 'Sub'ektivnyi faktor i sluchainost v voine', Voenno-Istoricheskii Zhurnal, 1965:6, and his 1971, Chap. VIII.

[33] In a study on the methodology of military research, the difference between necessity and fortuity is explained as follows: necessity is generated by the very essence of things, processes and events from their internal development, thus they inevitably proceed in a given way. Fortuity emerges from the development caused by secondary or external factors, the fortuitous events may occur, but they also may not occur, they may proceed in various ways; and they are secondary to the thing, process or event in question (Grigorenko, et. al., 1959, p. 47).

[34] Features of combat connected with the characteristics of individual soldiers which are accidental emerge on the external side of necessity (Tyushkevich, 1962, pp.104-105); the essence of modern combat is 'to attune nuclear strikes to actions of land forces and air forces with regard to aims, directions, boundaries and time, in order to destroy the enemy quickly. The necessary cooperation is accomplished in each particular combat (operation) in certain limits through its accidental form, caused by the specific situation. The more completely the accidental form reflects necessity, the greater the success of the combat' (p.117). On the other hand, combat may proceed more fortuitously if the troops do not know the main direction of development of the whole military campaign, and thus events develop independently of their will.

[35] Grudinin, 1971, Chap. VIII. Grigorenko, et al., write that in each real situation one has to do with the interaction of many laws; the action of any one of them may be examined only in the process of analysis when one also takes into account the influence of the others which can either intensify the given action or hinder and weaken it (p.35).

[36] Grundinin, ibid.; Savkin, 1972; Tyushkevich, 1975.

[37] Tyushkevich, 1975, describes in detail various sources and manifestations of accidental factors and analyses their place in the general 'necessary' tendency governing the military operations; he concludes that 'each accidental factor (event) is included in the system of factors of armed struggle and conditions (sic) its course and outcome' (pp.238 ff., p.256).

[38] Occasionally, some classifications of contingencies in war are presented. In one approach they are divided into external and internal contingencies. The former include the individual actions of commanders and soldiers which are fortuitous although they constitute a link in the necessary process resulting from the multitude of such individual actions; the external contingencies are exemplified by natural and environmental conditions, for instance good or bad weather, favourable or unfavourable terrain, etc. Another division distinguishes between the so-called statistical and non-statistical contingencies. The former spring from the individual characteristics of politicians and commanders who by their decisions affect the general course of events, and may accelerate or slow it down; statistical contingencies occur repeatedly and, as something average and recurring, may finally merge into a new necessity.

[39] Grudinin, the main theme of the Chap. VIII.4 ('Rol'sub'ektivnogo factora v neitralizatsii neblagopriyatnykh i ispolzovanii blagopriyatnykh sluchainostei'). In a similar vein, he discusses the problem of the relationship between spontaneity and consciousness and emphasises that, in spite of the frequency of spontaneous processes in war, the latter is a carefully-planned activity, and the spontaneity must be counteracted (pp.253-256).

[40] The close interaction of necessity and fortuity in war is often explained as stemming from the nature of twin categories. It seems, however, that in military studies the explanation, which is given in a very general and simplified form, tends to obliterate the boundary between these distinct categories.

[41] Respectively, Marxism-Leninism on War and Army, p.312, Grudinin, 1971, p.246, Savkin, 1972, p.57. Tyushkevich defines dynamic laws as essential and necessary ties between the relatively autonomous phenomena and processes which dominate over all others; fortuity does not play here any significant role (p.236).

[42] Dynamic laws reflect essential, necessary and stable ties which determine the course of each combat and operation. Statistical laws represent tendencies which can be observed only in a great number of operations and combats, waged over a longer period. They can be discovered through the analysis of many similar ('odnotypical') phenomena, facts and events (Grudinin, 1971, p.246). Statistical laws determine the behaviour of collectives, and their action constitutes a multitude of individual movements. They are the result of the regular repetition of a multitude of mass homogeneous phenomena. The behaviour of an individual, or the course of a single process, can be predicted only with some probability (Savkin, 1972, pp.57-59).

[43] Grudinin, 1971, p.246. In his view, no events are subordinated solely to dynamic or statistical laws.

[44] Marksism-leninism o voine i armii, 1968, pp.360-364; Krupnov, 1964, p.92; Sushko, pp.49-50.

[45] Marksizm-leninizm o voine i armii, 1968, p.361. An interesting proposal to relegate a part of the laws of armed struggle to a new type of laws, called 'regostatistical laws' was presented by Savkin, 1972. These should be statistical laws, whose conditions of action are subject to human control to a certain extent (pp.60-61).

[46] Tyushkevich, 1975. 'Laws and principles of armed struggle, as well as other social laws, are of a statistical and not dynamic character' (Krupnov, 1964, p.92). Voina i armiya, p.149.

[47] Marksizm-leninizm o voine i armii, ibidem; Sushko, ibid.; Krupnov, 1964.

[48] 'Therefore the phenomena and processes of armed struggle are characterised by some intermediary, resultant dimensions, and deviations from them are simply accidents, reflecting necessity' (Tyushkevich, pp.120-129).

[49] Comp. Savkin, 1972, p.61.

[50] 'The change in the character of socio-economic and political contradictions in the antagonistic society, of the sources and conditions of war, means and methods of armed struggle, inevitably causes changes in the laws of war' (Sovetskaya Voennaya Entsiklopediya, Vol. 3, Moscow 1977, p. 378). It is also pointed out that laws of war change with the change in the correlation of world forces, since victory depends on the international ties which the opposing parties can exploit.

[51] Laws of war have a historical character. As conditions change, certain laws emerge, others disappear. The scope of the action of some of them increases, of others decreases. As the impact of the factors of war changes, the form of the manifestation of the laws changes, they change their content depend-

ing on the character of wars and of the historical epoch' (Sovetskaya Voennaya Entsiklopediya, ibid.). Cf. Voina i armiya, Chap. VIII.3.

[52] Stalin in his famous thesis on the five permanently-acting factors determining the course and outcome of war, stressed that, in spite of the then unfavourable correlation of forces, the Soviet Union would win since it was superior in the potential correlation which it could and would create during the war.

[53] For instance, Wassily Leontief, 'Theoretical Assumptions and Non-observed Facts', *American Economic Review*, March 1971.

[54] Alfred O. Hirschman, A Bias for Hope, Yale University, New Haven, 1971.

[55] Karl R. Popper, Objective Knowledge. An Evolutionary Approach, Clarendon Press, 1972, esp. 'Of Clouds and Clocks: An Approach to the Problem of Rationality and the Freedom of Man'. Gabriel A. Almond, Stephen J. Genco, 'Clouds, Clocks, and the Study of Politics', *World Politics*, July 1977.

[56] 'K voprosu o kharaktere zakonov voennoi nauki', *Voennaya Mysl'*. 1953:9.

[57] Voennaya strategiya, 3rd ed. 1968, p.17. Cf. Popov, 1964, pp.103-4. However, the acceptance of the fact that laws operate also on the side of the adversary loses much of its value since Soviet scholars, as before, state that only the Soviet state and its army can fully exploit the possibilities which the laws of war create. In other words, the laws act on both sides by creating possibilities (opportunities); however, only one side can fully exploit them.

[58] This seems logical. It is difficult to be certain of the final outcome if there exists only a probability of the given course of events. In the terms used by some Western scholars, while the outcome of war, armed struggle, or battle have a deductive-nomological explanation, their course has an inductive-probabilistic one.

[59] The rescue is an alleged one. On the one hand, the absence of an effect expected from the action of a given law may be explained by the action of other laws which also operate in the given situation. On the other hand, if an expected effect does happen, we cannot also assert with scientific certainty that it has not been produced by the action of other laws or factors. Thus, the assertion that the simultaneous action of many laws may paralyse the action of one of them also makes the testing of laws very difficult. One cannot refute them, but this does not mean that they can be reliably confirmed.

Part II

The System

3 The system of laws

In recent years Soviet scholars have been mainly concerned to establish a standard set of laws of war encompassing all the phenomena and processes of war studied by military theory. They have aimed at creating a system of law subdivided into categories and groups.[1] The scope of such a system and the criteria for its classification are here the crucial questions studied.

Bases of the classification

Scope

In war a multitude of laws, from the most general to the most specific, operate; laws of war proper, i.e. laws of using armed violence for attaining political goals are only one kind of them. In the Soviet view, the phenomena and processes of war, like all phenomena in nature and society, are governed by the laws of materialistic dialectics; general sociological laws operate since war has its place in the mechanism of social development; likewise laws concerning human activity - psychological, biological, sociological - since men are the actors in war; and laws covering physical phenomena since men fight with weapons and military equipment. Theoretically, all these laws could be included in the scope of military theory, but this is hardly feasible and is unnecessary anyway, since they are dealt with by other sciences.[2]

The problem of scope can also be seen from another angle. Apart from the actual fighting there are other fronts in war: political, economic, ideological, etc. These too could all be included in the study in question, but again it is unnecessary for the same reasons.

Thus, in the prevailing Soviet view, laws covering war encompass its general conduct (the so-called general laws of war), and warfare proper (the so-called laws of armed struggle). All other laws are said to be taken into account when the mechanism of the action of laws of war is discussed. However, the problem of the scope has not been resolved with the above delimitation: another question has caused doubts and disagreements — namely, whether the laws of the origin of war should be included in military theory and in the system of laws of war?

Two main alternatives have been proposed. In one view, laws of the origin of war and laws of the conduct of war (or simply laws of war) constitute two quite different categories, and should not be united in one system of laws. They are related to the two different states of society, peace and war, and should be studied by two different disciplines.[3] Thus, in some studies, laws of war — the action of which begins when a war starts — are called laws of war proper.[4]

In the other interpretation, laws of the origin of war are an inherent part of laws of war as a whole. The problems of why and how a war breaks out, it is said cannot be separated from the questions of who wages war and for what aims.[5]

Some emphasise that individual wars, their origins, cause and termination constitute a single process, and it would be artificial to separate laws concerning the interrelated stages of that process. Parenthetically, the problem of the laws concerning the consequences of war has never been raised, although it seems to be in a sense a counterpart of the problem of the laws of the origin of war in the above context. Since the approach which includes laws of the origin of war in the system now seems to dominate in Soviet theory,[6] I shall attempt to analyse this in the following.

The basic division

Two categories of laws of war are usually discussed and presented as basic: general laws of war[7] and laws of armed struggle.[8] Both will be analysed below in detail; here only a preliminary description is given. The former concern the essence of war as an instrument of policy and its dependence on politics, economics, and other social activities and factors. The latter operate as the external and internal ties and relationships in armed struggle, the core of war.

In a usually adopted approach, the two kinds of laws are clearly differentiated. The origin of war aside, the essence and conduct of war as a whole on the one hand, and fighting, on the other, are two different aggregates of social activities, studied by different disciplines of science. The analysis of war as a sociopolitical phenomenon, as a part of the whole activity of state, nation, or class should be separated from the study of the laws of successful fighting. The former are dealt with by the teaching on war and army, the latter by military science.

This approach, though predominant, is not the only one. There are conceptual presentations in which the difference is negated or assessed as very relative, and in some studies both categories are combined in one.[9] These and other deviations from the prevailing view will be discussed in Chap. 8. Nevertheless, for the sake of analysis, I have taken this basic division as a working criterion.

The criteria for groups

The principal division into two categories according to the difference between war as a whole and armed struggle, which seems to be the prevailing one, is not a precisely-formulated criterion, however, which could serve as a basis for a scientific typology. It does not establish whether there is a difference between the laws governing political and military activities in war and if there is, the nature of it: whether it is a difference between the whole and its part, and whether laws classified in these different categories can be treated as of the same order (e.g. the same degree of generality) or not. Taking the separate treatment of these two categories as a basis for the working classification, one should mention that the lack of definite criteria for such a distinction cannot fail to result in confusion and inconsistencies in the body of laws presented. This will be discussed in Chap. 8, following a review of the laws.

There have been other proposals as to the basic division. In one approach the degree of generality seems to be the criterion: laws are divided into the laws of all wars in all times, and laws of contemporary wars.[10] In another view, which is more implied in some considerations than directly presented, the classification could be constructed according to the different types of war i.e. with laws concerning particular types of war as the classes. A variant distinguishes between the laws of wars fought by the so-called imperialist states and those waged in defence of the socialist states.[11]

A unique proposal is the division of laws according to their character: into genesis laws (the origin of war), structural-functional laws (ties between phenomena and objects of armed struggle), and laws of the development of armed struggle. However, the authors try to combine such a division with the division into laws of the first and second order i.e. general laws of war and internal laws of armed struggle.[12]

While interesting, the above proposals have not been followed by perspicuous classifications. The main difficulty seems to be that some laws would be common to all or a few of the groups e.g. in a classification based on the types of war.[13]

The difference between laws concerning the character of war (or armed struggle) and those concerning its course and outcome is used as another criterion for creating a set of groups of laws which is most frequently presented, and can be regarded as constituting a standard classification.

Thus we have laws asserting the dependence of the character of war on policy, and the dependence of the course and outcome of war on correlation of forces; we also read about the dependence of the character of armed struggle (i.e. of military art) on external factors, and the dependence of the course and outcome of military operations on external or internal factors.

Naturally, 'to base' is not the same as consciously to apply a scientific criterion. Here it is more an attempt to organise the laws which have hitherto been put forward - i.e. which have already been formulated - into some set of groups, taking as the basis obvious differences such as that between laws of war as a whole and laws of fighting, or between military art and the course and outcome of particular military operations. This leaves out of account many conceivable laws and groups of laws, a shortcoming which will be discussed after a review of the existing classification in the final part of our study.

The above-mentioned proposal to divide laws according to their character (laws of genesis, of structure and function and of development) was an attempt to create genuine scientific criteria for the system but it has not resulted in a more or less complete classification; it has been replaced by examples. Gaps in this quasi-classification are numerous.

The standard classification

We take as the working classification the following set of groups of laws, which can be regarded as standard:[14]

1 Laws expressing the dependence of the origin of wars, and of their aims, upon economic and political conditions (or in another wording, simply laws of the origin of wars).

2 Laws of the dependence of the character of war upon policy.

3 Laws of the dependence of the course and outcome of war on the correlation of forces of warring parties (or simply laws of the course and outcome of wars).[15]

4 Laws of the dependence of the methods of armed struggle on the mode of production and level of productive forces, on the scientific and technical progress and the spiritual forces of society (laws of military art).

5 Laws expressing the ties and relationships between phenomena and processes of armed struggle (or internal laws of armed struggle, or laws of armed struggle).[16]

Scholars who do not classify laws of the origin of war with laws of war naturally omit the first group from the classification.

This classification is frequently complemented by the indication that the groups belong to the two main categories described above. The usual approach is that the first three groups are called general laws of war and the latter two laws of armed struggle. However, some scholars point out that the third and fourth group are simultaneously general laws of war and laws of armed struggle. In such a case, laws of the fifth group are called laws of armed struggle proper.[17]

Further differentiations and groups under formation

In some presentations, the fifth group is divided into two groups, or simply replaced by them:

5a Laws of the dependence of the course and outcome of armed struggle upon external factors (e.g., correlation of forces of fighting troops).

5b Internal laws of armed struggle.

Two new groups seem to be under formation. This tendency can be observed in recently presented classifications and studies, and it concerns problems which are essential to any conceptual analysis of a possible future war. The first are the laws of the creation of military power.[18] In one presentation the following laws are included:

1 Laws of the dependence of military power on economic forces and capabilities.

2 Laws of its dependence on the character of the economic system.

3 Laws of its dependence on the moral and political forces and capabilities.

Another scholar notes the existence of objective laws of the dependence of a country's military power on the complex of the economic, moral-political, techno-scientific and military factors and the degree of their activity.[19] The term 'military power' has at the same time been introduced in some studies to the description of the third group: the laws of the dependence of war on the correlation of forces have been re-named laws of the dependence of war on the correlation of the military power of warring states (or coalitions). In the corresponding laws of armed struggle, the expression 'correlation of forces' has been replaced by the 'correlation of combat power'.

The other addition is the group of laws concerning the dependence of the course and outcome of war on the preparedness and readiness for it. That the formulation of such laws is in progress can be gathered from the many comments which have recently been made on the extreme importance of preparation and readiness for a nuclear war. Since from the very outset of war the principal military operations will be initiated by all kinds of armed forces, a complete preparation for them in peacetime is claimed to be necessary, and it is emphasised that a firm and continuous strategic control of troops and their groupings in the predicted future theatres of military operations should be maintained even in peacetime. Thus a high degree of readiness of war is posited as the main condition of victory.[20]

Search for the basic law of war

In their attempts to create a system of laws, Soviet researchers have also sought the so-called basic law of war. Such a law, they say, if it exists, must differ from all other laws by its direct relation to the essence of war: it must express what is basic in war, its defining characteristics. By expressing the ties and relationships between its main aspects, it would underlie all other laws[21] except those of the origin of wars. Thus, in a sense, such a law can be viewed as constituting a special category, of which it is the only representative. Proposals to establish a number of such laws - which will be mentioned below - would seem to be self-contradictory.

This problem was first raised after Stalin's death. In the years following World War II, the study of war was dominated by the thesis on the five permanently operating factors that determine the course and outcome of any war. This was formulated by Stalin (in Order No. 55, 23 February, 1942). Although it only re-stated old assertions, it was presented as of paramount importance - which was not surprising, considering the extraordinary position of its author.

The factors mentioned were as follows: the stability of the rear, the morale of the army, the number and quality of divisions, the armament of the army and the organisational ability of the army commanders. During the war it became the guiding policy to concentrate efforts on the above factors and scientists were ordered to focus their research on them (or rather to describe them in detail). This thesis was considered until Stalin's death the basic law of war. After 1953, however, it began to be called in question and even contested; the first proposals to present a genuine basic law of war were put forward, and the first formulations of such laws presented.

Two main proposals and their variants

Talenskii, in 1953,[22] was the first to call for a revival of military science and a search for objective laws of war. He was also the first to attempt to formulate the basic law of war: 'Victory in contemporary war is to be achieved by the decisive defeat of the enemy in the course of armed conflict, through the employment of successive blows accumulating in force, on the basis of superiority in the permanently operating factors which determine the outcome of war, and on the basis of the comprehensive exploitation of economic, moral, political, and military potentialities in their unity and interaction'.

Talenskii, as we see, took the position that the conditions of victory should constitute the essence of the basic law of war, and emphasised the importance of armed struggle as the essence of war, the successful conduct of which is the most important of the conditions. He also preserved in an altered form the idea of the primary importance of the permanently operating factors.

The very idea of a basic law of war and its proposed wording were both sharply criticised. Some opponents contended that no basic law existed and the social laws discovered by historical materialism were sufficient to explain all phenomena of war. The critics of the wording took issue with it from two perspectives.

Firstly, the adherents of the then still accepted thesis concerning five permanently-acting factors cautioned against the tendency to replace it by a new law. The formula, they said, expressed the main dependences of war, and it did so in clear and concise terms. Secondly, those who agreed on the desirability of some new formula argued that the basic law should express the dependence of armed struggle on policy. Some pointed out that since war was not confined to armed struggle and its essence was the political instrumentality of war, the basic law ought to express both sides of war, the political aims and the military struggle, and their interrelationship.

The two developments

The subsequent debates developed in the two directions mentioned above. The thesis on the five permanently-acting factors was many times modified and finally became the law of the dependence of the course and outcome of war on the correlation of forces of the warring sides (see Chap. 4). Some scholars called just this formula the basic law of war.

The critics who accused Talenskii of being so obsessed by armed struggle as to forget the essence of war as a political instrument proposed the dependence of war on policy as the basic law. As an example, one of the first proposals of this kind can be cited: 'The political content of war has a decisive influence on the general character of armed struggle, on the methods and forms of its conduct and on the employment of particular types of weapons. In other words, the political content of war determines the character of the armed violence in it'.[23] The contention that the relation between the political content and armed struggle is the basic law was supported by another contention that the action of this law permeates all the processes of armed struggle; all other laws of war were considered to be rooted in this law. In a later study this scholar asserted that his formula meets all criteria for a basic law of war: it is the closest one to the very nature of war; all other laws derive from it; and it is manifested in all phenomena of war from strategic operations to the actions of an individual soldier.[24] In a comprehensive study on the methodology of military affairs, the same formula is repeated and presented as reflecting the basic relation in war, which distinguishes it from all other laws.[25]

Two other proposals involve a combination of two laws. In one interpretation, this is accomplished in the form of a pair of basic laws complementing each other.[26] The scholars refer to Lenin who formulated two main laws of war, resembling the proposed pair - namely, the law of the dependence of war on policy and the law of the dependence of victory or defeat in war on the relationship of the military power of warring parties.

In another approach the two laws have been united in one formula[27] e.g. as follows: 'The political content of war and the correlation of forces decisively influence the origin of war, its character, its course and its outcome'.[28]

The above formula has recently been somewhat modified, and one sometimes reads of the 'law of the unity of the determining influence of political goals and of the correlation of forces of warring sides'.[29] This tells us more than a simple sum of the two component laws since it asserts the interaction and interdependence of both goals and correlation of forces. Goals depend on the correlation of forces, and both change in the same direction and affect war in the same direction, since both depend on the character of the socio-political system.

Here one additional but important aspect of the basic law of war enters the picture. It is basic not only because it manifests itself in all other laws of war and in all phenomena and processes of war, but also because it is tied up with the laws of the functioning and development of the warring social systems. The more progressive the socio-political formation, the more just are the aims of war and the more favourable the correlation of forces. For each warring side the action of the basic law of war corresponds to the action of the laws governing the given socio-political system. Thus the basic law of war links the complex of laws of war to the more general complex of sociological laws governing the warring socio-political systems.[30]

Other concepts

Other very different concepts have also been put forward. In one approach, three fundamental laws of war, all of them relating the basic law to the correlation of forces, are formulated: the law of the dependence of the course and out-

53

come of war on the correlation of military capabilities of the adversaries; the law of the dependence of the course and outcome of war on the correlation of the military - economic capabilities of the warring sides; and an analogic law of the dependence on the correlation of moral-political capabilities.[31]

In another approach, the basic law encompasses only contemporary wars. 'Wars are waged by peoples' and 'war depends on the economic-political organisation of society' may be cited as examples.[32]

Criticism

Traditionally, objections have been levelled against the assumption that a basic law of war exists. This criticism has gradually and tacitly been softened, however, since almost every military writer is eager to present his own formula. Criticism, therefore, has come to focus on the two above-mentioned laws.

The main objections against the proposition that the dependence of armed struggle on policy is the basic law of war are the following.[33]

1 Victory is determined primarily by the correlation of available military, military-economic, moral-political, and psychological forces and capabilities, which in the final analysis are rooted in the mode of production and its level.

2 Methods and forms of armed struggle depend not only on policy, but also on economics - on economic conditions as a whole, including the level of development.

3 The morale of the troops is determined not only by the political content of war, but also by the following complex of factors: the country's socio-political system in which policy is rooted, the people's moral-political condition, the quantity and quality of weapons at their disposal, the course of armed conflict, the level of propaganda work in the armed forces and so on.

4 The conduct of particular operations, especially the decisions taken by commanders, are based on military not political considerations.

The conclusion follows that the dependence of armed struggle on policy is not the most general dependence characteristic of all phenomena of war, nor does it permeate all ties and dependences in war.[34]

Critics of the view that the basic law of war asserts the dependence of the course and outcome of war on the correlation of forces raise two objections: the law is not related to the nature of war - i.e. to the relationship between policy and armed struggle, and it lessens the importance of the course of military operations; their effective conduct is, however, the main condition of victory.

Summing up: six views

To review the discussion briefly, six views may be distinguished.

1 The character of the relations between policy and armed struggle constitutes the basic law of war.

2 The dependence of the course and outcome of war on the correlation of

forces is such a law.

3 The above-mentioned laws are a pair of basic laws.

4 The same laws are treated as one law in a combined formula.

5 Other laws are presented as basic.

6 There is no basic law, or we have not hitherto found it.

It seems to me that the debate on the basic law of war has not been waged purely for theoretical reasons. Scholars who assumed the existence of a basic law of war perhaps wished to emphasise the independent and scientific character of military theory or in particular of military science. The existence of a basic law of war has been regarded by some scholars as a reaffirmation of the scientific status of military theory; it was always a part of the Soviet creed of science that each part of human activity is governed by one basic law from which all other derive. Perhaps there was also the underlying idea that military theory would appear more independent if it had a basic law of its own.

In any case, the dependence of war on policy *is* the law generally regarded as the basic one, even if there is no universal agreement on this, and even if it is sometimes combined with the law of the correlation of forces. The decisive criterion is said to be that it comes closest to the very essence of war as an instrument of policy.

Notes

[1] The existence of such a system of laws has often been asserted: '. . . war is one of the most complex phenomena in the life of society. This gives ground to speak about the existence of whole system of laws of war. In this system it is possible to isolate several groups of laws' (Metodologicheskie problemy, Ch.XIV); the whole chapter is devoted to an attempt to construct such a system. 'It is well known that war is governed by a system of laws' (Zemskov, 1972, p.15). Cf. Grigorenko et al., 1959; Metodologiya voennogo poznaniya, 1977; I. Zavyalov, 'Die Dialektik des Krieges und die Militärdoktrin', Militärwesen, 1976:1.

[2] All these problems have recently been discussed in a larger framework, including the scope and content of military theory (in particular, of military science) as distinct from other sciences that also deal with war. The prevailing view seems to be that which focuses the so-called teaching on war and army on the socio-political analysis of war and armed forces, on their role and use as instruments of policy and directs military science towards the problems of preparing and waging armed struggle. Both disciplines, together with military doctrine, constitute military theory. The latter should utilise the achievements of other disciplines analysing war, such as political economy and the theory of socialist revolution, but not replace them in this respect.

[3] V. Morozov, S. Tyushkevich, 'O sisteme zakonov voennoi nauki i printsipov voennogo iskusstva', *Voennaya Mysl*, 1967:3; cf. by the same authors: 'Ob'

ektivnye prava voiny i ikh otrazhenie v sovetskoi voennoi nauke', *Voennaya Mysl'*, 1971-5; 'war is governed by laws different from laws of peace. They constitute a system of laws of war' (Popov, 1964, p.44). Some scholars exclude laws of the genesis of war from the system of laws of war simply by not mentioning them in the classifications which they present. Savkin, for instance, reduces all (general) laws of war to four laws of its dependence on respective groups of factors (see note 2 in Ch.IV).

[4] Popov, 1964, p.44.

[5] Tyushkevich, 1975, presents war, from its origin to outcome, as such a unified process. In 1974 he wrote that the Marxist-Leninist teaching on war and army solved 'the philosophical-sociological problems of the origin, course and outcome of wars' (p.7). He elaborates this problem in more detail in 'Voina i armiya', Ch.VIII. Grudinin writes that in military affairs the dialectical 'principle of development' means to examine war in the whole process of its genesis, development, and termination (the same is related to each military operation) (1971, p.21). Dmitriev states that the most general problems concerning war and the army studied by historical materialism include the general sociological laws of the genesis and development of war, army and military affairs as historical, socio-political phenomena proper to all class-antagonistic structures (formatsii) (1975, p.11). Milovidov writes that there exist objective laws of the origin, course and outcome of wars, and objective laws (regularities) of the development of methods of armed struggle (1974, p.12). I. Zavyalov, when characterising the analysis of the 'dialectics of war' as one of the basic aims of military theory, states that the main problems include firstly, the emergence of war, its nature and content, and the laws of its historical genesis and development and, secondly, the causes and conditions of the origin of individual wars ('Die Dialektik des Krieges und die Militärdoktrin', loc. cit, p.12).

The two different views may perhaps be related to the two dimensions of war: war as politics and war as warfare. Laws which express the action of the generic element of war, politics, concern both politics preceding a war and carried out during it. Laws expressing the use of armed violence are limited to the time armed struggle is waged.

[6] As usually, there is also a compromise position which, on the one hand, assigns to historical materialism the study of the most general problems of war (and army), with the laws of the genesis and development of war (and army) and their relationship with policy and the totality of social factors but, on the other hand, regards these problems and respective laws as covered by the so-called teaching on war and army, the latter being considered part of a military theory. In other words, the teaching on war and army is considered to constitute an intermediate discipline, or a link between dialectical and historical materialism and military theory, belonging to both of them (Marxism-Leninism on War and Army, p.300). Some scholars, although they insist that laws concerning the socio-political essence of war are studied by historical materialism, write about the teaching on war and army, which deals with them, as being simultaneously a

part of historical materialism and military theory (Milovidov, 1974; cf. Kozlov, 1971).

[7] 'Laws of war are the essential, necessary and stable ties or relationships of phenomena and processes of war; ties and relationships among peoples and armies of countries participating in war and their governments, policies and goals of war; ties and relationships between war, the course of armed conflict, and state of the rear of states and their economic, moral-political, and military potentials' (Savkin, 1972, p.55). Cf. Zavizion, 1973; Metodologicheskie problemy, Chap. XIV.

[8] Laws of armed struggle include laws expressing the dependence of the forms and methods of warfare on external factors, and laws expressing the ties and relationships among phenomena and processes of military operations themselves, manifested on battlefields (Azovtsev, 1971, p.26; Zemskov, 1972; Savkin, 1972). Savkin calls them 'laws of armed conflict'. Terms like 'laws of armed combat', 'laws of warfare' and the like are also used.

[9] Kozlov, 1971; Milovidov, 1974.

[10] Tyushkevich, 1975.

[11] Another typology can be mentioned: it distinguishes between the general laws of war, laws of war of the contemporary epoch, laws of the aggressive wars waged by the imperialist states, and laws of wars fought in defence of the socialist states (after Tyushkevich, 1975).

[12] Morozov, Tyushkevich, 1967, 1971. Tyushkevich, 1975, writes that structural-functional laws regulate the internal relationships between the elements of the combined power of the fighting parties, the interaction of the aims of war with the means applied, the interaction between the adversaries, etc.

A special group is here included, the so-called laws of correspondence: the law of the correspondence of the actions of various troops fighting for the attainment of common ends; the law of the correspondence of military operations according to their levels (tactical operations correspond to the operational ones, the latter to the strategic ones, and these to the general conduct of war); the laws of the correspondence of the methods of fighting to the aims of the operations, etc. These groups also encompass laws which determine the methods of warfare and the effectiveness of military operations. In the collective study 'Voina i armiya' Tyushkevich presents a proposal of a typology of laws of war based on a division into genesis laws, structural-functional laws, and laws of development (Chap. VIII).

[13] One should also note the following typology, based on the dependence of war on various external and internal factors: (1) laws of the dependence of the genesis of war and its political content on the political and economic conditions; (2) laws of the dependence of war on the correlation of forces; (3) laws of the dependence of the course and outcome of armed struggle on the methods of military operations; (4) laws of the dependence of the development and change of methods of military operations on the material basis (after Tyushkevich, 1975).

[14] Krupnov, 1963, p.50; Marksizm-Leninizm o voine i armii, 1968, p.358.

[15] Grudinin calls them 'laws determining the course and outcome of war' and includes four items: the law of the dependence of the course and outcome of war on (1) the correlation of the economic power of warring states, (2) the correlation of the moral-political forces of warring sides, (3) policy, (4) correlation of armed forces actively participating in war (1971, p.90).

[16] Popov, 1964, pp.44-45; Rybkin, 1965, in a review of this book by Popov, in which he agreed with author's classification; Metodologicheskie problemy, p.320.

[17] Metodologicheskie problemy, p.320.

[18] Morozov, 1974, pp.3-4. He uses the term 'military might' (the Russian term 'voennaya moshch'), however in this study the term 'military power' as commonly used in political-military writings in the West will be applied. A. A. Grechko who in his pamphlet on the Soviet Armed Forces, 1971, postulated a complex of measures of increasing Soviet military power, asserted that 'the dependence of the military power of a state on the level of its economic and social development was formulated by K. Marx and F. Engels' and interpreted in this 'modernised' way the well-known Engels' proposition about the dependence of the organisation of armies and military art on material conditions.

[19] Prokop'ev, 1965, p.212, simply notes the operation of these laws. He places them in the following context: 'laws of the dependence of a country's military power and of the course and outcome of war', and then describes only the latter dependence (pp.212 ff.).

[20] Nauchno-tekhnicheskii progress, Ch.V and others; the military-technical revolution 'enriches the content of one of the most important laws of warfare, according to which the moral-political state of the civilian population and army determines not only the course and outcome of war but also the degree of preparedness for it' (Filosofskoe nasledie, p.259).

[21] Metodologichskie problemy, pp.324-5. The basic law . . . 'stands nearer than others to the essence of this or that phenomenon of nature and society, expresses it frankly (priamo) and directly'. The basic law of war 'expresses the ties and relations between its significant aspects - political content and armed violence' (ibid.).

[22] Talenskii, 1953.

[23] Popov, 1964, p.53. Rybkin, 1965, agreed with this formula. A formula connecting war with the economic system through policy was earlier presented: 'War . . . is a continuation of the politics of definite classes and states by violent means; the direction of policy is in the final analysis conditioned by the economic system of society. This is the basic law of the origin and essence of each war' (Marksizm-Leninizm o voine i armii, 3rd ed., 1962, p.53). This formula of a 'law' was criticised by Popov as being identical with the definition of war (1964).

[24] Popov, 1969, quotes Stalin's view of the basic criteria for a fundamental law.

[25] Metodologicheskie problemy, p.325. 'The relation between the political content and armed violence in war lies at the basis of all other ties and relations

both of war as a whole and of armed struggle. Therefore the basic law of war, permeating the action of all its other laws, is also the basic law of armed struggle' (p.326).

[26] Marksizm-Leninizm o voine i armii, 1968, p.366. The authors present two basic laws of Soviet military science. The law of the correlation of forces includes a number of 'tendencies . . . which can be considered laws in themselves' ('imeyushchikh silu zakonov') - namely, the laws of the course and outcome of war (the dependence of war on the correlation of military, economic, scientific, and moral-political forces of the belligerents).

[27] Filosofskoe nasledie, pp.137-9. The two above mentioned laws are presented as general and universal by Skirdo, 1970, pp.97-9.

[28] Morozov, Tyushkevich, 1971; Tyushkevich, 1975, writes: 'The law of the unity of the determining influence of the political goals and of the correlation of forces of warring sides can be regarded as the basic law of war, expressing its nature. It stresses the fact that war is waged by opposing sides for opposing goals, but these goals are founded on a certain correlation of forces as on their objective basis, that the action of laws of war is conditioned by two basic factors: by the political and military goals and by the correlation of material and spiritual forces at any given moment' (p.231).

[29] Tyushkevich, 1975.

[30] Ibid.

[31] Trifonenkov, 1962.

[32] Baz', 1958; Kozlov, 1961, pp.15-16. A. Strokov writes about the 'basic law of the imperialist epoch'. This states that 'wars are now conducted by peoples, by mass armies and millions of people in the rear'; and that 'the will to victory as manifested by the popular masses is of decisive importance' (V.I. Lenin i Sovetskaya Voennaya Nauka, in: Marksizm-leninizm o voine i armii, Voenidat, 1956, p.60). A proposal to consider the dependence of the outcome of war on the economic-political organisation of society the basic law of war was also made.

[33] Savkin, 1972, Ch.2.

[34] Ibid. p.81. It seems that, in consequence, this writer denies the existence of any basic law of war. Note that Savkin takes an extreme position by stressing that the political goals of war are fundamentally determined by production relationships (p.80).

4   General laws of war

Classification

To begin with the first main category of laws - those concerning war as a whole - neither a standard classification, nor subdivisions within particular groups have been presented. Sets of laws are occasionally listed, at times as informal proposals;[1] definitions and descriptions of what is called 'the teaching on war and army' only point out law-like regularities which have to be investigated.[2] Thus the set of laws and groups of laws which will here be outlined, as well as the subdivisions within the groups, are my own suggestion.

The law-like statements which will be taken into consideration include: (a) Statements called 'laws' by Soviet scholars, and analysed as such by them, e.g. laws of the dependence of the course and outcome of war on various external factors (b) Among them laws presented in a very general form only, such as the law of the dependence of the character of war on the political system. (c) Statements which, although not usually termed laws, should have the status of a law in Soviet teaching, since they correspond to the definition of a law of war, and are also of the same order as law-like statements concerning similar ties and relationships. For instance, the causes of national-liberation wars, like the causes of other type of wars are seemingly regarded as laws, although they are only occasionally termed laws by individual scholars. (d) In single cases I have considered statements which have not yet been formulated in a law-like fashion, but which will supposedly be called laws sooner or later since they are foreseen in the framework of Soviet military theory. Laws concerning the origin of individual instances of war are an example.

In other words, the set of general laws of war and their classification, which will be discussed here, should be viewed as deriving from various Soviet publications and lists of laws,[3] complemented by laws in *statu nascendi* or even in *statu desirandi*.

On the basis of the relatively standard classification of laws of war (see Chap. 3), with division of the second group into two parts, the general laws of war may be classified and reviewed as follows:

1   Laws of the origin of wars.[4]
2   Laws concerning the dependence of the character and conduct of war on policy.
3   Laws expressing the dependence of the course and outcome of war on the correlation of the economic, moral-political, techno-scientific and strictly military potentials of the warring sides.

The reasons for subdividing the second group of the standard set are that: (a) the laws of the two new groups seem to have different scientific origins - the second group is more a logical derivation from the determining characteristics of war (see below), while the third one has much more empirical roots - and also (b) they are actually discussed separately in Soviet writing.

Apart from these three groups, one law - that concerning the role of popular masses in war - occupies a special place, beyond all the above groups, and perhaps can be regarded as a group in itself. It will be described in the last section. And, finally, two new groups which seem to be in course of formation should be mentioned. Their provisional names are 'laws of the creation of military power',[5] and 'laws of the dependence of the course and outcome of war upon preparedness for it'.

Laws of the genesis of wars

This is the least elaborated group in the Soviet system of laws of war. The following reasons may be suggested. Laws included here were not traditionally regarded as laws in Soviet theory. They were termed 'causes of wars' and described in innumerable writings on historical materialism, and analyses of imperialism, revolution and contemporary international and civil wars without emphasising their law-like character or status.

Even nowadays Soviet students of international relations, who devote increasing attention to the analysis of conflicts and wars, and contribute more than military scholars to the study of the origin of wars, generally use the concept of causes of war rather than laws, and propose taxonomies of such causes rather than sets of groups of laws. Military scholars only recently have begun to restate the formulae in the form of laws. However, they have not managed to do any thorough study of these problems, nor have they added anything to the main ideas on the origin of wars (presented by Marxist-Leninist theorists of social development chiefly in their analysis of the two world wars), by an assessment of the military conflicts of our days.

An additional factor, mentioned above, may be that these laws have not until recently been regarded as an integral part of the set of laws of war and therefore have not been given due attention in military theory.[6]

The threefold causality

No classification of laws of the genesis of wars has been proposed. It can, however, be inferred from the analysis of the Soviet concept of the nature of war in which the problem of causality has been included. In this concept, the objective laws of the origin of wars have been conceived of as causal ones. Wars are begun in consequence of certain conditions and policies and in pursuit of certain aims by the states (classes, nations) which unleash or enter war: aims or motives are an aspect of the conditions and policies and thus also causes.[7] In other words, states, classes and nations undertake military action *in consequence* of the development of the given situation and political interaction *in order* to achieve desired gains.

Aims, as the second aspect of causality, are given special attention in the Soviet military literature. Social phenomena and processes are conditioned by conscious aims: men pursue definite aims on the basis of cognition of their interests and of the laws of social development. War is perhaps one of the most striking examples: the political aims of war are an inherent part of its nature.[8]

It seems that each aspect of this causality has a double nature. Both the conditions and actions which lead to war, and war-aims which are the motives for starting it, constitute a unity of the immediate, direct, and of the deep, and indirect. In the first place, wars have their immediate causes and deep roots. Conditions and policies which precede the outbreak of war (i.e. certain concrete differences of current interests and conflicts concerning them) constitute the former; the class system and class struggle rooted in the contradictions inherent in the given socio-economic formation and the international system constitute the latter.

The same can be asserted concerning the motives for, or aims of, fighting. Wars are fought for certain concrete political aims, but at the same time, according to Soviet teaching, they play a role in the general course of social development which proceeds just through conflicts and wars, towards a classless society. Thus, laws of the origin of wars as presented in Soviet theory, could (or rather should) express two kinds of law-like dependences. One would be the recurring direct causation of the given type of war by a certain set of conditions and actions as well as aims; the other the determination of the outbreak of war by the general course of social development.

To put it in another way, Soviet laws of the origin of wars could present a unity of two laws in each one: the one expresses the direct causes of the incidence of wars (or direct conditions, policies leading to war, and their aims), the other their roots in the character of the given socio-economic formation and/or in the shape of the international system. (The words 'should' or 'would' are used here because the actual wording of the given laws is far from including two such dependences.)

This double causality becomes a threefold one since 'roots' in this case can mean both the roots of all wars as a socio-historical phenomenon (i.e. as the expression of class struggle in all class societies), and sources of wars in a given epoch (i.e. the expression of concrete types of class contradictions). Students of international relations and of military affairs have recently presented various taxonomies of the causes of conflicts and wars which, in spite of the different number of classes, have one common feature; they correspond to the three principal kinds of causes, which will here be termed, for the sake of brevity, roots, sources and immediate causes (the latter concerning the outbreak of the individual instances of war).[9]

The main conceptual expression of the idea of the threefold causality is perhaps the treatment of the nature of a given war as an inner combination and dialectics of features it shares with: (1) war in general; (2) other wars of its historical type; and (3) features peculiar to it alone.

In such an approach, the notion of the nature of war comprises three notions: (1) that of the nature of all wars i.e. of war as a socio-historical phenomenon and a political act; (2) of the nature of the particular type of war with which the given war is classified; and (3) of the nature of the given war (cf. J. Lider, On the Nature of War, Chap.12). This corresponds to the three kinds of causes with a descending level of generality: of all wars in history, of the given type of war and of the given instance of war. For example, each war for a socialist revolution shares some general causes with all wars in history, some more specific causes with all revolutionary wars of the workers against the bourgeoisie, and it has also individual causes.[10]

The picture is simplified and at the same time complicated by the assertion that all sources of wars in our epoch have one common basis (which can also be termed 'primary' source): the existence and policy of imperialism. Thus, to explain the causation of the war of a particular type, one should not only point out the particular type of contradiction which leads to wars of this type, but also the way this instance of war is connected (more or less directly) with imperialism.

The idea of a threefold causality is only a simplified reflection of the fact that to account for all characteristics of a single event (not to mention a process) one has to include a multitude of causes of various degrees of generality and relation to the event in question. In a law-like statement one is compelled to choose between them and to point out one or several causes regarded as decisive and recurring in the given class of events, and also corresponding to the degree of generality of this law.

Thus, statements which express laws operating in all wars in history, should refer to the roots of all wars; accordingly, laws concerning the genesis of particular types of war can mention the roots of all wars, but they should emphasise the sources of the given type (for instance, laws of the genesis of contemporary revolutionary wars - the conflict between bourgeoisie and proletariat). Laws of science concerning the causation of individual instances of war within particular types can repeat the two more general levels of causation, but ought to concentrate on the individual causes shared with other instances.

One of the conditions which a cause must fulfil to gain the status of a law is its recurrence. To discover a law means to discover causes common to all wars, or to all wars of a certain type, or all wars within a certain type, which have common characteristics and constitute a sub-class. They may have in common a specific kind of war-generating contradiction within the whole type, or a very similar mechanism for their outbreak (the escalation of a crisis, a sudden outbreak or the like, which has profound consequences for the whole course of war). If some regularities concerning essential features or ties characteristic of these wars are detected, they may be regarded as laws.

Easier said than done. Up to now, while laws concerning all wars and some types of war have been presented, no law-like generalisations concerning the immediate causes of individual instances of war within these types, nor the characteristics of the mechanism that unleashes them with a law-like regularity have been put forward (see Ch.8).

Soviet scholars perhaps tacitly accept that it is very difficult to make generalisations which would cover the immense variety of contemporary wars and include statements about individual immediate causes and mechanisms that unleash wars; they focus on laws concerning the roots of all wars and the sources of their particular types. Recently, however, more attention has been devoted to the immediate (including accidental) causes of wars, which perhaps means that some new laws are emerging.[11]

In this connection, Soviet scholars have begun to point out the difference between causes and occasions or reasons: cause generates the effect i.e. war; distinct from this, occasion or reason only accelerates the action of the cause. Thus while cause is a factor of necessity, occasion expresses fortuitousness and cannot be included in the formulae of the laws.[12]

Finally, one should mention that while attempts have been made to present a taxonomy of causes of war on different levels of generality and to explain the interrelation between them, there have been no similar attempts with regard to the laws concerning these causes. Such interrelation between laws on various levels is only implied. Describing particular wars, Soviet scholars point out that their immediate causes express a law connected with the given type of contradiction, and add that in our epoch it is always connected with the policy of imperialism and also that, for a better understanding of the causation, one must consider the politics of the exploiting classes which, law-wise, are at the root of each war.

It would be desirable, naturally, to get a more conceptual analysis of the interrelation between laws on different levels of generality as regards the dialectics of the general, particular and individual, as Soviet scholars do when presenting their approach to the nature of war.

The classification

Taking the above ideas as a criterion for a working classification within this group, the following may be suggested:

1 Laws concerning the sources and origin of wars common to all wars in all times.

2 Laws concerning the main sources of wars in particular epochs, with focus on the laws of the main sources of wars in our time.

3 Laws concerning the origin of individual instances of war within particular types. This sub-group should deal with the more specific contradictions leading to wars and the way they are unleashed.

Laws in the first sub-group, when presented as laws, are formulae derived directly from expositions of historical materialism and are regarded as the basis of the so-called teaching on war and army. They state that the internal contradictions in each antagonistic socio-economic and political formation, and the aggressive and oppressive policy of the exploiting classes, lead to internal and external wars.[13] These formulae express the most general objective laws, which are said to operate in all wars. They state that any war, regardless of who caused it and who directly started it, is rooted in the very character of the class system and is generated by the politics of the exploiting class dominating that system.

They can be treated as logically interconnected with one of the main assumptions of historical materialism, that war as a social phenomenon first occurred when class societies had emerged - in other words, with the basic assumption about the origin of war in history.

Laws in the second sub-group indicate which classes, in pursuit of which aims, are mainly responsible for the outbreak of wars in particular epochs. They are usually mentioned as an illustration of the laws assigned to the first sub-group.

Among these laws, those concerning our own epoch deserve a special attention. Here the most general law states that imperialism is the primary source of all contemporary wars, whether international or internal. The other laws, which concern types of contemporary wars - namely, inter-systemic wars, inter-capitalist wars and wars of social and national liberation, are in some degree a manifestation of the aforementioned primary law. They refer to the types of contradictions that lead to these types of contemporary wars.

To take *inter-capitalist wars*, capitalist countries in the imperialist phase of capitalist evolution, with their uneven states of development and their tendency to redivide the world in order to obtain new sources of raw materials and markets, are said to generate not only inter-capitalist wars but also inter-imperialist world wars. In *wars of liberation*, the growing exploitation of the working class is alleged to lead to *revolutionary civil wars*, and the suppression of democratic movement to *democratic civil wars*. The growing antagonism between the colonial powers and their colonies and dependent countries, generates *wars of national liberation*, and the tendency to impose neo-colonial dominance over the newly-created states in the Third World leads to wars *between the imperialist powers and the young countries.*

After the emergence of the first socialist country, and then of the whole system of socialist states, which has meant the emergence of a new epoch - that of transition from capitalism to socialism - *inter-systemic wars* have become the most important type. A new law has emerged: one states that 'the military defence of the gains of socialism is a general law of transition from capitalism to socialism in contemporary conditions'.[14] This law refers to the war-generating policy of imperialism: imperialist policy rooted in the contradictions of its socio-economic system creates a constant danger of the outbreak of war between the two antagonistic systems.[15]

The emphasis in the presentation of the above sub-group of laws has been shifting from one type of war to another. The Marxist-Leninist theory of the genesis of wars was, in its earliest stage, focused on inter-imperialist wars and on the application of the law of the uneven development of capitalist countries. Then it shifted to the possible wars between the first socialist state and its capitalist environment. Since World War II the main concern has been with the possibility of a war between the two antagonistic systems. This is said to be the main contemporary content of the law which states that all wars nowadays are rooted in imperialism.

The present preoccupation with international wars, and in this category with the laws of war between the antagonistic systems, has brought about a lessening of concern with the laws of civil wars. This may be explained by the fact that in Soviet view class struggle has been transferred to the international arena in the form of competition between the systems. It seems that law-like regularities concerning wars of national liberation and wars between imperialist powers and newly-created states in the 'third world' are also examined mainly from the perspective of a possible war between systems.[16] A search is made for factors which may engender an intrsystemic world war, and for regularities in their operation.

Changes in the theory of the inevitability of war

All laws of the genesis of war have acquired a somewhat modified interpretation in consequence of a radical change in the Soviet theory of the inevitability of war.[17] In the late fifties it was declared that all wars, of all types, could be avoided. There was no fatal inevitability about the occurrence of wars between social systems, or even wars between capitalist states. A peaceful transition from capitalism to socialism in particular countries was said to be possible. The inevitability of war as a means to national liberation was denied.

Nevertheless, the assumption that imperialism generates wars has not only been preserved, but repeatedly re-stated. Thus laws of the genesis of war have not been 'renounced', and their wording has been only slightly modified, to replace the inevitability of wars with the constant possibility of their outbreak. The main change can be found rather in the interpretation of these laws. This runs as follows. Since laws of the origin of war are social laws, acting through and by the activity of men, they can occur only if the two following conditions have been fulfilled: (1) they are instrumental i.e. there is some chance that they will lead to victory and the achievement of desired political goals and their costs will be less than the resultant gains and (2) the forces which are interested in war are stronger than those which oppose it.

Both conditions are hardly fulfilled, however. In our times, although imperialism remains a source of wars, because it constantly generates and aggravates contradictions which push towards a violent resolution, the conscious activity against wars is a greater restraint than ever before. To summarise it simply, the change of the balance of world forces in favour of the progressive forces, and the advent of the new military technology, have made war unprofitable and even dangerous for the exploiting classes, since they probably would lose it. For the exploited classes and nations, as well for the socialist states, war has become unnecessary since in the long run they will achieve their progressive aims without armed violence.

Thus, while objective conditions for the occurrence of wars still exist, people are reluctant to fight them, and without people - without the subjective factor - laws cannot decisively affect the course of events.

To put it another way, in the Soviet interpretation these laws do not cease to exist, they still act, but the counteraction of potent factors hinders the outbreak of actual wars. The laws will disappear only with the conditions and relationships which they concern i.e. with imperialism and antagonistic class societies. Until that happens, the existence of laws of the genesis of wars ought to be repeatedly recalled, and the possibilities of their action studied, say the Soviet theoreticians.

In the Soviet view, the principal means of paralysing the action of laws of the genesis of war, which are described as 'the favourable correlation of world forces', are of a dynamic character; there must be a continuous fight for its maintenance. It is emphasised that even such a correlation does not ensure peace, and warmongers always have a chance to carry out their plans. Thus the socialist states must constantly be ready to defend their independence and socialist gains, and at the same time support all progressive forces fighting against imperialism.

Laws of the dependence of war on policy

Dependences, not laws

The dependence of war on policy was not presented as a law until the late fifties. The dependences and links which it specifies were included in the description of the problems of the nature of war as a continuation and instrument of policy, of the influence of policy on the conduct of war and of the determining influence of policy on the just or unjust character of war.

The analysis of war as a political instrument was based on the assumption that politics is the generic element in the nature of war.[18] Fighting that serves no political purpose could not be termed war. Because of such an intrinsic (conceptual) interrelation between the nature, socio-historical character and conduct of war and politics, no additional statement which would in a law-like form directly refer to the essence of war as an instrument of politics and to the dependence of its character and conduct on politics was regarded as necessary.

The primary law

However, in the course of time, not only has such a law appeared in Soviet writings, it has even been presented as the basic law of war (or one of two basic laws constituting a pair, or as a component part of a combined law (cf. Chap. III.2).

In an official exposition (in the Soviet Military Encyclopaedia) the dependence of war on its political aims is called the universal (vseobshchii) law of war.[19] The most influential and articulate theoretician of the problem of the relationships between war and politics, Gen. Y. Rybkin, writes that the universal (vseobshchii) law of war holds that 'war is a continuation of policy by violent means'. This *is* a repetition of the definition of war.[20] The formulation and reformulation of such a basic or universal law may be regarded as the second stage in the development of this group of laws of war.

The three component laws

Certain scholars are satisfied with the formulation of this law, adding only explanations of *how* policy determines war: policy generates war, determines its social character and its strategy. Others go further and transform these component dependences into laws: the latter constitute an example of the 'component laws' which complement (the term 'fill out' is sometimes used in the Western literature) the more general law. These laws may be stated as follows:[21]

> 1 War is engendered by politics, which determines the outbreak of a war and its timing.
> 2 Policy determines the social character of war and the historical significance of war - progressive or reactionary.
> 3 Policy decisively influences the strategy of war.[22]

According to the latter, law policy is considered to have a decisive influence on the strategic objectives of armed struggle, the means used to achieve them, and consequently on the general character of military operations. Just aims, for instance, are said to stimulate the armed forces to fight with greater determination; an element of acute class-conflict in war aims precludes any compromise and compels the use of all military means available.

Thus, because of the action of this law, wars between states with the same socio-economic and political systems are considered to be normally moderate, while wars between states with different systems are characterised by fierce military operations using all armament available and having decisive aims. A future war between antagonistic systems would be the most fierce, intense and grim of all conceivable wars. The political systems, policies and political aims of war would then combine in one 'political factor' to determine the character of the war.[23]

The fourth law and the change of name of the group

The fourth dependence, which in some studies is given the status of a law, is that of policy on the course and outcome of military operations (i.e. the reverse of the dependence of war on policy): policy is compelled to bring its aims and decisions into line with the course of armed struggle.[24]

Two ways in which this influence operates have been pointed out: the direct one, when the political leadership must take decisions directly resulting from the course and outcome of military operations, and the indirect one, consisting in the influence of the losses and sufferings caused by war on the economic and spiritual conditions of social life, which in turn generates new tasks for a country's policy.[25]

Obviously, the addition of this law changes the term given to the whole group of laws, turning them into 'laws of the relationship betwen war and policy'.

The variants

In different statements about the above dependences, both policy and war have been presented and interpreted in different ways. 'Policy' (or 'politics') has been used to mean either the political (socio-political) system, or the long-range policy of a state (class, nation) or the political aims of the given war.[26] 'War' has been interpreted as including either the general features of strategy, or its course and outcome, or its socio-historical characteristics. Thus these are a number of different formulations of both the primary law and the component laws.[27]

Changes in the nuclear-missile age?

Soviet scholars stress that the nuclear-missile age has not changed either the basic law in this group or any of the component laws.[28] (1) Imperialist policy has become even more aggressive and it engenders wars, although its possibility to unleash them is more than ever limited; (2) the social character of war remains to be determined by policy; if a nuclear war in unleashed by imperialists it will become even more unjust and reactionary than any previous war; (3) the directive influence of policy on war has become more complex and at the same time policy has become even more responsible for the direction of war; (4) finally, in the case of a nuclear war, the influence of war on policy would immensely increase and could lead to revolutionary changes.

In sum, all laws *remain operating* in a nuclear war. Because of the changed conditions only their concrete manifestation could be modified.

Laws of the dependence of the course and outcome of war upon the correlation of forces

This is the only group of laws which seems to be a result of a long conceptual development through many discussions and changes.

The description of the factors influencing war was from the early stages of the development of Soviet military theory dictated by political and ideological demands - to emphasise these factors which the Soviet state and its army could rely on; at the same time it reflected the actual state of the economic reality, the possibilities, inter alia, of providing the army with armament and equipment.

Thus, in the first post-revolutionary years, when the technology and armament basis were very poor, theory stressed the importance of the political and moral factors, which were presented as determining the course and outcome of war. When the armed forces grew in number but were still poorly equipped, scholars and politicians emphasised the value of their new revolutionary quality. As industry began to expand, the role of the economy and of the strength of the rear in the description of the 'factors of victory' also grew. Through the whole period the superiority of the Soviet state and socialist system in the aggregate of factors determining the course and outcome of war as a whole was emphasised.

The thesis of the five permanently-acting factors, when formulated by Stalin in 1942, was closely connected with the concrete contemporary political, military and economic tasks of the country and its army, it pointed out the direction of main efforts, and also aimed at raising the spirit of the people and army in a very dangerous situation. It was in fact a set of political and economic postulates and directives, called 'factors'. However, it was at that time considered, and afterwards really became, a basic theoretical proposition delimiting the scope and defining the main ideas of all military research and military theory. It was called a 'thesis', 'proposition' and the like, but was treated as a law and as the main one, since it pointed out the main dependence in war, the set of factors regarded as determining its course and outcome.[29]

After Stalin's death both the validity of the 'permanent-factors-thesis' and its law-like status as determining the scope of military theory, were questioned and many changes were gradually introduced. The term 'thesis' was replaced by 'formula', permanently acting was abandoned, determining was replaced by influencing and the five factors were soon reformulated and restructured into three: economic, political, and military (factors, potentials, possibilities, and the like). Another change was the admission of the role of so-called transitory factors, such as surprise attack, the current international political situation and others.

At the end of the fifties and during the sixties innumerable studies, articles and books were published, describing and reformulating the factors which affect the course and outcome of war. The following tendencies in the development of the theory can be identified:

1 The replacement of the five 'permanent' factors, which were very different as regards their scope, structure, and force of influence, by the more equal potentials representing the main fields of social activity the economic, techno-scientific, moral-political (sometimes called ideological) and military.

2 Changes in the content and structure of the potentials according to the conditions and requirements of the nuclear missile age (for instance, the emphasis in the techno-scientific potential on the possibilities of automat-

ing a good deal of human activity, the dominance of the nuclear missile armament in the military factor, etc.).

3 The increasing role of military potential proper, with emphasis on the nuclear missile 'forces in being'.

4 Rejection of automatism in the interpretation of the thesis: potentials do not ensure victory in an automatic way, they must be transformed into real factors, actual forces superior to those at the disposal of the enemy.[30]

5 Application of a more objective approach: laws and dependences have begun to be presented as acting on both sides.

6 Finally, the replacement of the absolute size of potentials (factors, etc.) by the correlation of forces.

As the number of publications devoted to the problem increased, new proposals were put forward concerning the formulation of a single unified law which would express all the given dependences as a whole.

In the sixties, the old formula on the five permanent factors, was transformed into a formal law after several modifications. The factors were regarded as dynamic and changing, depending on the degree to which the corresponding potentials were exploited; in other words factors were presented as potentials transformed into real forces.

The law was phrased in three alternative ways.

1 In the most general form, as the law of the dependence of the course and outcome of war on its material and moral basis, or on the correlation of military power regarded as representing the whole power of the state in war: 'The dependence of the course and outcome of war on the correlation of military force of warring sides, regarded dynamically, and taking into consideration the political aims of the parties, is the general law of war'.[31]

2 In a more detailed form, war was said to be dependent on the correlation of the whole of economic, scientific, moral-political, and military forces proper, and on the ability to change the correlation in one's favour.[32]

3 Finally, the new law was presented as a set of partial laws. For instance, in one presentation, the aim of the teaching on war and army was defined as the investigation of laws which express the dependence of the course and outcome of war on the correlation of the economic potentials of warring sides, their techno-scientific potentials, their socio-political systems, their moral-political potentials, and their military potentials.[33]

No final set of laws in this group has been agreed upon, and, in particular, no choice has been made between one law stating the dependence of war on the correlation of all forces (potentials), considered as the entire state power or military power, and a set of laws asserting a set of dependences of war on the correlation of particular forces (potentials).[34]

Nor has the terminology been finally established. The shift in emphasis from factors to potentials in the late fifties was followed by focus on 'forces in being', which was quite natural under the conditions of the nuclear missile age; but finally no clear priority was established, and up to now factors, potentials, and forces have often been used interchangeably.

The special place of the law of the increasing role of popular masses in war

Apart from the above three groups of laws of war, one additional law is sometimes presented as occupying a special place and is not classified with any other group. The growing role of popular masses (or: the people) in war is regarded as such a special law. It is also formulated as the law of the determining role of popular masses in war.[35]

In the above wording the law relates to all wars in history. In another wording it is confined to our time: it holds that the course and outcome of modern war depends on the attitude of the popular masses and their participation in it. Two arguments are presented to substantiate the validity of this law. One is the increased magnitude and intensity of wars which, after being 'wars of knights' for ages, have now in the Soviet view become 'wars of nations'. Not only are wars now fought by multi-million mass armies, but the rear too has become an object and subject of warfare. The attitude of popular masses towards the aims of war has become the crucial item in all components of the correlation of forces, especially in the economic and moral-political potentials (factors); popular masses also exert the decisive influence on the combat power of armies - inter alia, determining the possibility of introducing new armaments and new methods of fighting.[36]

Secondly, the socio-political essence of wars in our epoch is of a quite new quality: wars in defence of socialist countries, wars of national liberation often combined with wars of social revolutionary changes, and a possible war between antagonistic systems - all these actual or possible wars involve the active participation of entire peoples. These either support the war, thereby strengthening the justice of its aims, or - like the peoples of the imperialist countries - they compel the governments to limit or even abandon the unjust aims. Soviet scholars contend that in World War II the popular masses of the Western countries decisively influenced the change in the character of war from an imperialist to a just, anti-fascist one. Scholars who argue for such a law point out that the increasing role of the popular masses in war is only one aspect of the growth of the role of masses in politics and of their socio-political awareness, which has become one of the main motivating forces of social life.

The law has its corollary. The attitude of the popular masses (peoples of the socialist countries are here included) towards a war 'in the air' can prevent it from materialising. In the Soviet view, this situation occurred when a nuclear war was prepared by the imperialist countries against the socialist ones after World War II. And if a war breaks out, the popular masses can press for its quick termination. Given the great importance attached in Soviet writings to the deterrent influence of the popular masses on the initiation of a war (or the increasing influence of masses on the prevention of war), this corollary will probably, sooner or later, be presented as a law. Together with the law discussed in this section it could either constitute a special group in the category of the general laws of war, or be included in a group of laws on the prevention of war, which has not hitherto been formulated, but which, if Soviet scholars aim at completing the set of laws, will perhaps emerge.

However, there is far from any agreement on the so-called law of the increasing role of popular masses in war. Some go the extreme of calling it one of the most important laws of historical materialism,[37] others do not grant it the status of a law at all.[38]

Comments

On the set of general laws of war

To summarise, Soviet scholars devote much attention to the elaboration of a set of general laws of war, as one of the main categories of laws of war dealt with by military theory. In the prevailing view this set should encompass two problems, the origin of wars as a socio-historical phenomenon, and the character and general conduct of war.

It has not been easy to create a group of *laws of the origin of wars*. It was first necessary to re-formulate the statements on the recurring causes of wars into laws, and then to separate them from the theory of the nature of war as an instrument of policy (the latter has given rise to the laws of the dependence of war on policy). Nor has it been easy to combine them with the laws concerning the character and conduct of war in a single category. On the contrary, there are good reasons for treating the former quite separately from the latter, since they reflect another kind of social activity, a policy at the time of peace instead of war, even if that policy terminates in war. Therefore, it is no accident that some scholars exclude these laws from the set of laws of military theory.

On the other hand there are valid reasons for their inclusion. The very essence of war consists in the continuation of political aims; the breakdown of the continuous political interaction connected with the genesis and conduct of war into separate elements could become an artifical procedure.[39] Even the methods applied in peacetime, on the one hand, and in war on the other, which previously were clear-cut and radically different, have come closer together: the analysis of the military or semi-military methods used during a crisis which can develop into a war seems to be similar to the analysis of many methods applied in war.

Finally, problems of the prevention of war i.e. of the prevention of the escalation of conflict, are in some respects similar to problems of the escalation and de-escalation of war itself, and in all these cases politics, perhaps, is conducted in a way that is subject to more or less the same law-like regularities.

Another difficulty has arisen when *laws of the dependence of war on plicy* and *laws of the dependence of war on the correlation of forces* have been viewed as groups in the category of the general laws of war; laws concerning the character, as well as the course and outcome, of war as a whole (i.e. of the conduct of war as a whole) have thereby been separated from the laws of the character, and course and outcome (or conduct) of armed struggle; thus the whole has been treated separately from its part. This, however, is fully conceivable. Sciences usually separate the investigation of a whole from its parts; and war, as a whole, with its many fronts of struggle, not only military, but also economic, ideological, diplomatic, etc. must be governed by laws of a different kind from those governing armed struggle.

On the character of laws

Let us briefly look at the character of the general laws of war, using the working formula presented in the conclusions of Chap. 2, which states that the incidence, course and outcome of war follows logically from the occurrence of human actions (A) under the determining circumstances or conditions (C), according to objective laws (L).

With regard to the *laws of the genesis of war*, C means the conditions which lead to wars, and A the actions which under these conditions, according to the laws L, unleash wars. In other words, L expresses here lawlike regularities in the causation of wars, recurring relationships between conditions and actions, on the one hand and the outbreak of war on the other. The conditions are the variables most frequently described: the class system as the root of all wars, particular classes as the initiators of particular types of war, concrete social forces as unleashing individual instances of war, and crises as directly preceding wars. And it is a law that wars result from the exploiting classes' unremitting pursuit of higher profits, both at home and abroad and of more of the power that makes possible such profits, and on the other hand from the struggle of the exploited classes and nations against the exploitation.

However, such general descriptions and adumbrations of the initial conditions and laws connecting these conditions and human actions with the outbreak of wars, account for only some general features of this causation and tell us very little about the nature and pattern of the dependence or its mechanism. No values for the variables that lead to wars are mentioned here.

For instance, if we accept that war is caused by a growing conflict between social forces, and that its character is determined by the character of the political struggle - just or unjust, progressive or reactionary - it is difficult to establish to what extent and what specific content the social conflict has to assume, and what the politico-military situation in the region and in the world have to become, to bring about a war. The law which holds that inter-capitalist wars are generated by the uneven development of particular capitalist countries, or that the war between systems is generated by the aggressive policy of the imperialist powers, does not point out to what extent the 'unevenness' has to reach, or how intense the aggressiveness of the imperialist powers has to become, to inevitably cause the outbreak of a war (or at least to make it very likely). Similarly, if a law of civil war states that a revolutionary civil war can be explained by reference to the growing discontent of the working classes, it is difficult to establish the amount of discontent which really causes a war.

In all the above cases, the laws only indicate that, if certain initial conditions occur war will probably break out. To attain more exact timing or a higher degree of probability, the initial conditions have to be specified in the wording, which seems very difficult in such law-like statements. Consequently, it is nearly impossible to ascertain whether initial conditions of such a type really cause concrete instances of war. The laws only state that in our epoch, because of the given characteristics of the world structure, and of the existence of certain long-range socio-political tendencies in the world (i.e. the division of the world into two antagonistic systems, the evolution of their policies and the dynamic correlation of forces), and because of the action of the laws concerning all wars, wars in out epoch and particuar types of war, some such types can be expected with some degree of probability. Even a rough approximation of this degree has not been established though.

Thus the above formula does not assert that certain determined values of C, and A, and a formula of L which shows a determinate pattern of causing a type of war, or an instance of war *necessarily* lead to E, to an outbreak of a type of war, or of an individual instance of war. In short, the above formula makes an assertion concerning a certain probability of particular types of war, but not their inevitable causation.

The second comment is that in the actual interpretation of the above formula L means only those laws which operate in the direction of the outbreak of wars. However, at the same time other laws operate in the opposite direction. In descriptions of the politico-military situation and the probability of wars, the growing power of the so-called progressive forces is given more and more attention, and these are the main cause of the abandonment of the theory of the inevitability of wars and its replacement by the assertion about the residual possibility of wars. The interfering influence of the laws which act against the outbreak of wars, however, is not reflected in the phrasing of the general laws of war, and accordingly, not in the formula in question.

Perhaps the problem is even more complex. It is conceivable that the origin of war is affected not by *two* laws (or kinds of law) either stimulating or hindering its outbreak, but by one *combined* law (one kind of law) that expresses in the interaction of stimulating and hindering factors. The outbreak of a concrete instance of war of a concrete type may result from a complex of war-generating and war-impending factors, ot to put it another way, from the correlation of social forces pressing for war and preventing it. Such a correlation influences the probability of the ocurrence of wars; it can be hypothesised, for instance, that because of the actual correlation of world forces the probability of international wars decreases while that of internal war increases.

Both comments lead to the preliminary conclusion - to be discussed further in Chap. 8 - that Soviet formulae of laws of the genesis of war can be regarded as statements on probabilistic laws (or hypotheses) with an undetermined degree of probability. In other words, they state the possibility of the outbreak of wars without specifying more or less precisely the requisite conditions for this. The deterministic laws characteristic of Marxist-Leninist philosophy are here set in a probabilistic framework. This seems to be inevitable since the complex of conditions necessary for the outbreak of a war is perhaps too complicated to be fully cognised and thus precisely formulated.

Another kind of difficulty is connected with the application of the working formula of war to the group of laws that state the *dependence of the character of war on policy*. While out formula with respect to the laws of the origin of war comprises the main factors affecting the occurrence of war, it should here be related to war's characteristics or, more precisely, to its characteristics as a process.

The laws involved here must be regarded as probabilistic hypotheses of a special kind: they constitute a causal connection between two complexes of features attributed to two fields of human activity (the character of policy and the character of war) which, in turn, cannot be measured but only broadly characterised. In other words, the formula relates in this case to certain qualitative features of war, and therefore can serve only as a guide to a characteristic of the main tendency in war and the most general features of its conduct.

The problem is even more complex, however. Firstly, policy leading to a war should be treated not only as a unity of internal and external policy (which is a tenet of Soviet theory), and of the objective situation and subjective activity[26] but also as closely linked to the whole system of international political relations. The latter can profoundly influence the character of war, its role in social development and the way it is conducted.[40]

Secondly, policy of which war is the continuation is influenced, as a rule, by various internal factors, by diverse interests and the interaction of various social forces. As some scholars point out, 'the majority of the concrete instances of war present an extremely contradictory political character ... numerous different - often opposing - interests, political aims and historical tendencies are tied together, which leads to an entanglement of just and unjust elements in war'.[41] Both of the above peculiarities of political interaction add to the complexity of the relationship between the character of policy and the character of war.

Yet another use of the working formula can be noted with regard to *the laws of the dependence of the course and outcome of war on the correlation of forces*. The element (and the difficulty) in common with the previous groups of laws is that 'laws of the correlation' have a probabilistic character, stating that the general course of events can be predicted with some probability and also here the working formula has an obviously qualitative character.

However, perhaps the main difficulty is with the application of our formula (which, in fact, concerns the causation of an event) to *the continuous dependence of a whole process* i.e. the development of military operations and non-military actions. These, even in the most simplified form, consist of a multitude of subsequent dynamic and changing states of social processes, situations and actions i.e. combinations of variables (situations). The dependence of the value of each of them and of their change on the corresponding values and their changes in the independent variable (also a complex combination of variables) would be reflected in the formula in question, if it could capture the whole complex dependence. But apparently it cannot.

Moreover, the statement on a law should indicate not only the existence of the dependence but also the manner in which it is manifested. If we assert the dependence of the course of war on a certain factor, or complex of factors, we should point out *how* they affect this course - the duration of war, its escalation or de-escalation (in all aspects: participation, location, issues, intensities), its effects, its division into phases and its termination.[42] Laws of the dependence of the course and outcome of war, in fact, point only to its final outcome without specifying the mechanism of victory. The laws merely state that 'the more forces - the better' i.e. the greater chances of victory. Thus our formula may be used here only to get some general picture, to point out some general tendency, and to state a probability of the outcome, as was done concerning the outbreak of war.

A further difficulty with these laws concerns their social character. They state the probability of a course of events. The conditions which must be fulfilled include human actions which may or may not be performed. The inclusion of the causation of human action in our formula would be very useful, but even if it were possible, it would add to the complexity of the formula.

Moreover, according to Soviet premises, there are different probabilities of a determined and predictable course of action for the two sides in war. For instance, the Soviet system, policy and leadership can much better exploit the dependence of the outcome of war on social factors than the capitalist system. In fact, this dependence operates against the capitalist army. Thus the degree of the probability of a favourable course of war is different for different sides, and this makes the common formula concerning laws of dependence even less applicable. Thus, two separate formulae would perhaps be here required, one for either fighting side.

To sum up, the above two groups of Soviet general laws of war may be regarded as either probabilistic laws, or rather as 'dependence hypotheses' referring to a certain causation (since changes in the independent 'factor' cause changes in the dependent 'course of events') which is here asserted in a very general form. To become well-established laws, these hypotheses should be followed up by more explicit statements, supported by evidence, concerning what kind of change in the development of the dependent variable follows specific change in the development of the independent variable. In the absence of such statements, any such law remains merely a claim that the two variables are connected by causal ties which cannot be defined with much precision.

Thus, in a preliminary conclusion, all general laws of war as presented in Soviet theory, can be treated as different variants of statements about some probable course of events, probabilistic laws or, more exactly, hypotheses with different and indeterminate, degrees of probability.

On the premises of laws

The interpretation by Soviet scholars of the character of the general laws of war, and especially of the laws of the genesis of war, is strictly connected with the place they assign to the laws in the whole mechanism of social development.

To review the main ideas in this theme in a very simplified and shortened form, society is a developing system with an inherent regulating mechanism. The economic basis of a class society considered as the system of production, distribution and consumption combines two socially contradictory functions: it satisfies human needs and at the same time it ensures profits for the owners of the means of production. Production is a cooperative process necessitating maximal coordination, but distribution, consumption and the whole social political and legal superstructure are based on the private ownership of the means of production and on the social and political dominance of the owners.

The unequal allocation of resources and power within the social system means a basic and intrinsic contradiction of class interests, systematically generated by the structure of productive relations. It leads to periodic crises when the constantly developing means of production - or material forces - begin sharply to conflict with the socio-economic, political and legal relations. These relations, after contributing to the development of the forces of production, eventually come to fetter them. Class struggle, which is permanent, sharpens at a certain stage and under specific conditions (for instance, a combination of a severe economic crisis with a sufficient degree of class awareness and organisation of the exploited classes, and also a conviction that only a revolution can resolve the crisis) leads to a revolution in both the economic system and the superstructure. Armed violence is an instrument in this development, applied by both the forces resisting and those pressing for change.

All such processes are links in the constant and permanent development of society through constantly increasing productivity and the periodic replacement of each socio-economic formation by a higher one. This development moves in the general direction of a classless society with a just superstructure and maximal satisfaction of human needs. (There is here, perhaps, a distant affinity to the action of homeostatic systems with their feedback mechanisms. The main difference is that we have here a developing system, and the regulating mechanism serves not only to maintain temporary stability in the system but above all to preserve the possibility of development.) In this mechanism, men act because of the development of objective conditions. This is the necessary cause of their actions. Other conditions (mentioned above) are also needed to constitute a sufficient complex of causes but, in the final analysis, the other causes are also rooted in the objective development of the material base.

However, this sort of causation is not identical with that in the physical world, for instance. Laws and conditions motivate men to act, but their purposeful action, although it is probable, perhaps even very probable, is not mechanically determined. The motivation, although meaningful, should be 'translated' into an awareness of common class interests and the belief that there is a need to act. Theoretically, it can happen that men will not act e.g. if the revolutionary party fails to prepare the masses for a revolution or if superior forces counteract; nor can accidental factors be discounted.

If, however, no extraordinary circumstances supervene, men who know the laws and causes of social development and correctly assess the situation, will make history by pursuing aims based on this knowledge. They regard their actions as inherent in the functioning of society which, although it satisfies the current needs of men, at the same time necessarily develops towards an increasingly effective system of production and a more socially just superstructure. War is a function in such a development and has its place in it. On the other hand, reactionary classes when expecting an unfavourable development, try to check it, and wars then become a part of this 'checking' behaviour.

Similar reasoning can be applied to the discussion of international wars; in short, if just and progressive wars - in our times, the anti-imperialist wars - have been necessary for defending the rights of peoples and achieving progress for promoting independence of peoples at less social cost than the alternative means, to that extent they are waged by men conscious of the necessity to defend their rights and also to achieve progress. Laws of war will also in this case concern human activity springing from social consciousness, which will take place if it is required by the cause of the independence of peoples and of further social progress. And the reactionary forces, seeing in war a means of furthering their interests, of acquiring new territories, markets and natural resources, and also of suppressing the national-liberation and revolutionary movements and checking social progress, will also see in war a necessary means for their aims.

Parenthetically, the use of the word 'they', or 'social forces', or 'men' means, in the first place, the conscious elites - the political leaders - of classes, nations and states, which put forward both the ideology and the programme of action.

Some say that since, in the Soviet interpretation of the general laws of war, the aims i.e. the intentions, of men play the decisive role; and since wars are regarded as one of the mechanisms of social functioning which leads to further social development, or else arrests such development, the laws are teleologically oriented. Others regard them as based on fatalistic deterministic philosophy, since society is presented as a kingdom of necessity where people's thoughts and ideas i.e. the motives for their activity, derive from their economic class situation.

Two comments on such an assessment may be made. Firstly, it seems that much misunderstanding of the Soviet approach results from regarding it as 'teleological' in the sense used in other philosophies, assuming that the world and society are arranged purposefully and that social processes and developments are subordinated to some final aim. According to Marxist-Leninist philosophy, the aims men pursue are mental pictures of the future phenomena, processes, states of society, which express men's interests and motives. A knowledge of the laws of social development can promote awareness of the need to establish equitable social aims and to act in pursuit of them. This has nothing in common with teleology.[43]

In the Soviet view, teleology is implied in the assertion that the world is arranged with a purpose and society aims at some perfect state according to a grand design imposed by a supernatural thinking force (God). Accordingly, the aims men pursue are but a reflection of aims *a priori* established by that extra-societal will, and any laws recognised also express and follow the grand design. Regardless of whether what is regarded as a teleological view by Soviet scholars can be accepted as such by others (and it seems that many will not accept it) this constitutes the Soviet view of the relation between aims and causes in social development.

This leads to the second comment. One should beware of the tendency to attribute to the general laws of war in the Soviet exposition definite and unambiguous interpretations contrary to those which Soviet scholars insistently propose. The character of laws presented by an ideology - and in the Soviet view both the existence of the objective laws and the statements about these laws are a component of ideology with definite ideological functions (see Chap. 7) - cannot be assessed without taking into account the interpretation which its authors insistently and consistently emphasise. Soviet scholars obstinately try to bring together the indispensable creative elements of human activity and its causation by material conditions. The laws, together with their interpretation, are meant as deterministic yet allowing the subjective factor a creative role.

For instance, in the Soviet view, there is no doubt as to whether explanation by laws can be replaced by rational explanation (i.e. that men act when they think it rational) or by explanation by patterns of behaviour (men act as they are used to acting). It may be suggested that in the Soviet view all alternatives can be combined: men start a war when they think it *rational*, in accordance with their *interests* and in accordance with *laws* - since they are used to acting in pursuit of interests and in accordance with laws.[44]

The action of laws is implicit in the causation of human actions; and human intentions - corresponding to laws and interests - are also a component part of causation. We see here an attempt to avoid both over-emphasising and underestimating the role of laws of war on the one hand, and of the human will on the other.

Notes

[1] For instance, Dmitriev, 1975, presents several general laws as concerning

the class aspects of war and military affairs; 'In spite of the differences in the contrete formulations of these laws in the literature, their essence is common. They express relationships pointed out by the classics of Marxism-Leninism: a) the dependence of all aspects of military affairs on the method of production, on the economic basis; b) the conditioning of military affairs by the character of the political superstructure, the class-political relations in society; c) the conditioning of war by policy, the dependence of the character and forms of armed struggle on the political content of war; d) the dependence of the course and outcome of war on the correlation of military power (of the material and spiritual forces) of the warring sides; and some others' (p.12).

In the recently published military encyclopaedia, an informal set of 'laws of war' is presented: 1) the dependence of war on political aims (called the most general law of war); 2) the dependence of the course and outcome of war on the correlation of the economic strengths of the warring states (coalitions); 3) the dependence of the course and outcome of war on the correlation of the scientific potentials of the warring sides; 4) the dependence of the course and outcome of war on the correlation of the moral-political forces and potentialities of the warring states (coalitions), and 5) the dependence of the course and outcome of war on the correlation of the military forces (potentials) of the opposing sides. Other laws are then added, such as 'the law according to which victory historically goes to the side which represents the new, more progressive social and economic system, and which effectively exploits the possibilities which it includes.' ('Zakony i obychai voiny', in: Sovetskaya Voennaya Entsiklopediya, vol. 3, pp.375-7).

[2] Kazakov, 1965, pp.44-50; Marxism-Leninism on War and Army, 1972, p.1. Milovidov, 1974, among the main propositions constituting the basis of the teaching on war and army enumerates 'the relationship between war and policy', 'the interrelation between the economic, socio-political, and moral factors in war', 'the laws of influence of the military technique and man on the military art' etc. (p.13). The latter statement is usually classified with laws of armed struggle and included in the sphere of military science; see Chap. V.

[3] Sushko proposes the following four 'laws of the dependence of war on the whole of social life': (1) The dependence of war on policy; (2) The dependence of military power of states, and of the course and outcome of wars on economy i.e. on the level of productive forces and the character of the economic system; (3) The dependence of the military power of states on the level of development of natural and technical sciences; (4) The dependence of military power, and of the course and outcome of military operations and the whole of war on the politico-moral state of population and armed forces (1964c).

In the Dictionary of Basic Military Terms the list of 'objective laws of war' includes the following ones: 'the dependence of the course and outcome of war on the correlation of the military-economic forces and potentialities of the belligerent states; on the correlation of moral-political forces and potentialities of the adversaries; on the correlation of the military potentialities of the parties in conflict, and the quantity and quality of their armed forces; the dependence of the method of waging a war on the method of production, and in particular on its most mobile element - the means of production, which have a direct impact on change in means of armed conflict'. ('Ob'ektivnye zakony voiny', in: Slovar osnovnykh voennykh terminov, Voenizdat, Moscow 1965).

In a study, four laws of nuclear war are advanced:

1 The course and outcome of war waged with the unlimited employment of all means of conflict depends primarily on the correlation of available, strictly military forces of the combatants at the beginning of the war, especially of nuclear weapons and means of delivery.

2 The course and outcome of war depends on the correlation of the military potential of the combatants. Military potential defined as expressing the maximum capability of a state to maintain and improve its armed forces, is considered as derivative of economic conditions and scientific and moral-political potential.

3 The course and outcome of war depends on its political potential.

4 The course and outcome of war depends on the correlation of moral-political and psychological capabilities of the people and armies of the combatants.

In the same study, two additional laws have been maintained: (1) the law of the dependence of the course and outcome of war on the correlation of the military-economic capabilities of the combatants, and (2) of the dependence on the correlation of the levels of scientific potentials of the combatants. (Savkin, 1972, pp.89-92, 97-9).

In another representation, four laws concerning all wars have been listed:

1 The law of the dependence of all aspects of military affairs (voennoe delo) on the economic basis:

2 The law of the dependence of military affairs on the character of the political superstructure and on the class-political relations in society.

3 The law of the dependence of war on policy, and of the character and forms of armed struggle on the political content of war.

4 The law of the dependence of the course and outcome of war on the correlation of military power of the warring sides (Dmitriev, 1975, p.12).

In some studies, the set of laws has been reduced to the law of the dependence of war and methods of its conduct on policy, and the law of the dependence of the course and outcome of war on the correlation of military power of the warring sides (Skirdo, 1970, pp.97-9).

[4] In all presentations, laws of the origin of war are treated separately from all other general laws of war. For instance, in 'Marxism-Leninism on War and Army' the main chapters are devoted to the origin of war and to the dependence of the course and outcome of war on the correlation of the military power of the warring parties. It is said that laws connected with the former subject constitute the basis of the teaching on war and army and laws of the course and outcome of war should be studied on the teaching, and on the military science levels (p.310). In many studies, the origin of war, and the dependence of war on external fac-

tors (policy, the socio-political system, economics, moral-political conditions, and the military factor proper) are described separately as two fields of theory, which naturally suggests two separate groups of laws (Prokop ev, 1965; Popov, 1964).

[5] Morozov, 1974. The set of the four laws proposed by Sushko, 1964 (see note 3 in this chapter) constitutes an attempt to combine laws expressing the dependence of military power and expressing the dependence of the course and outcome of war on social factors in aggregate laws. Parenthetically, he uses the term 'voennaya moshch', i.e. 'military might'.

[6] This is reflected in a somewhat strange way of presenting these laws in some studies. For instance, in the first part of the hitherto most elaborate exposition of the teaching on war and army, which is devoted to the description of the causes and nature of war, several statements concerning these causes are neither put in a law-like form nor termed laws. But in the concluding part of the same study it is stated that at the beginning of the book 'the laws expressing the dependence of the emergence of wars, and their aims, on economic and political conditions' have been described (Marxism-Leninism on War and Army, 1972).

[7] Obviously, declared aims should not be equated with the actual ones e.g. the declared aims of war usually avoid mentioning the actual goals or even disguise them.

[8] Tyushkevich, 1975, pp.38-9.

[9] No unified terminology for the causes of different levels has been provided. In some publications the most general causes of wars, i.e. the common causes of all wars, which in this study are termed 'roots' are represented by the Russian term 'istochniki'. This can be translated as 'sources' but also as 'roots' since the definition is as follows: 'Sources of war: the genuine ('korennye'; 'koren' = root) fundamental causes of war, generated by the socio-economic system of the exploiting states and appearing as primary motivating forces' ('Istochniki voin' — in: Sovetskaya Voennaya Entsiklopediya, vol. 3, pp.632-3).

[10] One consequence is that particular wars may resolve particular contradictions but the more basic ones, which are the main source of all wars in the given epoch, remain unresolved, not to mention the root of all wars, i.e. in Soviet view, the class system (cf. Tyushkevich, 1975, p.9).

[11] The emerging interest in seeking the more immediate causes of the occurrence of wars is manifested in publications on the so-called conditions of such occurrence.

Tyushkevich lists three kinds of conditions: (1) conditions of the continued possibility of wars; (2) of their outbreak; (3) of their specific form. The first kind includes, in our times, the existence of a strong system of imperialist states, of military-political blocs, and militarisation of the economy, as well as the action of laws characterising the capitalist system: for instance, the law of the uneven development of capitalist states. The second kind is equated with the material means necessary for unleashing a war, which requires armament, armed forces, and an economy able to meet the needs of war. The third kind is exemplified by a surprise attack or by war emerging from the escalation of a conflict and the gradual involvement of new countries in it (1975, pp.101 ff.). The status of these conditions is, as we see, quite different, and the presented set can be viewed only as an indication of the increasing interest in the problem.

[12] Osnovy marksistskoi filosofii, 1959, Chap. 6; Grudinin, 1971, pp.217-8.

[13] Some scholars put it simply: the cause of war should be sought in the laws of class society (Seleznev, 1974, p.10).

[14] Kulikov, 1973. One theme in the Marxist-Leninist programme for the education of troops is the following: 'The defence of the socialist gains as a general law of the socialist and communist construction' (see: Sidelnikov, 1976). This statement, however, is most frequently formulated as a proposition: so long as imperialism exists, 'the armed defence of the socialist Fatherland is an objective necessity' (Dmitriev, 1975, p.15).

[15] See: Sovetskaya Voennaya Entsiklopediya, Vol.1, p.284.

[16] Some scholars contend that the 'globalisation' of local wars, which involve many countries and tend toward escalation into inter-system wars, has become a new characteristic of the contemporary epoch (Dshordshadze, 1976, pp.32 ff.).

[17] V Cf. On the Nature of War, by J. Lider, Ch.12.

[18] Filosofskoe nasledie, p.33; Seleznev, 1974, p.17 ('political struggle' is here the generic notion in relation to warfare). In both cases the Russian term 'rodovoi' is used, here translated as 'generic'.

[19] 'Zakony i obychai voiny', in: Sovetskaya Voennaya Entsiklopediya, Vol. 3, pp.375-6. In 'Filosofskoe nasledie' the discovery of this law is attributed to Lenin (p.138).

[20] 1973a, p.52. Laws of the determining role of politics in war are an almost perfect example of statements the truth value of which is a matter of logical necessity, because they assert ties included in the defining characteristics of war. If war is not waged for political aims it is not a war. And it is non-typical if policy does not determine and control the whole conduct of it. If war could not be fought with a justifiable prospect of attaining the political goals, it would not be waged at all.

Some scholars formulate this dependence in a 'law-generating' way: 'When speaking about the influence of policy on war, one must also consider the reverse: each war influences policy in varying degrees. Depending on the results of war, policy must change its aims during the course of war and after its termination' (Zav'yalov, 1976, p.14). Gareyev, 1977, enumerates the 'interrelation between policy and war' as one of the main subjects of the teaching on war and army (p.92). Many scholars give examples of a radical change of policy resulting from the course of war during World War II.

[21] Popov, 1964. 'Sootnoshenie politicheskogo soderzhaniya i vooruzhennogo nasiliya v voine', pp.46-62; Filosofskoe nasledie, pp.33-4. The authors explain the relation between politics and warfare as one between the 'generic and specific' elements in the essence of war. Politics is the principal, determining

aspect of the essence of war, while violence is the subordinated aspect. Cf. Rybkin, 1973a, Ch.II.

[22] 'The relationships between them are established on the principle of the complete dependence of military strategy on policy. Policy sets the goals for strategy, formulates its tasks, and controls its development. Moreover, policy creates the conditions favouring the fulfilment of these tasks - mobilising and employing the material and spiritual forces of the state. Policy in a definite way influences the composition and structure of the armed forces, the training and supplying of the troops, with military equipment, and the selection of the methods and forms of waging war'.

The bourgeois military theoreticians are wrong, 'No weapons can change the essence of the interrelationship between policy and military strategy. Moreover, the appearance of modern means of destruction is increasing the determining role of policy in relation to strategy' (G. Kulikov, 'Mozg armii', *Pravda*, 13.11.1974).

[23] Skirdo, 1970, pp.98-9. It should be asked, however, whether another Soviet assertion does not contradict this interpretation of the law in question. It is maintained that in just and progressive wars the nature of the goals prompts the avoidance of extremes in armed combat; only such methods are used which are directly dictated by military necessity (Bochkarev, 1965). The Chinese civil war with its low intensity may serve as an example.

[24] Popov writes that this is the relation between aims and means: if the means do not correspond to the aims, the latter must be changed; e.g. if armed forces are assigned unrealistic tasks, defeats ensue, and the aims must be changed (1964, pp.59-60).

[25] Rybkin, 1973a, devotes a whole section to the description of this law (Chap. 2.2, pp.69-75), and also deals with it in his introduction (pp.9-10). Note that Rybkin uses the term 'regularity' interchangeably with 'law'.

The authors of 'Filosofskoe nasledie' contend: 'When war begins, the subsequent destiny of policy is in an inverse relationship to victory or defeat in the course of armed struggle. War serves as a tool of politics but it can effectively carry out its role only if victory is achieved. Finally, politics is in an inverse relationship to the spontaneous effect of armed struggle on society as a whole. Armed struggle puts society into a special state, sharply aggravates all processes inherent in that society and produces victims and destruction, which as a rule have a negative effect on historical progress' (p.34). Two propositions are here combined: the impact of the course of warfare on international policy - that is, on enemies and allies; and the impact on domestic policy - that is, on social classes.

Some scholars formulate this dependence in a 'law-generating' way: 'When speaking about the influence of policy on war, one must also consider the reverse: each war influences to this or other extent policy. Dependently of the results of war, policy must change its aims during the course of war and after its termination' (Zavyalov, 1976, p.14). Gareyev presents the 'interrelation between policy and war' as one of the main topics of the teaching on war and army (1977, p. 92). Cf. Morozov, 1975. Many scholars quote examples of a radical change in policy resulting from the course and outcome of military operations during World War II.

[26] This may partly be explained by the fact that politics (policy) in Soviet theory is treated as a many-sided phenomenon which can be approached from different angles. For instance, one can focus either on its objective side (the objective relationships between classes, nations and states, also termed the objective situation) or the subjective side (the political line, the methods and forms of actions, termed the political strategy and tactics). See Rybkin, 1973a, p.8.

[27] Individual scholars also include in this group the law of the dependence of war on the attitude of the popular masses toward it (Skirdo, 1970, has elaborated this problem in detail). This law is however closely linked to the law of the dependence of war on the moral-political factor, which belongs to another group of laws.

[28] Rybkin, 1973a, pp.68ff.

[29] O sovetskoi voennoi nauke, 1964, p.292. Cf. Popov, 1964, pp.34 ff. for the criticism of this thesis.

[30] 'Potential means the true possibilities of a country (coalition) which can be exploited for the conduct of war. War constitutes a very complex set of phenomena and processes, and the possibilities may be transformed into reality, or may not ... The notion of the "factor" is very broad, it means the role of each material and spiritual element of the objective world in war phenomena and processes'. Thus each effort or condition which in some way affects the course and outcome of war can be regarded as a 'factor' (Prokop'ev, 1965, pp.212-3); 'Potentials and their elements, set in motion when aggression by an opponent is possible, or in the course of war, becomes factors i.e. driving forces, and conditions of victory or defeat' (Marksizm-leninizm o voine i armii, 1957, p.246); 'The moral factor ... is the moral potential in action' (Il. in, 1969, p.8; in the same words: Tabunov, p.30).

[31] For instance, 'The dependence of the course and outcome of war on the correlation of military force of warring sides, regarded dynamically, and taking into consideration the political aims of the parties, is the general law of war' (Marksizm-leninizm o voine i armii, Voenizdat, Moscow, 1957, p.245). Lenin presented the law of the dependence of the course and outcome of war on the correlation of the material, moral-political and military potentials (Azovtsev, 1968, cf. 1971).

[32] Metodologicheskie problemy, the chapter entitled 'Dialektika sootnosheniya sil v vooruzhennoi bor-be', pp.297-318. Lenin pointed out that all components of the correlation of forces, all material and spiritual forces of both fighting parties, had to be taken into account (S. Ivanov, 'V.I. Lenin i sovetskaya voennaya strategiya', *Kommunist Vooruzhennykh Sil*, 1970:8). The law has also been described as the dependence of the victories and defeats on the correlation of military power of the warring sides; its discovery has been attributed to Lenin

(Filosofskoe nasledie, p.138). Here military power is seemingly considered the entire state power engaged in war.

[33] 'Voina' in: Sovetskaya Istoricheskaya Entsiklopediya, Izd. 'Sovetskaya Entsiklopediya', vol. 3, Moscow 1963, p.622.

[34] Note that other dependences have also been formulated as laws - for instance, the dependence of the course and outcome of war on the correlation of the 'condition of the rear' in the warring countries (Skirdo, 1970, p.97). Several laws stating the dependence of the course and outcome of war on particular external factors (and among them - on the correlation of particular potentials) are presented in Voina i Armiya, pp.153-7.

[35] Baz', 1958; Skirdo, 1970, Chap. II; N. Kulikov, 1978. Baz' contends: 'Wars are now conducted by the peoples. This is so universal that it is true of all significant wars of our times despite all the differences between them ... It should be emphasised that, as facts testify, throughout the entire course of the twentieth century this objective law, diffusing its action over all wars of contemporary times, has been displaying a tendency toward exerting ever-growing influence on the character of war'; the mass character of armies, the tremendous territorial and strategic scale of armed conflict, its comparatively long duration are different expressions of this general law (1958, pp.91, 93). Kulikov presents 'the objective law of the growing role of the people in war', but also writes: 'the popular masses decisively influence the course and action of wars' (p.9).

[36] Kulikov writes that the increased role of the popular masses in war is determined by their participation in military operations and their personal contribution in spheres such as the economy, policy, and ideology. Their participation in armed struggle includes the guerilla struggle behind the enemy lines (1978, p.10).

[37] O sovetskoi voennoi nauke, 1964, p.315.

[38] They regard, however, the attitude of the popular masses towards war as one of the most important factors affecting it (Marxism-Leninism on War and Army, 1972, Ch.II:6. 'The Role of the Popular Masses in Wars in the Modern Epoch', pp.97 ff.).

[39] This has been expressed in the presentation by some scholars of a group of laws described as 'laws expressing the dependence of the emergence of wars, and their aims, on economic and political conditions' (Marxism-Leninism on War and Army, p.310).

[40] Günter Rau, et al., Gerechte und ungerechte Kriege, Militärverlag, Berlin, 1970, pp.19. The authors repeat the Soviet theory of the subject. Cf. Rybkin, 1973a.

[41] Rybkin, 1973a, pp.16-18.

[42] The problem is even more complex, since particular factors variously affect different aspects of warfare - its material basis, conditions, actors, strategy. For instance, the economic potential brings a direct bearing on armament and logistics, less direct of the quality of personnel, and only indirect on strategy, etc.

[43] See: Kratkii ocherk istorii filosofii, Moscow, 1960, Ch.XXIV; Kazimierz Ajdukiewicz, Zagadnienia i kierunki filozofii, Czytelnik, Warsaw 1949, Ch.II, IV.4 'Mechanizm i finalizm', Zdzisław Cackowski, Główne zagadnienia i kierunki filozofii, IV ed., KiW, Warsaw 1970, 'Ontologia', Ch.X, 'Kauzalizm i finalizm'.

[44] In other words, it seems that because in Soviet theory to act rationally means to act according to laws, even if unconsciously, the usual presumption that people act for sufficient reason means that they act according to laws.

5 Laws of armed struggle

The concept

To turn to the second main category of laws of war, no standard classification or set of laws of armed struggle (also called laws of armed conflict, of armed combat, of warfare) has been presented. It might be inferred from the fragmentary definitions and descriptions of these laws, from various groupings and lists that have occasionally been proposed (see below), and also from general and combined sets of laws and groups of war (i.e. general laws of war *and* laws of armed struggle) (Ch.3). Let us briefly examine these sources.

The definition

That laws concerning the way men fight and the outcome of the fighting *do* exist has often been asserted in Soviet writings.[1] As with all social laws, this should mean that the fighting troops act according to certain laws which determine the main trend of their actions, and under certain conditions which create the framework of armed struggle. These conditions are the following:[2]

1 Armed forces pursue definite aims, which spring from the policies of the warring sides, which are in turn conditioned by their socio-economic systems, and the politico-military situation.
2 Armed forces possess means of combat that are limited by the power of their countries, and they have to use forms and methods of armed struggle which depend on the level of the economic and scientific potentialities.
3 Their actions are restrained by the power of the actions of the enemy.

These conditions generate recurring necessary ties and relationships between armed struggle and external factors, as for instance the dependence of the effectiveness of fighting on the means available for the armed forces.

But armed struggle has its specific internal ties and relationships, as for instance those between the various combat levels - strategic, operational, and tactical - or between the means and aims that can be attained through fighting.

The definition of the law of armed struggle should reflect both the above kinds of relationship. However, up to this point, it encompasses only the second of them: laws of armed struggle are usually defined as the deep, inner, essential, stable, necessary, repetitive, and objective ties and relationships between the phenomena and processes of armed struggle manifested on the battlefield in the course of armed struggle.[3]

Divisions and lists of laws

A subdivision of the laws of armed struggle as a separate category of laws is usually made within the sets of the laws of war in their entirety. In these sets, two groups are presented which fit the concept of the laws of armed struggle: laws of *military art*, and *internal* laws of armed struggle (cf. Chap. 3, p.47).[4]

An unorthodox distinction is sometimes made between general and specific laws of armed struggle. The former encompass laws covering all wars in all times, the latter laws proper to the particular socio-economic formations. Each formation is considered to generate specific laws of war, including those of armed struggle.[5] These proposals, however, do not go beyond making a general division; they are not complemented by more detailed descriptions of the proposed groups and they do not correspond to the usual description of the laws of armed struggle.

To turn to the *informal* sets of laws of armed struggle, these are very diverse, with regard to the number of laws and to their wording. For instance, in one of the earliest propositions, four laws were presented;[6] in a collective work on the methodology of military affairs, three laws as follows:[7]

1 The law of the dependence of the means and forms of armed struggle on the properties of weapons and combat equipment.

2 The law of the dependence of the course and outcome of armed struggle on the correlation of combat power.[8]

3 The law of the relation between politics[9] and armed violence in war.[10]

In an officer's handbook four laws were adduced:[11]

1 The law of the determining effect of policy on armed struggle, its methods and forms.

2 The law of the determining influence of the means of armed struggle on its course and outcome.

3 The law of the dependence of the course and outcome of armed struggle on the correlation of forces of the warring sides, and - as its component - the law of the concentration of superior forces and means at the required time in the decisive direction.

4 The law of the determining effect of strategy on operational art and tactics.

Two laws have been presented by another researcher:[12]

1 The methods and the forms of armed conflict depend on the material basis[13] of the battle and operation.

2 Any battle or operation at any given moment of its development takes shape in favour of the side whose armed forces possess the greatest combat power in comparison with the enemy.

The latter law has been stated occasionally in other articles.[14]

In many studies and articles, which do not explicitly specify sets of laws, these can be inferred from the exposition. For instance, in an article on 'laws of battle',[15] the following laws of the dependence of the course and outcome of battle (and - to extrapolate - of all kinds of military operations) are apparently assumed:

1 The law of the dependence of battle on the means employed.

2 ... on the balance of forces participating in the combat.[16]

3 ... on the concentration of efforts and achievement of superiority over the enemy in the decisive place and at the decisive time.

4 ... on the correspondence of the aim of battle to the true situation.

At first sight, the above proposals and others, are so different and encompass such different groups and problems of varying scope that their usefulness as a basis for working classification seems very limited. However, some common ideas can here be hypothesised.

Firstly, most of them distinguish between laws concerning the methods of fighting i.e. military art and those concerning the course and outcome of armed struggle. Secondly, most of them present laws expressing internal ties between phenomena and processes of armed struggle (the relationship between strategy, and operational art and tactics, the importance of the concentration of efforts and achievement of superiority, etc.). Thirdly, concrete groups of laws are mentioned which can be useful for devising a working classification.

The very concept of armed struggle which suggests the key dependences of military art and the course of fighting may also be of use.

In any instance of war, armed struggle is regarded as: (1) dependent on the material conditions of fighting (2) dependent on the political content of war and (3) interrelated with all other forms of struggle in war.

The classification

To sum up, the laws of armed struggle as a whole may be divided into two main sections which, in turn, consist of certain groups. The first section includes laws of military art (or laws of the determination of military art). These may be divided into: (1) laws of the development of military art as a whole in history, and (2) laws determining the methods and forms applied in the individual instances of war.

The second section includes laws of the effectiveness of armed struggle and can be divided into: (3) laws of the dependence of the effectiveness of armed struggle (or its course and outcome) on the external conditions, and (4) internal laws of armed struggle.

Laws of military art

The subject

Traditionally, the interest of Soviet scholars was centred on the dependence of the development of military art on its material basis, and many recent presentations are still confined to this. However, other relationships have also been mentioned, if only in single studies, and it would be appropriate to distinguish between two different dependences: (1) The dependence of the *development* of military art on the development of the material basis and (2) The dependence of military art applied in *individual instances* of war, or particular types of war, on a complex of factors characteristic of the contemporary epoch (the political aims of war or type of war, the level of the economic and technological development, main system of military art in the epoch) and of the given war (its political content, the correlation of forces, the pecularities of the theatre of military operations and so on).[17]

An intermediate problem connected with the above two dependences is the dependence of the main system of military art *in a given epoch* on it material basis.

In some respects, the above relationships are interconnected: for instance, factors that affect the development of military art in history, also affect, if only slightly, its state in the given epoch, the choice and application of particular methods in individual instances, or particular types of war, and the change of methods in the course of armed struggle. In consequence, both main dependences are hardly to be distinguished in the analyses or descriptions hitherto provided; they will however be treated separately in this presentation.

Laws concerning the development of military art

The dependence of the development of military art on the development of the material basis of the conduct of war has been presented either as one law, and generally in exactly the above wording, or as a set of laws.

The traditional formula In all the traditional views presented, the material basis was described as the unity of the economic conditions under which wars were fought and of the people who fought them, and in a reduced form as the unity of means (armament and military equipment) and fighting men. All these views related to Engels' statement that weapons and the composition, organisation, tactics and strategy of armed forces at any given time in history depend primarily on the level of production and means of communication; and also to his other statement that methods of military operations depend on armament and the quality of personnel (human material). This was the point of departure for many versions of the so-called 'law of the development of military art'.[18] A corollary formula stated that military art changed in a revolutionary way with the transition of the socio-economic and political formation to the subsequent higher one. Since such a transition involved a change of the whole economic basis and of the 'human material', a revolutionary new military art also emerged.

Thus the manner of interpreting the law in the first post-war period was as follows: a new, higher system produces a new, higher military art, the rate of development of which is also higher. To put it in another way, essential changes can result only from the socio-economic and political revolutions, and changes which occur within one formation are of merely evolutionary character. For instance, changes in bourgeois art in the imperialist period cannot be radical, they are limited to changes in the techno-military aspects of fighting. The

92

October Revolution, on the other hand, generated a wholly new military art, superior to any bourgeois one.

While the historical evidence for the law in question was rather poor, one example has always been presented as most convincing and as a confirmation of the law. This example concerns the basic difference between Soviet and German military art and the superiority of Soviet military art generated by the October Revolution as evidenced by the Soviet victory in war.

Modifications In the course of time, however, individual scholars expressed the opinion that the initial interpretation was simplified and at times in disagreement with the facts. They pointed out the following inconsistencies.[19]

1 There existed no direct and exact correspondence between the systems of military art and the respective socio-economic and political formations; for instance, there was no purely feudal military art or standard bourgeois military art (especially if bourgeois history is considered as a whole together with the imperialist period).

2 Nor did changes in the material basis and in military art always correspond to each other. The revolutionary transition of one formation to the subsequent one was not reflected in a simultaneous transformation of military art.

3 Revolutionary transformation of military art occurred withon one and the same formation as, for instance, the emergence of nuclear-missile military art in the imperialist period of capitalism.

4 The antagonistic formations - especially when they coexisted - frequently employed similar methods.

Consequently, a revision of the presentation of the law in question was made in the form of certain changes in wording of the law, and different interpretations and emphasis on various components, and at times in a modified form of exposition. Although by no means common to all studies and descriptions, the modifications are characteristic of the tendency to adapt the law to the new conditions.

To make an inventory of these various interpretations and modifications I should like to think of the law as expressing a sequence of two dependences. The first (lower) dependence is that of military art on armament and human material. The second and higher, dependence is that of the armament and human material on the socio-economic system (often including the level of production, but in some presentations disregarding it) and on the socio-political structure.

In other words, the two dependences are as follows: (1) military art depends on armament and human material; (2) armaments and human material depends on the socio-economic system; (including or disregarding the level of production), and on the socio-political structure, or in a graphic form:

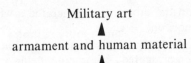

Military art

▲

armament and human material

▲

socio-economic system (including or disregarding the level of production and the
socio-political structure)

In different presentations either the lower or the higher dependence is emphasised. In some cases, the intermediate member of the two (i.e. armament and
human material) is omitted, and only the direct dependence of military art on
the socio-economic system and on the socio-political structure is asserted.

Another view (or rather modification) sometimes presented involves the separate treatment of the two determinants, components of the highest degree of the
sequence (i.e. of the socio-economic system and socio-political structure). Thus
the impact of (a) the socio-economic revolutions (together with the revolutionary changes in science and technology) on changes in military art, and (b) the
effect of the socio-political revolutions are treated separately.

In other words, two sequences of dependences are asserted:

military art ▲ armament and human material ▲ changes in the socio-economic system incl. economic level

military art ▲ armament and human material ▲ changes in the socio-political system

Similarly, the impact of the changes in the two determinants which are components of the intermediate member (armament and human material) have at
times been treated separately:[20]

military art ▲ armament

military art ▲ human material

A number of separate dependences have resulted.[21] In particular studies, such
separate and partial dependences have been used to explain or illustrate the reasoning connected with them. The most far reaching modification introduced by
some scholars, consists in a formal replacement of the above law by two partial
laws; this was accomplished in two ways.

In one presentation, *two laws correspond to the two dependences* presented
above: the lower and the higher ones. One law asserts the dependence of military
art on armament and human material, the other holds that changes in armament
and human material depend on changes in the socio-economic system and on

the socio-political structure.

The other kinds of pair laws is much more complex: two separate law-like sequences are presented: (1) social revolutions lead to radical changes in the human material which, in turn, bring about radical changes in military art and (2) radical techno-economic changes lead to radical changes in armament, which, in turn, involve radical changes in military art.

In graphic form:

social revolutions	techno-economic revolutions
▼	▼
new human material	radical changes in armament
▼	▼
radical changes in military art	radical changes in military art

The first sequence, and the corresponding law, have usually been exemplified by the radical change in military art which emerged from the French Revolution and the October Revolution.[22] It was the new 'human material' with its high moral-political qualities and the new organisational abilities on the command level, which were able to apply the revolutionary new military art,[23] although no immediate revolutionary changes in technique and armament occurred.

The second law is evidenced by the modern nuclear missile revolution which has occurred *without* any social revolution. It was the revolutionary change in armament and military equipment, a consequence of the revolutionary development of science and technology, which caused the emergence of a quite new military art.[24] The importance of the 'human material' is mentioned only as a factor which makes possible full utilisation of the new armament.[25] In several studies the first of the laws is completely omitted.[26]

One prominent scholar states that all revolutions in the system of warfare have emerged from the revolutionary inventions of new sources of energy: the invention of gun-powder and fire arms, the combination of automatic fire-arms with a motor (plus the simultaneous introduction of electricity), and finally the invention of new sources of energy by modern science - the force of a nuclear explosion and rocket vehicles.[27]

Role of the social revolutions restated As usual, however, no modifications are allowed to underestimate, or — what would be even worse — to negate the decisive role of social revolutions in history. Parallel to the long descriptions of the decisive impact of the techno-scientific revolution given in more professional writings, the traditional thesis about the dependence of revolutionary changes in military art on socio-economic revolutions and changes in the technical basis of war are restated.[28] The term 'bourgeois military art' is in common use.[29] Here and there, the role of social transformations[30] is recalled, even if the focus is on technical developments. It is said that only a higher socio-economic system meets all demands made by the modern techno-military revolution: the equipment of mass armies with the enormous amounts of modern armament and technology required, and the preparation of entire societies for total engagement in war.[31]

However, even in this orthodox approach two modifications can be noted. In the notion 'human material', the political awareness is now less emphasised than the ability to manage modern techniques;[32] and the new quality of the human material is regarded rather as a condition that makes possible the application of the new military art than as a primary cause of its emergence.

A new question is the impact on military art of the new kind of international relations, which is presented by Soviet scholars as a revolutionary transformation of the international system. The emergence of the system of socialist states means a restructuring of the whole international community. It influences military art by making possible the effective exploitation of all human resources within the socialist system and consequently the effective application of the new weapons and new military art.[33]

Changes not revolutions While many of the previously-mentioned modifications have implied that social revolutions are not a necessary condition for a revolution in military affairs, which in turn has prompted some scholars to a restatement of the crucial importance of the revolutions, others have taken a compromised position: they do not write about revolutions determining the transformations in military art, but about radical changes, which is a much more modest expression. While a socio-economic and political revolution means a change of the whole formation, socio-political (or simply political) changes may occur within one formation or, as happens nowadays, in the relations between two coexisting formations. Thus, in one view, the main factors causing changes in military affairs can be presented as follows: (1) changes in the political relations between states or between classes within states; (2) basic changes in the determining means of armed struggle on the condition that they are introduced on a mass scale.[34]

Accordingly, the revolutionary changes in Soviet military art can be explained as follows: radical changes in the correlation of forces between the capitalist and socialist systems prompted the imperialist countries to a bellicose policy and to the invention of weapons of mass destruction. This compelled the Soviet Union to make a great techno-scientific-military effort. In other words, while defence requirements have provided the politico-military basis of the revolution in Soviet military art, the radical changes in military technology have constituted its military-technical basis. Such reasoning salvages the essence of the law concerning the double dependence of the changes in military art on socio-political and techno-military changes, by replacing social revolutions by changes in the alignment of socio-political forces.

Dialectics of the development

The law of the dependence of the development of military art on its material basis is regarded as an expression of the more general law operating in the whole gamut of social life: that of the dependence of all social activities on the material basis of society. It could be expected that *the way* in which the development of military art proceeds would also be presented in a law-like form, as an expression of the laws of dialectics determining the source and mechanism of any social movement. There are many references to these laws in the description of the development of military art; however they are confined to comments on the manner in which laws of dialectics can be used to explain the mechanism of this development.

The law of contradictions in action According to Soviet philosophy and methodology, the main internal root of each development is to be sought in the contradictions inherent in each phenomenon; their mutual interaction and the competition between them are the motivating and driving force of movement and development. Thus to explain how the law of the development of military art operates, one has to demonstrate the effects of the inherent principal contradiction of the way of fighting.

In military art, the contradiction between the rapid and continuous development of the means of armed struggle and the slower development of the methods of fighting is usually pointed out as such a principal, or primary, contradiction. Means develop much more speedily than methods and their different rates of development result in periodical emergence of a lack of correspondence between them. Consequently, after some time, methods have to be radically changed.[35]

Other contradictions are considered to arise from this principal one. The list of these begins with the contradiction (and in some sense competition) between the means of attack and of defence.[36] Means of attack usually develop first and means of defence are adapted to them. This leads in turn to a further perfection of the means of attack, which aim at overcoming means of defence. The contradiction - and at the same time mutual influence - is said to sharpen in the nuclear missile age, when means of defence cannot successfully counteract means of attack - or, at least, have not done so up to this time.

Closely related to the above contradiction is that between offensive and defensive operations, the two contrasting but at the same time interdependent kinds of military action.[37] In some periods in the past, the defensive form of fighting seemed to be more effective, but the opposite is nowadays true. The offensive operations are able to achieve the decisive goals of the battle, operation and the whole warfare and they aim at a total defeat and destruction of the enemy.[38]

Then comes the contradiction between the new means of combat and the traditional methods of management of armed forces. An interrelated contradiction is that between the centralisation of the management of forces and its decentralisation. The former enables forces to act according to one central strategic plan, the latter meets the needs for maximal activity, initiative and the ability to act in isolation from other units.

The contradiction between the new means of armed struggle and the traditional forms of organisation and structure of armed forces is of a similar character. The forces should be organised in a simpler way which would enable them to increase their mobility and act independently, but they also must have at their disposal modern diversified and complex means of combat which require a more sophisticated structure. They should be able to concentrate forces for the purpose of maximal attack but at the same time be able to disperse quickly in order to avoid the enemy's counter-attacks.[39] Many other contradictions are listed.[40]

The search for internal contradictions as the driving force behind the development of military art reflects not only the attempts of Soviet researchers to prove that the law of contradictions is universal, but also the way in which they apply this law.[41] However, the contradiction between means and methods of fighting is hardly a contradiction in the sense intended by the law. The material basis of fighting and the way it is conducted cannot be regarded as opposite aspects of a single phenomenon, or as two counteracting things or processes of the same order, for instance, two physical poles or two antagonistic social classes. Their interaction is that of instruments and methods. Naturally, if instruments change, methods change too, and change of methods involves change of instruments, but such coupled changes can hardly be called an interaction of two opposite and contradictory aspects of a phenomenon.

Attempts with the law of transition Similar attempts are made to apply the law of transition from quantity to quality; this law states that a radical change in the quality of a thing (phenomenon) results from an accumulation of quantitative changes, and proceeds in jumps. In other words, instead of regarding development as a gradual evolutionary process the law maintains that the gradualness in the development is disrupted by qualitative jumps, by sudden radical changes. Since the Soviet view implies that the law of the dependence of military art on the material basis is a sequence of two dependences, many different interpretations of the action of the dialectical law of transition may be conceived. For instance, one can contend that on the highest level quantitative changes in economic science, or technology, lead to a qualitative jump i.e. to a revolutionary invention or to a quick expansion of the economy. At the same time quantitative social changes result in a social revolution. A similar transition from quantitative to qualitative changes may occur on the middle level, in the development of armament and transformation of the human material. And parallel to such changes and interrelated with them in the field of military art, the accumulation of quantitative improvements leads to a radical change in the whole way of fighting.

Alternatively, one can regard the action of the dialectical law as a sequence of two pairs of jumps.[42] A jump on the highest level, in economy, science, and technology - prepared by the quantitative changes - together with social revolution leads to a jump on the middle level in armament and human material, and this, in turn, involves a jump in military art. The jumps on the lower levels are prepared by quantitative changes corresponding to those of the higher levels.

Both, however, would be ideal models. In fact they have been reduced in some respects. The first reduction consists in omitting the social jumps. Social revolutions and revolutionary changes in the human material are often excluded from the descriptions: jumps in economy, etc., lead to jumps in armament and, in turn, to transformations of military art.[43]

The second reduction concerns quantitative changes: the quantitative development presumed to precede and prepare the qualitative jump is omitted. For instance, a new system of armaments is said to appear concurrently with a new source of energy, nuclear energy and ballistic missile technique providing the outstanding examples.[44] The process of preparing the jump in armament by means of the preceding quantitative changes in the armament itself, however, is not mentioned.[45] On the lowest level of the sequence of dependences, the quantitative changes are sometimes mentioned, but they too are presented in a highly-reduced form. For example, it is occasionally mentioned that revolutionary weapons can evoke revolutionary changes in military art, if used in significant quantity in the armed forces.[46] Here, however, the accumulation of quantitative changes relates solely to the number of new weapons.

If the exclusion of social changes from the development process means a serious deficiency from the viewpoint of historical materialism, the exclusion of the quantitative changes means negation of the law itself, since it stands and falls with the idea of transformation of 'quantity' into 'quality'.

In the classical view, such a transformation should proceed in the form of 'jumps' i.e. revolutions in the whole way of fighting, occurring either suddenly or within a very short time. However, the history of the development of military art has not provided unambiguous examples of such jumps. On the contrary, revolutionary changes in military art have been accomplished gradually, over long periods of time: the period between the introduction of firearms and their use as the principal means of armed struggle lasted more than four hundred years, about three centuries were required to develop rifled weapons to the point where they began to play a decisive role in warfare.[47]

For this reason, Soviet scholars decided to present such jumps as having a special character: jumps which mean a radical change of quality can be accomplished not only through single lightning acts, but also through slow processes lasting decades and centuries.[48] New methods of waging war become predominant through a long process of the gradual replacement of the old methods by new ones. Only in individual cases were jumps accomplished more rapidly and this occurred when great techno-scientific changes went with profound social transformations.

It follows, therefore, that jumps can be divided into two kinds: a rapid elimination of the old quality and the consequent emergence of a new one; and a relatively long gradual change as a cumulative effect of many changes which at one point bring about the emergence of a new quality. Even such an extremely radical jump as the modern techno-military revolution in military art may be included in the gradual class since, according to Soviet scholars, it has been carried through over a considerable period and its accomplishment can be divided into three stages.[49]

Apart from this conclusion, another modification has been put forward: jumps may differ with regard to their range, size and significance. Some jumps may encompass the whole realm of military art, others may lead to qualitative changes only in single fields.[50] The modern techno-military revolution in military art is an effect of a gradual change, but at the same time it has a most radical and all-encompassing character, which confirms the contention about the diversity of jumps.

The application of the law of transition from quantity to quality has posed more problems than it has solved, if it has solved any at all. This has led to two further modifications, which in fact amount to an abandonment of the explanation of the mechanism of change in military art by this law.

Some scholars present the ties between quantitative and qualitative changes instead of the leap-like transition of the former to the latter. They say, for instance, that the increase in the number of soldiers and in the quantity of equipment in a certain unit, means transferring it to a higher level in the military hierarchy (a platoon is transformed into a company, a company into a regiment etc.) which means an ability to perform new functions i.e. a new quality.[51] Some go even further and replace the law with a statement asserting that only the correspondence between the quantitative and qualitative characteristics of things and phenomena - their harmonious unity - allows them to perform their functions.[52]

The trivial character of such relationships is obvious, however, and in both cases - especially in the second one - the core of the dialectical law, the leap-like occurrence of most radical qualitative changes, preceded and prepared by the accumulation of quantitative ones, disappears.

Negation of the negation This law, we may recall, states that process of development goes through succeeding stages. Each new stage begins when the previous one is liquidated by the so-called negation, and lasts until it, in turn, is negated. Unlike the mechanical elimination of the old quality (in principle, by external factors), a dialectical negation means a transformation of the old quality into a new one (basically, resulting from internal development), and not a complete destruction of the former. It is a combination of two processes: of replacement of the old by the new, and of retaining the valuable elements of the old which, transformed, are included in the new quality.

The application of this law of negation of negation to the analysis of the dependence of the development of military art on its material base has been reduced, however. Only the interaction between the means and methods of fighting (i.e. only problems in the lower dependence) has been considered in the light of this law. A simplified formula concerning this interaction states that new weapons and new methods of fighting periodically replace (=negate) the outmoded ones, but those elements of the previous military art which can be useful are included in the new quality. In turn, the new becomes old after some time, and therefore is negated by a yet newer military art. In other words, the development is presented as a chain of succeeding stages, where each new stage is a negation of the previous one, except that all valuable elements from the past are preserved.[53]

In another version, the process of development of means and methods of fighting is presented as a kind of dialectical cycle in which the initial accordance between means and methods is followed by discordance (between new means and old methods or between new methods and old means), which can be treated as a negation of the previous accordance. This discordance, in turn, is replaced by a new accordance (new means and corresponding new methods), which can be treated as a new negation i.e. as a negation of the negation.

These are two different pictures or interpretations. In the former (accordance - new accordance - still newer accordance) periods of a lack of correspondence between means and methods are but short crises leading to revolutionary jumps, negations, after which the new stage in development brings a new correspondence between means and methods. In the latter (accordance - discordance - accordance) periods of discordance are not confined to crises leading to the immediate leap-like transformations, but are like separate stages in the development of military art, characterised not by unity of components distinctive with regard to their essence (means-methods), but by a unity of the old and the new, even if only temporary. This is an unorthodox approach, but it perhaps better corresponds to the real picture of the development of military art, in which we find many periods of coexistence of the old methods with new armament, of gradual accumulation of new armament and transformation of old methods, and in which periods of military art based on a correspondence between means and methods alternate with the above 'transitional' periods. This, however, requires a modified presentation of the manner in which the dialectical law should be applied to the explanation of development.

As we see, the laws of dialectics serve to explain certain features of the mechanism of the development of military art, its motivating forces, and the forms of development. In the latter, the emphasis is on revolutionary (or at least radical) changes, little attention being paid to periods of stagnation and decline, and to the mechanism of the development of methods of waging war, which occur continuously and in some periods slowly and gradually.

Other laws of the development of military art

The law of the dependence of the development of military art on its material base, which has always been in focus in the presentation of laws governing military art, can be regarded as primary in a whole group of laws which is perhaps in the course of formulation. The above law defines factors which determine the development of military art, but does not touch on the direction in which military art changes, or the characteristic features of this development.

101

These features have frequently been presented as assertions about the constantly increasing size, intensity, and other characteristics of wars. Recently, some scholars have begun to present them as laws or regularities. In the collective study on the revolution in military affairs three such laws (regularities-zakonomernosti) have been advanced.[54]

1 The increasingly active methods of military operations, designed to achieve ever more decisive results.

2 The increasing scale of combat and operations in terms of the number of forces participating in them, the power onslaughts employed, as well as the depth and pace of actions of all types of armed forces.

3 The increasing diversity and complexity of the methods of conducting military operations.

In another collective study, other laws have been presented, for instance, that stating that, with the development of the material basis, the costs of war continuously increase.[55]

While the number of these laws (regularities) may increase and their wording may change, the trend seems obvious: features of the two world wars, as well as of the possible future nuclear war, are treated as a lawful result of the whole development of military art through its dependence on the development of the material basis, and these processes should be 'codified' in corresponding laws.

Laws of the dependence of the methods and forms of fighting used in individual instances of war

This section deals with laws which have not yet been presented as a separate group. Particular dependences either have not been called laws, or have been included as components in other laws (for instance in the law of the dependence of the character of war on policy, or of the course and outcome of war on the correlation of forces, or in laws of the development of military art); some of them, however, have occasionally been mentioned or suggested. Such a law-group would appear to call for at least a brief presentation here because of its role in the Soviet concept of the set of laws. The latter purports to encompass laws concerning war in general, particular types of war, and individual instances of war, their socio-political essence and the military picture. Military art is here a case in point.

Three sub-groups of laws suggested Like the set of factors which, according to Soviet theory, influence war as a whole, the factors influencing the methods and forms applied in individual wars can be divided into three sub-groups:

1 The political content of a certain war, and, in particular, its political aims.

2 The economic, techno-scientific and techno-military conditions in a certain epoch, as well as the level of military art in that epoch, which is dependent on these conditions.

3 The correlation of forces of the warring sides and especially of armed
forces employed in armed struggle

Accordingly, three sub-groups of laws can be suggested: laws of the dependence
of military art applied in individual wars (1) on policy and the political aims of
war, (2) on the complex of conditions in the given epoch and (3) on the correlation of forces.

The first sub-group is only a direct reflection of the law of war which states the
dependence on policy of the main features of war in the first place, the main character of armed struggle, i.e. the general character of strategy.[56] The latter concerns the characteristics of forms and methods applied in military operations
(see Ch.8 for comments on the 'adjacent' law-groups).

Laws of the second sub-group have rarely been mentioned. Popov, when writing of the dependence of the change and development of military art on the
change and development of armament and military technique, presents as an
interrelated law the law of the dependence of the general character of armed
struggle, of the methods and forms of its conduct on the properties of armament
and combat technique (it is implied that this concerns military art applied in a
certain epoch, or even an instance of war).[57]

The third set has never been mentioned as a sub-group, nor have particular
laws in it been presented as separate laws. However statements about the dependences in question have been advanced - for instance, that a substantial superiority in numbers usually permits armed forces to launch offensive actions, while
inferiority necessitates defensive forms of warfare.[58]

Change of methods It should be mentioned, however, that these laws concern
methods and forms of conducting armed struggle chosen by the leadership at the
beginning of war. The determining factors may change, however. For instance,
the development of armaments and the accumulated experience of fighting can
affect military art, which thus can change in the course of a given war. However,
radical changes usually cannot be carried out during a war, because a relatively
long time is needed to produce a new weapon in sufficiently large quantities, to
transform the structure and organisation of the armed forces and to radically
transform military art as a whole. Therefore changes in the forms and methods
of fighting often extend into the subsequent peacetime as in the case of nuclear
weapons on into the beginning of the next war.

It is not certain whether in the near future a law-group like that suggested in
this section will be formulated. But even if its absence up to now in the Soviet system of laws has shown nothing else, it has surely indicated the incompleteness of
this system.

Common laws Laws of the dependence of military art are often formulated in
such way that they may be included in both of the above groups. For instance,
the law which states that forces and weapons (or men and armament) exert the
determining influence on the means and methods used in armed struggle, applies

both to the development of military art in history and to the conduct of each specific war.[59]

Laws of the effectiveness of armed struggle

The second main division of the laws of armed struggle has been called variously: laws of the effectiveness of armed struggle (or armed combat, armed conflict, warfare); internal laws of armed struggle; the 'proper' laws of armed struggle; laws of the dependence of the course and outcome of armed struggle on methods and forms of fighting; laws of the dependence of the course and outcome of armed struggle on the internal and external factors and the like. Some descriptions of the laws on particular levels of fighting provide additional terms, such as laws of battle.[60]

Suggested classification

Many particular laws, or sets of laws, classified with this group have occasionally been presented. Almost every new description makes a new proposal differing in the terms given to the variables, the wording of the laws and their classification. In effect, no systematic and generally accepted classification has been worked out.

However, three groups of factors on which the course and outcome of armed struggle depend (i.e. the effectiveness of armed struggle) recur in many proposals: (1) the external factors (conditions), (2) means and methods applied, and (3) interrelation of various levels and kinds of military operations.

A resultant, if only provisional and temporary, list of laws can be suggested as follows:

1 The law of the dependence of the effectiveness (or course and outcome) or armed struggle on the political aims of war.

2 The law (or group of laws) of the dependence of the effectiveness (course and outcome) of armed struggle on the correlation of strengths of the opposing forces.

3 Laws of the correspondence of means and methods used in armed struggle to the missions which the forces are to carry out, and vice versa.

4 Laws of the unity of action of all divisions of the armed forces.

5 Internal laws of the particular services and branches of the armed forces, and branches of arms.

Law of dependence of the effectiveness of armed struggle on the political aims of war

The operation of such a law has been illustrated by examples taken from past and present wars (especially the wars in Korea and Vietnam), and also supported by the logical procedure: since the dependence of the course and outcome of war as a whole on its political aims is one of the basic laws of war, permeating all phenomena and all fronts of war, it cannot fail to be reflected in a corresponding law of armed struggle. The mechanism of its action, apart from the examples given from particular wars, has been explained cursorily and summarily. The political aims affect military art and thereby the course and outcome of armed struggle; they affect the attitude of people towards war, their moral condition, and thereby the course and outcome of armed struggle; they affect the correspondence of the means used in war to the military-strategic aims, and thereby . . . etc.

Dependence on the correlation of forces

Two interpretations Two variants of the basic law in this sub-group have been presented. According to the narrower concept, the course and outcome of the armed struggle - operation, battle, or combat - depends on the correlation of the combat power of the troops directly participating in it.[61] In other words, the chances of victory are the dependent variable. The law holds that at any given moment in the development of any operation, battle or combat, the shape it takes will favour the side whose forces have greater combat power than the enemy's.[62] Both versions seem to assume that the correlation of forces on a particular sector of the front at a certain time may differ from the global correlation of the armed forces fighting against each other.

In a much broader interpretation, the respective general law of war is directly applied to armed struggle: other things begin equal, the winning side will be that which is superior in means and forces i.e. the complex of all political, economic and strictly military factors.[63] Here, however, there is no clear difference between a general law of war which operates with all socio-political and economic forces and a law of armed struggle which concerns only the factors which affect combat power.

Proponents of this law consider it the principal law of armed struggle, since only superiority in combat power enables the forces to assert their own appropriate methods of combat, to exploit fully the terrain and the time factor, to seize the initiative and to achieve further changes in the correlation of power to their own advantage.

The correlation of forces is presented as determining the whole course of development taken by the combat and also affecting conditions for the action of other laws of armed struggle.[64] Other laws serve the attainment of a favourable correlation of forces. One such law holds that in any combat, battle or operation the troops which forestall the enemy in deploying forces into combat and operational formations and outpace him at the beginning of the active combat operations, will gain a considerable advantage.[65] Another law asserts the essential dependence of the course and outcome of each combat, battle or operation in the concentration of main efforts of participating forces on the decisive axis.[66]

105

Correlation of forces. The statement about the determining influence of the correlation of forces is perhaps the most representative example of elevating the common experience of fighting to a law. The key problem is obviously the interpretation of the term 'forces'. In most descriptions based on the narrower concept of the law it is held that 'forces' here means the combat power of the troops directly engaged in the given action,[67] which encompass all quantitative and qualitative characteristics of means and forces, including the level of military art applied by them.

In a more detailed presentation the quantitative indices are said to embrace the numerical strength of the forces, the number of units, and the quantity of weapons and equipment; among the qualitative characteristics the political aspect includes such moral-political features as the world outlook, political awareness, morale and discipline of the soldiers, while military aspect covers the level of training, the efficiency of the weapons and technical organisation, the grouping and combat readiness of troops, the system of control, the organisational talent and the operational training of officers, etc.[68]

Some scholars observe that even such a narrower interpretation of the concept of forces does not contradict the assumption that the size of combat power depends on the political content of the given war as a whole and on the country's economic and moral potentialities.[69]

Changes The mechanism of the law (laws) discussed in this section has profoundly changed under nuclear conditions. It is not the initial correlation of combat forces which determines, or at least greatly influences, the final outcome, but the ability quickly to change it in one's favour through fighting. This is now considered possible and necessary because of the availability of nuclear weapons and the high mobility of troops; the former can destroy the combat power of the enemy, the latter makes it possible quickly to take advantage of the results of nuclear strikes. Changes in the correlation of forces can now be achieved in minutes, and even seconds.[70]

Such changes in the mechanism of this law can perhaps affect its objective content. If previously it could be expressed by the formula: correlation ——► outcome of fighting, it should now, perhaps, be replaced by a more complex one: initial fighting, partly depending on the initial correlation ——► the resultant correlation ——► outcome of the fighting as a whole.

Correspondence between means and missions

With this sub-group of laws, several dependences presented as laws can be classified, and two of them will be briefly described.

Firstly, there is the law of the dependence of the effectiveness of armed struggle (or of its course and outcome) on the correspondence between the means and methods applied, on the one hand, and the missions assigned to the forces, on the other. This is a two-way correspondence: means and methods have to correspond to the mission and, on the other hand, the mission must be chosen in full correspondence to the available means and methods which can be applied.[71]

The other law maintains that the effectiveness of armed struggle depends on correspondence between the mission which the troops are to carry out (i.e. the goals of military operations) and the situation at the moment. The latter is to be interpreted as the ensemble of conditions under which armed struggle (combat, battle, operation) is conducted.[72] In a simpler wording, only such missions can be assigned to the troops as can be carried out in the given situation.

Unity of military operations on all levels and in all dimensions

The basic law in this sub-group has been formulated in three alternative ways. (1) The law of the unity and interdependence of actions in all dimensions - land, sea and air[73], (2) The law of the unity and cooperation of actions of all services of the armed forces[74], (3) The law of the unity and interdependence of actions on all three levels of military operations: strategic, operational and tactical.[75] Since these laws partly overlap, they may be regarded as a set of three complementary laws.

The third formula is usually complemented by the law of the subordination of military operations on the operational-tactical level to the interest of strategy.[76] It was previously held that strategy depended on the results of particular battles and operations; but in a nuclear missile war strategic blows may determine the outcome of the whole armed struggle, or determine the situation in which armed forces on the tactical and operational levels can successfully carry out their missions.[77] This law has also been presented in a somewhat different version: under modern combat conditions a higher level of military art directly influences a lower one.[78]

Laws within the services of armed forces

Laws expressing relationships and dependences within particular services and branches of armed forces and arms, constitute a separate sub-group. As a sub-group, or class, they have not been elaborated, and only single laws are presented. Their systematisation goes beyond the aim and scope of this study.

Other laws

Occasionally, in this or that study, various other laws have been presented, either within the above-mentioned sub-group, or even beyond them. For instance, Grudinin mentions, in connection with the laws of the effectiveness of armed struggle, the law of the dependence of this effectiveness on the character, force and directness of combat strikes.[79] In the other variant, a whole new sub-group of laws is indirectly suggested: in the comprehensive history of military art, in the Officers Library series, mention is made of the laws of the preparation and conduct of warfare, 'laws indicating in what way, and by what methods, the armed forces are trained and victory is achieved in contemporary war'.[80]

Various versions of particular laws of armed struggle, which may in some instances amount to different laws, have been quoted above, on the occasion of presenting informal sets of laws (see p.90). As can be noted with regard to other parts of the set of laws and principles, these additional laws, sub-groups of laws, or different versions of them, confirm the view that this set is in a state of constant evolution.

Search for one fundamental law

As with the laws of war, attempts have been made to formulate a basic law of armed struggle. A prominent scholar proposes the following formula: 'The direct basis determining the direction of the development of military operations, and their subordination to laws, is the correlation of forces of the warring sides'. He substantiates the formula by the fact that the outcome of the interaction of fighting armies, which is the main front of war, depends on the correlation of forces i.e. on the correlation of the quantity and quality of fighting troops, and on each side's possibilities of changing the initial correlation in its own favour.[81]

It seems, however, that the above formula is far from complete, since it says nothing about the key factors which influence the course and outcome of armed struggle for instance, the political content of war including its political aims.

The criteria for a basic law of armed struggle have not been discussed. One such criterion, however, seems obvious: the law should be most general in this category, and cannot be a combination of particular laws, or a law of the same order as particular laws.

Consequences of the action of laws: characteristics of current military art

Soviet scholars, discussing the characteristics of the military art of our epoch, state that these provide evidence of the correct exploitation of the laws of armed struggle in Soviet theory and practice. The general characteristics of military art reflect the determining influence of all the factors and conditions stated by the laws of the development of military art, particularly the revolutionary changes in armament and equipment. They also reflect the operation of the laws of the effectiveness of armed struggle under the new conditions. The characteristics in question may be summarised as follows:

1 All dimensions of war keep expanding to an enormous extent: the zones of all kinds of military operations are undergoing a vast extension, their depth is increasing, the pace quickening, the destructive power of weapons acquiring an annihilating character. As regards military operations, the situation is changing with lightning speed.

2 Military art is adapting itself to the all-important roles of the first period of war and the surprise factor.

3 The whole relationship between strategy, operational art and tactics changes, since all kinds of tasks can be solved at one and the same time and the use of strategic nuclear weapons can bring decisive results.

4 The conduct of future warfare must be based on the premise that the offensive will be the decisive type of combat action, and even defensive tasks will be solved by vigorous offensive operations.

5 Military art re-assesses all kinds of military operations, taking into account the possibility of conducting them with or without the use of nuclear weapons. Two arts of warfare are being worked out, not counterposing each other but closely connected: even if only one category of weapons will actually be used, the existence of the other one and the possibility of its use at any moment will be calculated in each action.

6 Military art is re-examining the role and place of different services and branches of armed forces and arms. The air force, for instance, will not only be able to participate in the combat operations of the land forces and navy, but also independently to carry out operational-level and strategic missions. The navy will be able to extend operations over vast ocean expanses and make powerful nuclear missile strikes not only against enemy naval groupings but also against its major objectives on the continents. The land forces will have favourable conditions for conducting offensive operations to a great depth and at enormous speed, and for achieving decisive goals in a very short time; this will be made possible by strategic missile strikes against major enemy installations.

7 All principles of military art are being re-examined and re-formulated, according to the above premises.

This brief survey suggests a comment. While the specified characteristics of current military art reflect formulae on the new techno-military situation, presented by Soviet scholars as laws of armed struggle, they insufficiently reflect the new socio-political conditions which in Soviet theory are said to play such an important role.

Comments

System of laws of armed struggle

As with the general laws of war, it has not been easy to present the second basic category of laws of war as a coherent and consistent whole. While general comments will be made in Chap. 8, a few preliminary remarks may be advisable here.

This part of the set is heterogeneous, the two main components differing significantly with regard to their scope and character.

1 As to the scope, laws of military art concern general features of the way wars

are waged; therefore their scope likens that of the general laws of war. This similarity has resulted in their overlapping with certain groups of the general laws of war, and in other inconsistencies of the general division of laws, discussed in Chap. 8.

2 On the other hand, the scope of most laws of the effectiveness of armed struggle is very similar to that of the principles of military art. Both concern the relation between means and methods of fighting and both concern the conditions to be fulfilled for victory. Although a necessary conceptual correspondence is alleged here, since principles should reflect laws, the result involves some confusion. This will be discussed in Chaps. 6 and 8.

3 The laws of the effectiveness of armed struggle constitute a heterogeneous group: the external and internal factors on which the effectiveness of fighting depends involve quite different kinds of relationships: policy and combat power express the factors decisively affecting war as a whole and here, in particular, armed struggle; while the internal factors represent specific structural-functional aspects of armed struggle. The former, although changing, maintain a definite and relatively stable shape, at least during particular stages of war; the latter are always in the state of reproduction in the course of fighting.

Character of laws

The differences between the character of the two main parts of the set of laws of armed struggle, as well as between their subdivisions, are also significant.

1 The laws of the development of military art resemble those general laws of war which operate as dependences of the processes of war on a complex of material and spiritual factors. They share with them all deviations from a strictly unequivocal and thus fully predictable causation, which are connected with their character as law-tendencies (Ch.4), and with their functioning as general dependences without quantitative measurements and with different degrees of probability.

According to our working formula, the development of military art and its application in particular epochs (E may here be replaced by M) follow logically from social activity (A) under the determining conditions (C), according to objective laws (L): the specifics of the formula in this case is that the conditions, C, which here mean the development of the economic basis and social-political superstructure in history, and their shape in the particular formations, epochs, and periods, are the main determining variable although, as in all social laws, they influence war through human action.

Both this determinant variable and the dependent one, the development of military art, are processes, with a very complex relationship: one cannot obtain an exact determination of the state of military art from the contemporary economic and socio-political state. The periods in which changes in the dependent variable occur and develop do not necessarily coincide with those in which changes in the determinant occur. Revolutionary changes in the former do not inevitably and immediately follow similar changes in the latter; these may occur even without economic and socio-political revolutions and be caused only by radical changes in science and technology. This confirms the judgement that laws (L) express merely general tendencies.

2 Apart from this, the dependence of the forms and methods applied in individual wars on a complex of external factors may be treated as a necessary and recurring relationship between two social activities at a given moment although, like other laws of armed struggle, it lacks any quantitative measurability. The development of military art as well as the development of the external factors during war further complicate the dependence, however.

3 While in the development of military art C is the main determining variable, in the general operation of the laws of the effectiveness of armed struggle human activity in fighting A plays the main role. Only the law of the dependence of armed struggle on policy, which is a direct application of the corresponding general law of war, is an exception.

In the operation of the law of the dependence of armed struggle on the correlation of combat power human actions aiming at creating a favourable correlation in each concrete military operation are of extreme importance. This can also be said about the operation of other laws concerning the dependence of the effectiveness of armed struggle: on the proper means and methods applied, and on the proper relationship between levels of combat, parts of armed forces and other aspects of combat. Terming these dependences laws means that the probability of correct and therefore effective actions is regarded as high. While the mechanism of the dependence has been described, the degree of such probability has not been established - indeed, seems impossible to establish, since the effectiveness depends on simultaneous observation of many principles and individual character of action (see Chap. 6, p.133).

Summing up the common characteristics in the very heterogeneous category of the laws of armed struggle, one may say that they concern qualitative ties between phenomena and processes and the probabilistic causation of events, with a very rough estimate of the degree of probability.

Notes

[1] The basic propositions of dialectical materialism here usually constitute the point of departure: that the world and its phenomena do exist, they occur and develop according to the laws of dialectics and are cognisable. Thus 'all phenomena of armed struggle, on the strategic and operational-tactical scale, are subordinated to the action of the objective laws, and all of them are cognisable' (Grudinin, 1971, pp.179-80).

'Indeed, armed struggle is an exceedingly complex, many-sided and at times contradictory phenomenon. Nevertheless, it has its "inner logic', its objective laws' (Morozov, 1974, p.2). 'The laws of armed struggle are essential relationships which exercise a most profound influence of the course of armed struggle and on the victories and defeats of the forces' (Popov, 1966a, p.4).

[2] Morozov, ibid.

[3] Kozlov, 1971; Savkin, 1972. Many laws presented as laws of armed struggle do not fit this definition since they relate phenomena on the battlefield to various external factors for instance, the methods of fighting to the level of economic development of society. Note that while in Soviet writings the term 'laws of armed struggle' (zakony vooruzhennoi bor'by") is that commonly used, in English translation the terms 'laws of armed conflict', 'laws of warfare', and 'laws of armed combat' are most frequently applied.

[4] Marksizm-leninizm o voine i armii, 1968. Among four groups of laws of war, two concern laws discussed in this chapter: laws of the development of military art, and laws of military operations (i.e. laws of the effectiveness of armed struggle) (p.358). Popov, 1964, terms them laws of armed struggle as a two-sided process of the military operations of the forces (Ch.3). Cf. Ch. 3, p.50.

[5] A.A. Strokov, at the discussion organised by military historians, 1.03.1965 After: 'Sov'eshchanie voenykh istorikov 'O metodologii voenno-istoricheskogo issledovaniya', in: *Voenno-Istoricheskii Zhurnal*, 1965:7,p.100.

[6] Popov, 1964, includes the following as laws of armed struggle: the course and outcome of battle (operation) depend on the correlation of combat power of the armed forces which directly participate in it; the main efforts by the forces must be concentrated on decisive axes; military operations on an operational-tactical scale are subordinated to the interests of strategy, which in turn depends on the results of particular battles and engagements; in any battle, engagement, or operation the advantage goes to the side which is able to forestall the enemy in deploying its forces and beat him to the punch at the beginning of combat operations.

[7] Metodologicheskie problemy, Ch.XIV.

[8] The law is also formulated as follows: the development of the battle, or operation, essentially depends on the correlation of the combat power of the opposing armed forces.

[9] Here 'politics' means the political content of war - in other words, the whole of the political interests and goals of warring parties and of the contradictions between them.

[10] Cf. Gare jev, 1977. (See note 20 to Ch.4).

[11] Kozlov, 1971.

[12] Savkin, 1972.

[13] This includes forces and means of armed struggle, armament and combat equipment, and people who use them.

[14] Law 'of the dependence of the course of hostilities and battles on the correlation of the combat might of the troops on the battlefields' (Morozov, 1974, p.4).

[15] Zamorsky, 1975.

[16] Cf. laws mentioned in note 6.

[17] Savkin called it 'the first law of armed conflict' and formulated it thus: 'Methods and forms of armed conflict depend on the material basis of the battle and operation' (1972, p.99).

[18] 'The recent development of military art completely confirms Frederick Engels' brilliant conclusion that the entire organisation of armies and the methods by which they wage war are dependent on material i.e. economic conditions: on human material and weapons' (Derevyanko, 1967, p.21). Cf. Strokov, 1965, p.658; Nauchno-tekhnicheskii progress, p.127.

'The dependence of the methods and forms of armed struggle on the economic conditions, armament, technology and human personnel is an objective law, operating in all formations and all wars' (Istoriya voin i voennogo iskusstva, 1970, p.8). Lototskii, 1973, formulates this law in almost the same words, Cf. Istoriya voin i voennogo iskusstva, p.9.

Sushko formulates this law (whose discovery he also attributes to Engels) as follows: 'The law of the correspondence of the methods of waging armed struggle and of the organization of armed forces to the level of the development and character of military technology, and also to the social nature and moral-political spirit of the army' (1964c). He enumerates several laws operating on the basis of the above law (using the term 'law' interchangeably with 'regularity').

'For the first time in the history of social life Engels regarded wars not as a chaos of chance occurrences but as processes governed by definite laws and expressing the dependence of the course and outcome of a war on economic, scientific, technical, moral, and purely military factors. Neglect of the laws of warfare leads to adventurism, to a defeat in war' (Babin, 1970b, p.11).

[19] The impact of social revolutions consists in a radical change in the aims of wars, in the moral spirit of armies, and in methods of fighting. The impact of the French Revolution and the October Revolution are said to confirm the statement of this lawlike dependence (Istoriya voin i voennogo iskusstva, 1970, p.9). Cf. Strokov, 1965, p.660, about the influence of the French Revolution.

[20] Marksizm-leninizm o voine i armii, 1965, Ch.VI.5: 'We have a full right to speak of the slave-owning, feudal, capitalist or socialist system, but we shall not find in history a slave-owning, feudal, capitalist or socialist system of conducting war and military operations' (Pukhovskii, 1965, p.26).

However, in the History of Military Art, edited in the 'Officer's Library' series we read: 'Basic changes (revolutions) in military affairs are connected with the replacement of one socio-economic formation by another and with new characteristics of weapons and military equipment. They arise from social revolutions and changes in the technical basis of waging war' (Strokov, 1966, Ch.17). Some scholars take an ambiguous position, however. The authors of 'O sovetskoi voennoi nauke' on the one hand contend that it would be wrong to think that the replacement of one socio-economic system by another one automatically and immediately involves the entire replacement of one system of propositions in military science by another one. Each period in the history of military theory is strictly connected with the preceding historical process and based on the accumulated knowledge. On the other hand, they write that the military thought of the slave-owning, feudal and capitalistic formations represents the main periods of its development. 'Each formation has its armed forces, wars of specific character with specific goals, and its own way of waging armed struggle' (1964, pp.91, 96). In the textbook for military academies, the history of war and military art is presented according to socio-economic formations, but it is pointed out that military art also develops within particular formations (Istoriya voin i voennogo iskusstva, 1970, p.7).

[21] Savkin, pp.99-100. In some cases, only one dependence is mentioned: 'The law of the dependence of the character of armed struggle and of the methods and forms of its conduct on the properties of armament and military technique' (Popov, 1964, pp.63-68; Zakharov, 1967, p.48; Metodologicheskie problemy, Ch.XV).

[22] Savkin, 1972; Lototskii, 1973. Cf. note 19.

[23] 'The forms of military conflict employed by the Red Army in using the same equipment employed by the enemy bore an innovative, advanced character. The new social nature of the Red Army, which was fighting for Soviet power, determined the essentially new features of the methods of waging combat operations which it used' (Savkin, p.100); 'Profound changes in the methods and forms of armed combat are also brought about by social revolutions. They radically change the goals of war, the personnel and the morale of the armed forces; they give rise to new methods of military actions or substantially change the old ones. For example, a radical transformation in military art was brought about by the French bourgeois revolution' (Lototskii, 1973).

In a more general form: '. . . the other material basis of the development of warfare - man - also changes. This change, although less noticeable, is very important. It is mainly the spiritual qualities of man who uses the weapons and controls the operations that change. The new complex equipment requires the fighting man to have extensive scientific knowledge, while modern fighting requires high moral and fighting qualities. Here, too, we see a connection between military and social problems. The moral and fighting qualities of the soldier are determined by his consciousness and the aims of army's struggle. History attests that the revolutionary changes in the methods of armed struggle may be based not only on techniques, but also on high moral and fighting qualities of an army fighting for a just cause' (Derevyanko, 1967, p.21).

[24] Metodologicheskie problemy, ibid.; 'The appearance of nuclear weapons and other modern weapons of war have caused a total revolution in military affairs' (Zakharov, 1970). 'The qualitative leap in military affairs today has as its immediate cause progress in science and technology. It is this that determines the development of weaponry and material and, *through them*, gives rise to new forms and methods of warfare' (Zav yalov, 1971, p.2). (Italics added.)

In many studies, the formula of this law stating both dependences is followed by the statement that 'the contemporary revolution in military affairs is connected with the appearance of nuclear weapons and missiles and the equipment of the armed forces with them' (Strokov, 1966, Ch.17). Cf. Voprosy revolutsii v voennom dele, 1965.

[25] S. Shtemenko, 'Nauchno-tekhnicheskii progress i ego vliyane na razvitie voennogo dela', *Kommunist Vooruzhennykh Sil*, 1963:3; G. Semenov, V. Prokhorov, 'Nauchno-tekhnicheskii progress i nekotorye voprosy strategii', *Voennaya Mysl'*, 1962:2; Strokov, 1966; Bochkarev, Prusanov, Babakov, 1966.

[26] Nauchno-tekhnicheskii progress i revolutsiya v voennom dele, Ch.V.1.; 'Scientific-technical progress, being the direct source of the modern qualitative leap in military affairs, determines the development of weaponry and combat equipment and through them brings to life new ways and means of conducting warfare. The same process can be observed particularly clearly in the example of the emergence and development of nuclear weaponry and the changes in military affairs to which it led' (Zavyalov, 1970, p.2). It seems to me that this is why some Soviet scholars quote *only* Engels' words about the dependence of military art on economics and ignore the thesis on the dependence of the latter on 'human material' (Voennaya strategiya, p.40). Engles 'proved that the level and character of the material production in society form the deepest basis and root of development of the methods of armed struggle' (M. Ivashchenko, Y. Lemeshko, 'F. Engels o dialektike razvitiya sposobov vooruzhennoi bor'by', *Kommunist Vooruzhennykh*, 1972:14, pp.9-1'); Cf. Grundinin, 1971; Zemskov, 1972.

Popov, 1964, argues that the two determinants of the change in military art should be separated, since the dependence of military art on 'human material' is but a manifestation of the dependence of the character of war on its political content (p.63). 'This discovery by Engels of the law of the dependence of the art of warfare on economic factors marked a genuine revolution in military theory' (Strokov, 1966b, p.45).

[27] 'Only such innovations, which are associated primarily with the new sources of energy, exert a truly revolutionary influence on all military development' (Derevyanko, 1972, pp.2-3). Therefore some scholars contend that no great differences nowadays exist between military art in the capitalist and the socialist countries. In World War II many kinds of military operations on the tactical and operational levels waged by the Soviet army and the armies of its allies and enemies were similar. This resulted from the similar armament (Metodologicheskie problemy, p.349; Marksizm-leninizm o voine i armii, 1964, p.383. Cf. Popov, 1964; Savkin, p.81). The latter writes: '. . . in spite of the presence of the effect of the political content of war on the character of armed conflict, the methods and forms of combat operations of both warring groupings, even with diametrically opposed political goals of war, may in a number of cases be more or less identical. For example, in the Great Patriotic War the methods of employing tank and rifle troops of the Soviet Army and of fascist German units had no fundamental distinction in number of cases; the character of armed conflict often was one of manoeuvre; both sides employed offence under some condi-

tions and defence under others as the fundamental forms of combat operations'.

[28] Strokov, who attributes the revolutionary changes in military affairs both to social revolutions and changes in the technical base of waging war (see note [20]), then writes, however: 'The contemporary revolution in military affairs is connected with the appearance of nuclear weapons and rockets and the equipment of the Armed Forces with them'. It means that social and technical revolutions are treated not as complementary sides of one revolution determining changes in military art, but as two alternative determinants; the technical revolution suffices to bring about revolutionary changes in the way of fighting.

[29] See, for instance, 'Voennaya nauka' and 'Voennoe iskusstvo' in: Sovetskaya Voennaya Entsiklopediya, vol.2, pp.208-11, 218-23; O sovetskoi voennoi nauke, 1964, Ch.III; Milshtein, Slobodenko, 1961; Grechko, 1975.

[30] V.K. Avramov, Chelovek i tekhnika v sovremennoi voine, Voenizdat, Moscow 1960; Il'in, 1969; Istoriya voin i voennogo iskusstva, 1970, p.9; Seleznev, 'V.I. Lenin osnovopolozhnik sovetskoi voennoi nauki', Kommunist Vooruzhennykh Sil, 1970:6; Ivashchenko, Lemeshko, 1970; Lototskii, 1973; at times, however, the assertions on the determining role of social revolutions in the development of military art sound artificial: '. . . rapid scientific and technical progress, the quckly-developing productive forces and the equally rapidly changing social conditions in the world as a result of socialist revolutions and the national liberation movement had led to a fundamental change in our ideas concerning the nature of armed combat and its methods' (Nauchno-tekhnicheskii progress, p.132).

[31] 'Naturally, the change in character of the personnel, the rising level of the general education and culture of youth in the process of the development of Soviet society, and the most modern armament, create the chief premise for the elaboration of new methods of armed struggle. The nature of army personnel, its quantity and quality, may widen or narrow the potentialities of military art' (Ivashchenko, Lemeshko, ibid., p.14); '. . . the stronger the economy of the state, the more numerous its population, the higher its cultural level, the more developed its industry, agriculture, science, and technology, the better able it will be to maintain armed forces and provide them with the latest weapons and other military equipment. The economy, through its influence on weapons and personnel, also affects the methods of conducting war - the tactics, operational art and strategy' (Voennaya strategiya, p.266).

'These weapons and equipment are created and controlled by a new Soviet man, a man of socialist society. This comprises one of the main bases in forming the new methods for conducting military operations' (Nauchno-tekhnicheskii progress, p.5); 'The main thing is the people in whose hands these weapons rest. Under present-day conditions as before, victory to a no lesser degree depends on the state of the combat morale of the warring armies. The men who have mastered the military equipment and who are strong in political morale terms will ultimately determine everything. Our army consists of such men' (A.A. Grechko, in Pravda, 3.04. 1971).

It is also often said that the political awareness of people, and their moral postures, which are directly related to the character of the socio-economic and political system, decisively influence the preparedness for a war, and its course and outcome (I. Zavyalov, 'Dialektika sredstu i sposobov vedeniya voiny', *Voennaya Mysl'*, 1969:10); Azovtsev contends that although Lenin stated the dependence of the methods of combat on armament and military technology, he attributed the main role to man (1971, p.17).

[32] Istoriya voin i voennogo iskusstva, 1970, p. 552.

[33] Krupnov, 1964, pp.72-5.

[34] Lomov, 1965, pp.115-24; some scholars point out the following external factors which constitute the material basis of military art and influence its development: economy, science and politics (V. Bondarenko, 'Sovremennaya revolutsiya v voennom dele i boevaya gotovnost' vooruzhennykh sil', *Kommunist Vooruzhennykh Sil*, 1968:4).

[35] 'The contradiction between the new means of combat and the old methods and forms of its conduct is the basic contradiction in the development of military art' (Krupnov, 1963, p.136); 'when a new weapon radically changes the combat capacities of the armed forces so that they cannot be reconciled with the old ways of waging war i.e. when weapon and ways of waging war are not in correspondence, a contradiction between them arises' (Voennaya strategiya, p.275); cf. Metodologicheskie problemy, p.349.

[36] Krupnov, 1963; Zav'yalov, 1969; Nauchno-tekhnicheskii progress; Voennaya strategiya, pp.273-74; this and other contradictions have been listed in Ogarkov, 1978, p.117.

[37] Krupnov, ibid. Soviet scholars observe that in military operations other internal contradictions are also inherent for instance, those between the means of combat and techniques for their use, between fire and movement, the rate of offensive action and possibilities of supplying troops, the amount of information available to the commanders and possibilities of analysing them in due time, etc. (Zav'yalov, 1969, pp.8-10; Ogarkov, 1978, p.117. The latter writes about the 'dialectical contradiction in the management of armed forces'.)

[38] '. . . nuclear weapons have established even more firmly the role of attack as the decisive form of military action and have made it necessary to accomplish even defensive tasks by active offensive actions' (Zav'yalov, 1970). 'A strategic nuclear rocket strike . . . combines in itself, simultaneously, the function of attack and defense' (Krupnov, 1966).

[39] G. Fedorov, 'Dialekticheskii materializm i sovetskaya voennaya nauka', *Propagandist i Agitator*, 1955:18, p.15; Krupnov, 1966, contends that each improvement in troop mobility solves this contradiction.

[40] In World War II, infantry could not quickly enough exploit the results of artillery and air force bombardments. Air forces did not manage to support the attacking tanks.

[41] Another example of the alleged unity of opposites is found, according to some Soviet scholars, in the contradiction between the objective and subjective

sides of military affairs, presented as one of the main contradictions of armed struggle. These can be resolved by correct action by the commanders (Grudinin, 1971, p.229). Ogarkov writes that among the contradictions of armed struggle, the contradiction between the adversaries and their strategic aims plays the main role (1978, p.117).

[42] V. Voznenko, 'Dialektika razvitiya i smeny form i sposobov vooruzhennoi bor'by', *Kommunist Vooruzhennykh Sil*, 1966:11.

[43] 'In our country, the revolution in military affairs has been carried out on the basis of progress in the development of the productive forces as well as scientific and technical achievements which have provided for the creation of such powerful weapons as nuclear weapons, and jet-propelled and radio-electronic military equipment . . . This comprises one of the main bases in forming the new methods for conducting military operations' (Nauchno-tekhnicheskii progress, p.5); cf. Strokov, 1966.

[44] Bondarenko, 1966.

[45] In various presentations, there is a general assumption that the development of military art goes on continuously and that at some point a noticeable jump takes place: the old methods disappear and radically new ones emerge. This assumption, however, relates only to past changes, and not to the modern nuclear missile revolution (e.g. Voznenko, ibid.). The latter is rarely presented as being preceded by a gradual quantitative development; and, when mentioned, it is never described in detail.

[46] Krupnov, 1966. The fact that improved weapons lead to changes in military art only when they are introduced in sufficient numbers is called 'the most important law' (Istoriya voin i voennogo iskusstva, 1970, p.8). 'Weapons do not always introduce basic changes in the conduct of war or in the organisation and development of the armed forces. This only happens when a new weapon possesses fundamentally different and better military properties than older types, when it is produced and supplied to the armies en masse and thus becomes a basic, or one of the basic, combat weapons' (Voennaya strategiya, p.275); 'One of the natural laws also establishes that the most highly perfected weapon exerts a substantial influence on changing the methods and forms of waging war only when it is available in great quantities. Thus, only the mass employment of machine guns and artillery during World War I resulted in the appearance of the position form of warfare. In World War II only the extensive employment of armed and mechanised forces supported by aviation resulted in overcoming the dilemma of position warfare and contributed to the development of manoeuvreing actions and an increase in the scale of operations. Nuclear weapons and missiles began to exert a substantial influence and brought about radical changes in the methods of conducting combat operations after the capability was acquired to supply significant quantities of these weapons to the forces' (Lototskii, 1973).

[47] It took 10 to 20 years to develop machine-guns, aircraft or tanks into very important weapons. It also took some time (10-20 years) to develop nuclear weapons to the point where they became the main means of warfare (Voennaya

strategiya, p.277; Zav'yalov, 1969, pp.10-11; Metodologicheskie problemy, p.70; Lototskii, 1973).

[48] Krupnov, 1963, p.108; Voennaya strategiya, p.277.

[49] More precisely, the post-war development of weapons and military art has been divided by many Soviet scholars into three periods: from 1945 through 1953, as a period of conventional weapons and conventional war doctrine, but preparing the nuclear jump; from 1954 through 1959, as the period of building up the nuclear arsenal and shaping the doctrine of nuclear war; and the period beginning in 1960, when parallel to the build-up of nuclear missile armament the doctrine of the nuclear missile war has finally been established. (Sokolovskii, Cherednichenko, 1965; cf. M. Povalii, 'Razvitie sovetskoi voennoi strategii', *Voennaya Mysl'*, 1967:2; N. Lomov, 'Osnovnye cherty sovetskoi voennoi doktriny', *Krasnaya Zvezda*, 7.10.1964; Strokov, 1966, pp.590-92; Savkin, 1972, p.167).

Some scholars consider the second and third stages as constituting a single one (subdivided into two sub-periods), since they wish to stress the unity of the nuclear rearmament and doctrine (M.I. Cherednichenko, 'Ob osobennostyakh razvitiya voennogo iskusstva v poslevoennyi period', *Voenno-Istoricheskii Zhurnal*, 1970:6).

Some scholars contrast the contemporary revolution in means of warfare with the older ones. Larionov, 1964, states that the mastering of atomic energy represents a revolutionary jump in the means of armed combat in contrast to the evolutionary process of change of means of war in the XIXth and early XXth centuries (in: Problemy revolutsii v voennom dele, 1965, pp.125-26), however he overlooks that the above changes have also been termed jumps, by other scholars, only prolonged ones . . .

[50] Krupnov, 1966.

[51] Rybkin, 1975, p.17.

[52] Grudinin, 1971, p.112. Another exposition of this problem also reduces it to the correspondence between the number and quality of armed forces (O sovetskoi voennoi nauke, 1964, pp.296-7).

[53] Some scholars point out that the new armament and equipment as a rule were initially adapted to the hitherto existing forms of organisation of armed forces and to the old methods of fighting; new organisation and new methods arose only gradually, as the number of new armament types and experience of their use increased. (Grudinin, 1971, suggested the examples of tanks and missiles. He gave several reasons for the vitality of the old methods of fighting: their effective use in past wars; the ability of troops to use familiar techniques of fighting, their lack of experience with the use of new armaments; the insufficient preparation of personnel for the use of new weapons; last but not least, conservatism - pp.125-26.)

Others stated, however, that it was always impossible to couple the new weapons and the old military art, and the latter had to be radically and completely changed ('. . . any attempt to use a new weapon within the framework of obsolete combat methods, or to use these obsolete methods without reference to the altered combat capacity of the troops will be doomed to failure, or at best will not produce the required effect ... The history of war and military art demonstrate that when a weapon no longer matches the ways of waging war, the discrepancy will not be remedied by using the new weapon with the old techniques: this would be a step backward. Instead, methods of armed combat and troop organisation must be sought which will make possible the most complete and effective use of the new weapon's combat potential' (Voennaya strategiya, p.276). But the authors are at variance with themselves when they continue: 'New forms of troop organisation and combat methods do not develop at once, but gradually within the framework of previous types. As a rule, older forms of troop organisation and ways of conducting combat operations are adapted to the new weapons, or *vice versa* (italics added); gradually, new methods are developed and improved until they give rise to other, still more effective weapons' (ibid.).

Since not all developments fit the classical interpretation of the law, this has been described in a modified form. Like the two kinds of jumps in the previously mentioned law, two kinds of negation have been invented: one is the liquidation of the outdated elements of the previous state in a certain field of military operations with the preservation of its basis (sic); the other kind is the replacement of the old basis with a new, of a quite new quality. The former kind of negation is exemplified by the development of the organisational structure of the armed forces, the latter by some leap-like developments of armament (Ogarkov, 1978, p.119). Indeed, this is a very 'elastic' application of the law.

[54] Voenno-tekhnicheskii progress, p.135.

[55] O sovetskoi voennoi nauke, 1964, pp.314-15. The authors assert that all these laws (regularities) manifest the dependence of the development of military art on economic conditions. Kulikov proposes another law: 'The more powerful and perfect are the weapons used by the warring sides, the greater is the number of human casualties' (1978).

[56] Istoriya voin i voennogo iskusstva, 1970, p.9; Metodologicheskie problemy, pp.325-26; 'the forms and methods of armed struggle are determined in large degree by the content and nature of the political goals which are pursued in war. The more radical this goal, then usually the more decisive the actions of the troops and the more fierce the battle' (Bochkarev, Prusanov, Babakov, 1966); '... the political content of war has an important effect on the morale of troops, on the general character of armed conflict and on methods and forms of combat operations; the decisive political and military goals of a future world war, if the imperialists unleash it, will predetermine the destructive, and annihilating, character of combat operations' (Savkin, 1972, p.79).

[57] Popov, 1964, p.65. He writes that the law of the dependence of military art applied in a war on the armament and military technique involves in the nuclear missile age the emergence of other laws (or 'manifests itself and expresses in them'); the law which states that the course and outcome of battles will be

decided by nuclear strikes may serve as an example. He later formulated this law as follows: 'There is thus an intimate relationship between the characteristics of arms and military equipment on the one hand and the methods and forms of fighting on the other. A change in those characteristics inevitably, and often contrary to people's wishes or will, produces changes in the methods and forms of battle, of fighting. This is one of the most important laws of armed struggle' (1966a, p.3).

[58] Lototskii, 1973; Istoriya voin i voennogo iskusstva, p.9. The methods applied are also said to depend on geographic conditions (climate, terrain, waters, weather, etc.).

[59] Zemskov, 1972; Milovidov, 1974, p.15.

[60] Popov, 1964, Ch.3; O sovetskoi voennoi nauke, 1964, Ch.VI; Marxism-Leninism on War and Army, Ch.VIII.3; Metodologicheskie problemy, Ch.XIV; Tuyshkevich, 1975; Trifonenkov, 1962; Savkin, 1972, Ch.2; Zakharov, 1967; V. Zamorsky, 'Laws of battle'. *Soviet Military Review*, 1975:3.

[61] Popov, 1964, p.77. He also presented a complementary law which related victory to the concentration of the main efforts on the decisive axis (p.81). In a later study, both laws received a modified wording: 'The course of a battle, engagement, or operation depends on the relationship of the material and morale of the belligerents; this, too, is a basic law of armed struggle', and 'The course and outcome of battle, engagement, or operation depends on achieving superiority over the enemy in the decisive sector at a decisive moment; this, too, is a law of armed struggle' (1966a, p.3).

[62] Metodologicheskie problemy, p.323; Savkin, p.110.

[63] O sovetskoi voennoi nauke, p.316.

[64] Metodologicheskie problemy, p.323; Savkin, pp.110-11.

[65] Popov, 1964, p.97. Zakharov, 1967, pp.48-9, contends that this law, which he regards as one of the basic laws of armed struggle, underlies the principle of surprise.

[66] Metodologicheskie problemy, p.335; '. . . the effectiveness of the actions of troops depends on the nature, strength and direction of strikes delivered by them' may also serve as an example (Marxism-Leninism on War and Army, p.318). Cf. Tuyshkevich, 1968, pp.13-14.

Popov contends that the law of the dependence of the course and outcome of each military action on the concentration of the main efforts on the axis of the main strike is universal in the sense that it is exploited by the commanders not only when the correlation of forces is unfavourable or when the forces are equal, but also when one of them has a clear superiority over the enemy on the whole front (1964, p.84). Thus the character of this law as a corollary to the law of the correlation of forces is here negated.

[67] Tyushkevich uses the expression 'balance of military power' (1968), Zamorsky 'correlation of forces', Savkin terms it 'correlation of combat might', or 'combat power' (p.111), Morozov, 'correlation of the combat might of the troops on the battlefield' (1974, p.4).

[68] Tyushkevich, 1968, pp.13-4. In some writings particular features of the correlation of forces as a relationship in armed struggle are described.

1 Although the correlation of forces on a tactical scale is part of an analogous balance on an operational scale, the latter being, in turn, a part of the global strategic balance of military powers, such a relationship is valid only 'in principle'. The correlation of forces on any lower level, and especially on the tactical one, is relatively independent of the more general alignment, and a situation may arise when a favourable tactical correlation of forces is created in spite of an unfavourable global balance.

2 Since armed forces consist of various components and various combinations of them, different components play the decisive role in different situations. Numerical superiority is frequently the determining factor, but in many situations other components e.g. combat morale, may prevail.

3 The correlation of forces is extremely dynamic. It changes as conditions change, for instance as a result of successful or unsuccessful combat operations. The higher the level of fighting, the greater the influence of social, economic, scientific and other conditions, and on the strategic level of the international politico-military situation. The size and rates of the change also depend on the form of combat and the weapons used. The correlation of forces changes more quickly and dynamically in air and tank battles, and it may change extremely rapidly and radically in any combat involving nuclear missile weapons. These enable the troops to alter the correlation of forces suddenly from an unfavourable to a favourable one, also simultaneously on the operational and strategic scale, and not only on the tactical one.

[69] Tyushkevich contends that the correlation of forces (balance of military power) is determined, in the final analysis, by economic conditions and circumstances; therefore it is a reflection of the law of the determining influence of the correlation of forces of warring sides on the course and outcome of war (p.74). Engels is quoted as stating that victory or defeat depend on the size and quality of population and on the equipment available (Marxism-Leninism on War and Army, pp.317-8).

[70] One of the main themes in Voennaya strategiya, Nauchno-tekhnicheskii progress and other monographs.

[71] O sovetskoi voennoi nauke, p.318.

[72] Marxism-Leninism on War and Army, pp.317-8.

[73] O sovetskoi voennoi nauke, p.318.

[74] Marksizm-leninizm o voine i armii, 2nd ed., Voenizdat, Moscow 1961, p.353.

[75] Popov, 1964, pp.87-92; Krupnov, 1963. The latter writes that it is necessary to maintain a due proportion in the development of particular branches of the services of armed forces and arms, and to promote close cooperation between them (p.89).

[76] Tactical actions must correspond to the operational goals, and the latter should be determined by the strategic aims (Voennaya strategiya, p.15).

[77] Strategy finds its own material strength; this will permit the strategic leadership to have a direct influence on the course of armed conflict with its own autonomous means (Larionov, 1965, p.127); 'Operational and tactical successes will depend on strategic nuclear missile successes. (In the past, war was the other way around; the strategic successes were achieved or built up gradually, according to the tactical and operational successes)' (Sbytov 1965, p.91); cf. Voennaya strategiya, p.332; Nauchno-tekhnicheskii progress pp.138-39; 'Nuclear weapons make possible the simultaneous accomplishment of tactical, operational, and strategic tasks ... the employment of strategic nuclear weapons can have a direct effect on the nature of the tactical actions of troops' (Zav'yalov, 1970).

[78] Nauchno-tekhnicheskii progress, Ch.V.1.

[79] 1971, p.310. Grudinin uses the term 'napravlennost'.

[80] Istoriya voennogo iskusstva, A.A. Strokov, ed., Voenizdat, Moscow 1966, Ch.XVII.

[81] Tyushkevich, 1975, p.74. The correlation of armed forces depends on the global correlation of forces and on economic and political conditions and circumstances; therefore, this law reflects the law of the dependence of war on the global correlation of the forces of the warring parties.

6 Principles of military art

In traditional military theory, those who denied the existence of laws of war, frequently set principles of military art[1] against such 'non-existent' laws. Principles were regarded as cognisable rules according to which one should fight in order to win. Scholars who accepted the existence of laws, made various claims about the relationship between laws and principles: some identified laws with principles, others made a clear distinction between these two structures without, however, pointing out the close relationship between them. Still others stated that while principles concern repetitive patterns of behaviour in similar situations, which can be cognised and applied, laws of war are very elusive and difficult to cognise.[2]

Nor has any common view been expressed concerning the eternal or changeable character of principles. A gamut of opinions exist, from considering principles of military art to be logically worked out patterns of rational behaviour, and thus relatively stable, to treating them as generalisations of methods of fighting which change with technical and social progress.[3]

In contradistinction to the traditional and present non-Soviet disarray of views and a number of unanswered questions, Soviet theory asserts that it has solved the scientific problem of the concept of principles of military art and presented a set of principles based on experience and scientific analysis. As directives for the preparation of armed forces for fighting, several principles are proposed which are derived from the laws of armed struggle and resemble a translation of them into the language of action.

The concept

Definitions and functions

Principles of military art are defined in several Soviet publications as basic ideas on the successful conduct of armed struggle and basic recommendations for its organisation.[4] Their doctrinal character is confirmed by the fact that they are recommended by manuals, regulations, orders and directives for armed forces.

Thus the definition (as well as various descriptions) of the principles of military art states that they are guidelines to action. The interaction between the objective and subjective in armed struggle, briefly commented on in Chap. 2 and Chap. 5, is partly based on the application of principles: the commander makes his decisions on the basis of, and in accordance with, (1) the concept of the action ordered by the higher chain of command, (2) the assessment of the situation and (3) the laws of war and principles of military art as reflected in manuals, regulations and instructions.

On the one hand he must take into account these three determinants. Among them, principles of military art are presented as a most valuable 'scientific fund' which enables the commander to accomplish any military operation; they indicate the premises of organising military operations, directions that must be followed in order to achieve victory. They are presented as a reliable basis for correct decisions by the commander.

On the other hand, the assessment of the situation is individual, the combination of principles which the commander considers it appropriate to utilise in the given situation is individual, as well as the way in which they are used, and the interpretation of the order from the higher chain of command is also individual. The general plan of the operation is determined by others, but the particular version of it is his own. Obviously, a commander acts 'freely' in the sense that he may wrongly assess all the determinant factors and act wrongly; the determinants of successful action are determining only if correctly interpreted.

What makes this creative contribution by the commanders all the more important, the theorists emphasise, is the fact that the principles are only general guidelines. Not only the choice of the complex of principles regarded as the most appropriate in the given situation but also their skilful application depends on the knowledge and the abilities of the commanders.

The executive part of the use of principles is the most difficult, one of the reasons being that the requirements of some principles often contradict those of the other principles, and at times the conditions for applying the proper principles are unfavourable. Besides, the commander must take care to apply the principles as 'cheaply' as possible, with regard to the cost/effectiveness ratio, which is especially important under the conditions of nuclear missile war.[5]

Principles and laws

Reflection, complement or notion of a higher order? In the interpretation most widely accepted by Soviet scholars, principles of military art are considered to be a direct reflection of the laws of armed struggle. They are said to spring from the laws and to correspond to them exactly.[6] For instance, the law which holds that the course and outcome of armed struggle depend on the correlation of forces of the belligerents, and its corollary statement that victory will be won by the side which succeeds in concentrating superior forces and means at the decisive place and at the decisive moment, have the corresponding principle of concentration of forces and means superior to those of the enemy at key sectors and at appropriate times.

In another approach, however, principles are not treated as direct reflections of laws, and some essential differences between them are pointed out. While laws interpret causes of the most appropriate mode of action, but tell us nothing about the mode itself, principles give recommendations for action, without indicating reasons for such recommendations.

In a variant, while laws of military science express our knowledge of the objective essential ties and relationships in the process of armed struggle, independent of people, principles constitute the knowledge of the ways and forms of fighting worked out and accomplished by people.[7] Accordingly, laws can be treated as the objective side of the action, principles as its subjective side; laws and principles complement each other.[8]

Finally, in a quite different interpretation, the principles of military art are regarded neither as a direct reflection of laws only, nor as their complement, but as a concept of a higher order than laws ('bolee vysokie poniatiya').[9] They go beyond the laws, because they couple the cognition of the essence of fighting with the directives for action. To the laws which constitute the objective component, principles add conclusions of the human mind, springing from activity and from experience i.e. the subjective component.

These conceptual differences, however, do not involve differences in the wording of the principles e.g. the above-quoted example with the principle of concentration of forces fits all three approaches.

The scope: similar or different The relationship between principles and laws can also be approached in another way: by comparing their scope. Three alternatives are here possible.[10]

1 If the scope is identical, one principle corresponds to the respective law.

2 More often, one law of armed struggle is connected with, or reflected in, several principles. For instance, the law of the dependence of the course and outcome of armed struggle on the correlation of forces (or of the dependence of the development of a battle or operation on the correlation of combat power of the fighting forces) is reflected in the following principles: the principle of concentration of efforts, that of surprise, that of the massive use of artillery, tanks and aircraft, of seeking fire superiority over the enemy, of economy of forces and some others. In other example, the law of the dependence of military art on armament generates several principles in particular services, and other divisions of armed forces.

3 It may also happen that one principle stems from the aggregate action of several laws as, for instance, the principle of high combat-readiness or the principle of coordination (interaction) of the efforts of all parts of the armed forces.

Change of principles

Soviet theory answers the question of the changeability of principles in the affirmative: principles change since the conditions of fighting change.[11] In the Soviet view, the change of principles consists first in the change of their content. Content is the main and determining component in principles and the most dynamic one, while the form of their expression remains relatively stable. In other words, the same formula, presented under new conditions, may mean something new.[12]

Such a position is reflected by the view that principles of military art are initial standards, and in no way overall patterns, and have significance only under typical circumstances or under certain conditions. This means that, since the actuality of armed struggle is much richer than any theoretical considerations, the commander has to apply the principles variously depending on the situation.[13] Even in one and the same war, under similar conditions of combat, the interpretation of principles, although these are formulated in a standard way, is highly flexible.

However, the formula given to a principle sometimes changes simultaneously with the content. For instance, the principle of the concentration of superior forces and means at the decisive point has been transformed into the principle of concentration of main efforts.[14]

Set of principles of military art

In the Soviet view, principles of military art are only part of an expanding system of principles, which now also includes:[15] (1) principles of the direction of armed forces,[16] (2) socio-political principles of Soviet military development (construction), (3) organisational principles of Soviet military development and (4) principles of the education and training of armed forces.

Here, principles of military art and of the direction of armed forces will be briefly reviewed. The others are more closely linked with the theory of armed forces.

Structure and content

No definite structure of the set of principles of military art has been worked out. A general distinction between the basic and specific principles has at times been mentioned, the former being valid for all levels of military art (strategy, operational art and tactics), the latter for the particular levels, different services and other divisions of armed forces, and also for specific actions in different combat situations.

A different distinction is at times proposed i.e. between the general principles which operate in all wars and are valid for all parts of armed forces and all levels of military art, and specific principles (and also rules) which reflect the peculiarities of particular kinds of war and operate as long as the peculiarities that have given rise to them.[17]

In most non-classified studies both approaches seem to be combined. The focus is on basic principles, which are discussed only with regard to the strategic level;[18] they are related to a nuclear war, being specific in the second of the above-mentioned approaches.

As regards the sets of principles, the number of the latter varies in the writings of different researchers.[19] Unlike the majority of Western military writers, who tend to limit the number of basic principles,[20] Soviet scholars state that the number cannot be limited since it must always be adjusted to current conditions of warfare. The nuclear missile age has brought about many significant changes both in the number and content of the principles, and it has generated many new ones.

A brief review of the principles presented by Soviet scholars in the three periods of the history of Soviet military theory will be followed by comments on the changes and the way in which they are being accomplished.

The following principles are mentioned in Soviet descriptions of military art in the civil war of 1918-1920:[21]

1 the right choice of the main axis of strike, and the concentration of superior means and forces on it
2 decisive action
3 surprise
4 variety of combat methods
5 high rates of combat operations
6 offensive action, changing directions of strikes
7 centralised and flexible management of operations conducted according to a unified plan
8 cooperation of all units on all levels
9 favourable correlation of forces
10 maintenance of a high moral-political condition in the armed forces and the entire population
11 large-scale operations at the enemy's rear.

Before World War II, the wording of the principles was not changed, but their content was modified. For instance, (1) new services and branches of services (air forces, airborne troops, tanks, mechanised units) were included in the content of the principle of cooperation, (2) In all principles, the actions against groupings of enemy troops, of which the destruction could be decisive for the outcome of the whole war, was given the highest priority, (3) In all principles, actions on the operational level were emphasised.

In the nuclear missile age, the following principles seem to be those most often presented:[22]

1 concentration of main efforts and creation of a superiority in means and forces over the enemy at the decisive place and at the decisive time
2 constant high combat-readiness
3 mobility, high manoeuvreability and high rates of combat operations
4 decisiveness and combat activeness
5 surprise
6 correspondence of the goals and missions in war to the means, forces and planned methods of military actions (in a variant, to the actual situation)
7 coordination of the combined efforts of all services and other divisions

of the armed forces with the decisive role of nuclear weapons

8 simultaneous action against the enemy to the entire depth of his deployment, and against objectives far in the rear[23]

9 continuity of combat operations

10 comprehensive security of combat operations

11 timely consolidation of successes achieved

12 economy of forces at the expense of secondary theatres of military actions or operational directions

13 combination of the centralised direction of troops with rational initiative and independence of subordinates in fulfilling their tasks

14 creation of reserves and their maintenance in a condition of constant readiness

15 provision of techno-material support.

While no separate principles for conventional warfare have been adduced, individual scholars point out principles that are equally applicable to operations with both nuclear and conventional weapons.[24]

How the changes have been made

In comparison with the previously-adopted principles, the latter set contains profound changes; these have apparently been made in the following way.[25]

Some principles have retained the same wording or have undergone only slight modification, but in fact their content has been significantly changed or expanded. For instance, the principle of coordination of the combined efforts of all the services and branches has acquired a new content: cooperation is now organised primarily for the most effective exploitation of the effects of nuclear strikes.

Another example: to achieve security in combat operations, protection against nuclear weapons should be ensured; this has become a condition *sine qua non*. In still another example, the constant struggle against means of nuclear attack has become the main content of the principle of continuity of combat.

Some wordings have been changed. The principle of the concentration of means and forces has been modified: 'means and forces' have been replaced by 'efforts', the latter being interpreted as the use of nuclear weapons. Many scholars emphasise the need to combine the ability to concentrate efforts with the ability to disperse units along the front and in depth, in order to reduce losses from nuclear attacks as much as possible. The concentration should be a timely one, performed secretly and rapidly, directly before the strike or even during it; and immediately after the strike the units should again disperse. Therefore some scholars add dispersion to the wording of the principle: 'concentration of basic efforts on decisive area: at the decisive moment with subsequent dispersion of troops under the threat of a nuclear attack by the enemy'.[26]

Some principles formerly adequate, but rendered obsolete by a new military reality have disappeared, at least from the set containing the main and universal principles. One of the principles of the past, stating that victory in war consists of a number of partial successes on various fronts and in various spheres of military operations - in other words, that strategic victory is the sum and outcome of tactical and operational victories - has, in fact, lost its universality, since modern strategic weapons make it possible under certain conditions to achieve decisive results without resort to the tactical and operational units and formations.

Certain former principles, now regarded as such general premises of any social action as do not qualify as principles of military art e.g. the former principle of the variety of methods, have been omitted; others, now considered to belong to other parts of the theory such as the high morale of armed forces and of the population, have also been excluded.

New principles have been added. The principle of simultaneous actions is a new one. The principle of dispersion (part of the principle of concentration) is sometimes presented as a separate one. The principle of high combat readiness, which has no parallel in the earlier set of principles, is now regarded as one of the main principles.

Emphasis on particular principles has altered. The earliest set of principles, for instance, emphasised the necessity of a centralised and unified plan of war, which was quite natural considering the irregular and - in many periods and many places - improvised nature of military operations in the civil war of 1918-1920. Nowadays, this condition is regarded as obvious, and the emphasis has shifted to the need to combine it with the initiative and independence of subordinate units, which is regarded as very important under conditions of nuclear operations.

In the earliest set of principles, operations at the enemy's rear were assigned great importance; nowadays in the wording of the principle they are replaced by nuclear strikes against the rear (e.g. in the principle of simultaneous action).

To sum up, the achievement of maximal correspondence of the principles of military art to the conditions of the nuclear missile age has been the main aim of the development and change in the set of principles. In order to attain it, principles have been excluded which either are too general and too obvious, or else outmoded, or not concerning military art; new principles, which reflect the condition of the new age, have been included; the traditional principles have been modified; new emphasis has been given to some principles, while others have lost their primary importance.

Comments on the changes

The fact that new formulae given to many principles are based on the old wordings as well as the re-affirmation of the core of the orthodox set of principles, may testify to the fact that the review of the whole problem has been insufficiently thorough. Most of the concepts - such as attack and defence, victory and defeat, combat and campaign - which dominated military strategy throughout history, have significantly changed their meaning in the age of nuclear strategy.

Thus a quite new set of principles should perhaps be worked out separately for nuclear and conventional wars.

A distinction may be made between two categories of principles of military art. The first includes those which are a direct application of the general principles of social action, based on common experience in all kinds of social activity, such as the principle of economy of effort, or of the correspondence of goals and missions to the available means (the principle of maintaining the aim, one of the most important in the Western sets of principles of military art, could also serve as an instance). The second category includes principles specific for military operations i.e. principles of the effectiveness of military action which vary from epoch to epoch. It seems that while the former are changing very slowly, the latter must change in step with the conditions of fighting.

The process of constructing a generally accepted set of principles of military art has not been completed. Individual researchers occasionally formulate new principles (but present them as accepted ones). For instance, among the general principles of military art Grudinin enumerates the following, which seem to be his own invention: the principle of the all-out effort (concentration) of all forces and means for the achievement of victory, or the principle of the maximal destruction of the enemy's forces with minimal losses.[27] The authors of *O sovetskoi voennoi nauke* (1964) enumerate a number of new and old 'principles of armed struggle' (also called by them 'principles of military science') which are not among the generally-stated sets. The new ones include, for instance the principle of the immediate exploitation of the effect of nuclear missile strikes. As old principles the following are presented: the principle of careful planning and comprehensive provision for military operations, the principle of combining all methods and forms of armed struggle, etc.[28]

Principles of the direction of armed forces

A recent study by Grechko, which has become a guide for both theoreticians and commanders, complements the principles of military art by the so-called principles of the direction of armed forces and of command and control of them.

Although given a different name and presented as a new aspect of theory, they seem, in fact, to constitute the same principles of military art, seen in a different perspective and complemented by specific requirements: if principles of military art lay down the rules of successful fighting in general, principles of the direction, command and control refer these rules directly to those in command. By the direction of armed forces is here meant the political and strategic direction of armed forces as a whole, command and control being relegated to the operational and tactical levels.

Let us quote a brief list of these principles,[29] which are said to have been applied in World War II:

  1 purposefulness, flexibility, and realism in strategic, operational and tacti-

cal planning

2 innovative approach to the development of new forms of military operations on all scales

3 great skill in massing men and material at the decisive axes

4 skilful achievement of surprise in offensive operations

5 timely preparation and skilful use of strategic and operational reserves

6 achievement of decisiveness and manoeuvreability in military operations

7 organisation of continuous mutual support

8 careful and thorough support of all operations on the combat and techno-material levels.

These principles are said to remain valid; but new factors, such as the increase in the scale of combat operations, their remarkable decisiveness, intensity and brevity, and the complexity of interaction and control have resulted in new requirements and new principles[30] viz.:

9 the fight to win time

10 the improving quality and command and control

11 high combat-readiness of all directing elements and of the entire system of command and control and communications as a whole

12 firmness in command of troops and control of forces

13 flexibility in command and control

14 continuity and regularity in command and control

15 secrecy in command and control

16 the central, dominant role in command and control is played by the commander-in-chief and commander.

However, in some studies the principles of the political direction of war as a whole (not only of armed forces) are discussed separately and in the form of political guidelines similar to those in other fields of social activity. In these studies, the following principles are enunciated:[31]

1 close ties of the leadership with the popular masses

2 unity of political and military leadership

3 scientific foundation and justification of the aims of war and planning of the conduct of war

4 objective assessment of the correlation of forces

5 principle of the main link (i.e. of focusing on the critical tasks)

6 transformation of the possibilities of victory into reality.[32]

In another variant, these principles are called principles of the conduct of war (or of the military-strategic conduct of war) and constitute a quite different set:[33]

1 the principle of party leadership

2 the unity of political and military leadership

3 the principle of collective leadership

4 the scientific approach in evaluating the correlation of forces of the warring parties - particularly class, political and military factors.[34]

This terminology points to the probability of the creation of a separate group of principles concerning the conduct of war as a whole. This should logically be done, if the laws of war and the nature of war as a whole are to be distinguished from those of armed struggle, and assigned to a special department in military theory. A new theoretical problem will naturally arise: that of the relation between the general laws of war and the principles of the conduct of war as a whole.

Two comments on the relationship between laws and principles

Subjective principles and objective laws

One may ask whether the application of the principles - new groups of which are constantly invented and presented - is conceptually derived from the laws and what is the place of principles in the Soviet complex of ideas of laws.

While the main explicit functions of laws of war in the Soviet view would appear to be explanation and prediction, so far as those are possible, the main function of the principles of military art (and other interconnected principles) seems to be that of helping men to act on the basis of knowledge of these laws and of historical experience.

Soviet scholars emphasise that a knowledge of the laws of armed struggle, although theoretically signficant, does not suffice for successful action. It should be combined with knowledge of how the laws operate under typical complexes of conditions and circumstances and, accordingly, how to exploit them, or counteract them, the latter knowledge being embodied, it would seem, in the principles of military art and other principles.

For instance, the law of concentration of forces which explains the reasons for, and the significance of, such concentration, is reflected in a principle of military art in similar words, the latter being a guide for action. This principle, in turn, is complemented by the principles of command and control which state the need for centralisation, for a skilful use of reserves, and other measures and which are intended for use by the controlling bodies which will implement them through concrete military preparations and operations.

Consequently, *the laws and the system of principles constitute one combined chain leading from the theory of action to action itself.* The codification of principles can therefore be regarded as part of the attempt to make military theory a science. On the other hand, one practical reason for codification cannot be discounted: principles can be regarded by the leadership as highly condensed commands, which comprise the main propositions of military art and as an extract from experience acquired in the direction, command and control of armed forces.

A comment (see also Chap. 2) may be made concerning the relation between the objective and subjective in war. The concept of the principles of military art as a reflection of laws of war and as a guide to action is an attempt to combine the primary principle of Marxism-Leninism about the determining impact of objective (laws and conditions) with emphasis on the great potentialities of the subjective factor i.e. the creative activity of man, here, of the commander.[35]

Although the concept of principles of military art as a subjective reflection of the objective laws seems to be the doctrinal one, some confusion in this matter can be detected in particular studies. The tendency to emphasise that principles of military art are not wilful intellectual constructions but reflect objective laws has led some scholars to assert that both laws and principles are objective i.e. exist independently of human consciousness.[36]

Others have compromised by taking a more intermediate position and noted that 'the content of principles is objective and does not depend on human consciousness, but there are no principles in objective reality itself'.[37]

However, there are also attempts to combine the incompatible assumptions and attribute to the principles both an objective and a subjective nature. One example here is the following run of thought. Savkin, in his book on the principles of military art, reiterates two statements, one on the primarily and essentially subjective character of the principles as ideas which always remain in the sphere of awareness, and the other on their objective character as reflecting objective laws. In the conclusions to the book he writes: 'There are no principles outside the consciousness of people. They are deduced by man with the help of abstract reasoning and in this sense are subjective . . . (they are, however, objective because they reflect the demands of objective laws) . . . Thus one can state that the genuine principles of military art stemming from the laws of war and of armed struggle are primarily objective (sic) but at the same time are also subjective.[38]

It seems that here the difficulties connected with the attempt to combine scientifically the objective with the subjective in the interpretation of laws of armed struggle and principles of military art lead to an extreme position. According to Marxist-Leninist philosophy, the subjective does not exist objectively beyond the human mind. It is subjective just because it reflects the objective world, the objective phenomena and relationships in the human mind, by human senses and abstract reasoning. To reflect the objective is not to be objective. To be at the same time subjective (as a reflection of the objective) and objective is self-contradictory.

It may be that the researcher is here expressing in an unfortunate way the idea that principles of military art should not be voluntary and arbitrary rules but should be objective in the sense of being scientific i.e. the expression objective is here used as opposed to unscientific and incorrectly reflecting reality. Such use, however, is characteristic of the confused way in which certain Soviet researchers explain the concept of principles.

Are these laws?

The difficulties with the interpretation of the relation between the subjective and objective in most of the laws of the effectiveness of armed struggle and principles of military art has brought to the fore one doubt which can be presented as a question: are these statements which relate success in military operations to the observation of some principles in human action really laws?

The determining feature of an objective law in Soviet science is that it manifests itself in a necessary (or at least highly probable) recurrence of events (phenomena, processes) under the same (or rather similar) conditions.

The so-called laws of the dependence of the effectiveness of armed struggle on several internal factors (which, in fact, means dependence on the observation by the armed forces of several principles of military art) do not seem to express such a necessary (or highly probable) recurrence.

If, in accord with the laws of historical materialism, it is inevitable, or highly probable, that the internal ties and relationships of armed struggle are reproduced in each military operation, because armed forces under similar conditions act similarly, they will be reproduced in each of the contending armies. Soviet scholars admit that non-Soviet military science has reached a sufficient level of military art to operate correctly in certain typical situations; they accept that laws of war operate correctly in certain typical situations; they accept that laws of war operate in the actions of all armies, and the main principles of military art are well-known everywhere. This means that the internal ties and relationships of armed struggle and the correct application of principles of military art will necessarily, or very probably, recur on both sides of the front-line: tactics will be subordinated to strategy, all parts of the armed forces will closely cooperate, both adversaries will attempt to achieve superiority of forces on the main axis of fighting, and so on.

However, while such action according to the principles of effective fighting will increase the absolute combat power of both contending armies, it cannot lead to a simultaneous increase in the effectiveness of their combat, since if one side fights effectively, the other fights ineffectively, if one wins the other loses; and the outcome of the combat must have contrary value to the adversaries: both cannot win simultaneously.[39]

Thus, in the present form, the statements about the laws of the effectiveness of armed struggle which concern its internal ties and relationships, in fact represent principles of rational action which should be observed in order to create possibilities of victory, however they do not determine the outcome of the two-sided struggle. The actual impact of such correct action by a certain army on the outcome of its operations is uncertain. The outcome depends on which side carries out the correct action better. In other words, only the correlation of the two ways of acting applied by both adversaries determines the outcome which is of contrary value for both.[40]

For instance, one can assert that each military operation tends to go in favour of the side which better organises the cooperation of all parts of the armed forces. However, even a statement of this kind which takes into account the correlative value of one aspect of rational action is insufficient. Only the achievement of superiority in all other aspects i.e. a better application also of other principles of rational action (or a complex or combination of them) is an important determinant of success in combat.

In fact, the achievement of all these 'superiorities' results in superiority of overall combat power at the point (direction, axis) where the achievement of some military aim is planned; and only such global superiority in combat power, *ceteris paribus*, determines victory. Perhaps all laws which connect the effectiveness of armed struggle with the observation of principles of military art should be reduced to one resultant law, stating the dependence of the effectiveness of fighting (or of the achievement of any military aim) on the ability to secure superiority in combat power. This, however, would constitute a repetition of the law of the correlation of combat power.[41]

The last comment is that the question whether such obvious principles of rational human action as the correspondence between means and aims, or cooperation between various parts of an acting collective, should be termed laws at all is here disregarded. The only criterion for assessment, in accordance with the aim of this study, is whether the tie or relationship in question fits the Soviet concept of a law.

Notes

[1] In a Soviet text-book for commanders, the chapter on principles of military construction begins with a definition of the principle as the basic position of any teaching or basic requirement or required norm made of behaviour of men. (Kozlov, 1971, Part I). Some Soviet scholars point out that the notion of principle has a double meaning: in theory, or teaching, it means a fundamental, initial thesis, while in practical activity it is used for a fundamental idea or rule according to which men act (Savkin, 1972, p.119). Grechko, who usually applies the notion in the latter sense, writes, however, about Lenin's 'principle' of dividing wars into just, progressive, and unjust, reactionary (1975, Ch.10). Here the notion of principles will be used to mean a statement about the proper mode of action and a guide to it.

[2] The variety of the Western approaches to the causal relationship of war cannot be reduced to a common denomination and no agreed position can be discerned. This disarray has a long history. Military thinkers have always tried to discover regularities or rules governing military operations, whether in the form of laws expressing causal relationships between phenomena and processes of warfare or simply guiding principles for its successful conduct. However, basic

premises concerning the very existence of the law-like regularities, or - more often - principles of fighting, and their wording, differed from one theorist to another. No habit of tabulating lists of laws or principles formerly existed, but since they began to appear, a wide range of presentations, including a great number of laws or principles with various wordings and content, has been accumulated.

Differences in views have always reflected different interpretations of the nature of war, whether or not it is subjected to laws or not, and whether or not the theory of war is (or, at least, may become) a systematised body of knowledge i.e. a science or an art. The analysis of the enormous literature on the rules governing military operations enables us to discern three main views of the theory of the conduct of war.

> 1 The theory of the conduct of warfare is a science; it has presented laws of war, or it should do so. Some contend that principles of war formulated by many scholars should be regarded as *sui generis* laws.
>
> 2 The conduct of war may be approached both as science and art. The former deals with laws of governing warfare, the latter with rules of successful combat, or guidelines to such combat.
>
> 3 The conduct of war is solely an art, and the lack of success in presenting immutable laws governing the processes of combat is evidence of this.

All three approaches have their optimistic and pessimistic versions. The optimists assert that laws of war and/or principles have been discovered and formulated. The pessimists contend that (a) even if the theory of warfare could be regarded as science, it could only be a very imperfect one, since it concerns a kind of human activity that is full of individual and fortuitous events in which the regularities cannot be fully cognised; (b) the conduct of war as an art is also very imperfect; in fact, no rules can be discovered; in the variety of unique situations the commanders' assessments of them and their individual skill decide the choice of methods and success in combat; (c) even those who accept the possibility of establishing principles of military art frequently question the hitherto-presented sets of such principles, pointing out that no commonly agreed view exists.

[3] The officially dominating view is that rules of successful fighting have been discovered and formulated. Rules of the conduct of war (strategy), termed 'principles of war', are officially presented - for instance, by Field Manual 100-5 of the US Army - as 'fundamental truths governing the prosecution of war'.

These rules give a simple summary of the basic business of war and are said to be of invaluable assistance to any professional military man today who has many subjects and a vast material to study, and to every commander who in the course of fighting is perplexed by conflicting factors and complex missions and has to take account of all the immensely complicated realities of contemporary warfare.

The rules provide guiding principles, it is said, because they correspond to the internal logic of armed struggle; this compels the commander to act in a determined way if he wants to win. Thus principles can be considered rooted in the very nature of warfare and they can be exploited by the commander in appropriate conditions. Principles are valued in many armies as an excellent device for the commander to use in analysing all aspects of the situation and planned action, and they are considered applicable in all kinds of warfare, including limited, counter-guerilla, psychological and other warfare.

To emphasise the universal validity of the principles, many scholars ascribe the connotation of 'law' to the word 'principles'. This connotation is explicable, inter alia, by the fact that, in scientific language, principles are hardly discernible from laws. In physics, the term 'principle' is often used concerning the law of gravity, and in microbiology concerning the law of spontaneous generation. This usage is reflected in many dictionaries which equate the term 'principle' with 'law' - for instance, the Oxford Dictionary which defines principles as a 'primary element, force, or law which produces or determines particular results', and the International Encyclopaedia of the Soviet Sciences, which defines science as a body of systematic principles (vol. 13, p.591). Naturally, one should also observe that military writers are not very precise in the use of terms, which only adds to the confusion.

At the same time, adherents of the principles point out that these are not rigid and dogmatic commandments; they should be applied creatively, according to the actual conditions. Principles should be treated as considerations that are in the minds of commanders when they plan or conduct a military operation, but they require an individual interpretation in accordance with the specific time and circumstances of the actual situation. They should reflect rational methods of acting according to the conditions, as the commander sees them.

They are presented by some scholars as 'refinements on common sense', or 'common sense propositions' which serve as a guide to action. The US Army Field Manual 100-5 states: 'Their proper application' (i.e. of the principles — JL) 'is essential to the exercise of command and to successful conduct of military operations. These principles are interrelated and, depending on the circumstances, may tend to reinforce one another or to be in conflict. Consequently, the degree of application of any specific principle will vary with the situation.'

[4] Popov, 1964, p.122; O sovetskoi voennoi nauke, 1964, p.324; Marxism-Leninism on War and Army, p.321; 'the principles of military art are to be understood as the basic ideas and most important recommendations for the organisation and conduct of battles, operations, and war as a whole, suitable for practical use in all basic forms of troop combat activity. It is accepted that the basic principles of military art include those which are valid for all three of its parts - tactics, operational art, and strategy' (Savkin, 1972, p.1).

[5] Savkin, pp.147 ff., 279-80.

[6] Savkin, 1972, p.52. Marxism-Leninism on War and Army, p.321-2. 'Laws of military science answer the question, what are the conditions and ways, the forces and means of conducting armed struggle. Principles answer the question of what to do and how to do it, in order to exploit the laws of armed struggle.

Therefore, principles are recommendations, directives for action ... and are formulated on the basis of the cognised laws of armed struggle' (Azovtsev, 1970, p.30).

[7] A principle does not mean only the recognition of an essential tie between phenomena and processes of armed struggle. It conveys the idea of how to act; and ideas, according to Lenin, are notions of a higher order, more complicated and more 'true' just because they contain conclusions on how to act (Popov, 1964, p.125).

[8] Metodologicheskie problemy, p.332, cf. Popov, 1964; principles of military art 'make it possible to translate scientific formulae, the content of the laws, into the language of practical activity, of military practice. For example, the law stipulating that victory will be gained by the side concentrating superior forces and means at the decisive place and the decisive moment, finds its expression in the principle of massing of forces: to secure success in battles and operations it is essential to concentrate forces and means at key sectors and at the correct time, superior to the forces and means of the enemy' (Marxism-Leninism on War and Army, p.321). While laws are basic relationships existing independently of the human intellect or will, relationships inherent in the phenomena and process of armed struggle themselves, the principles are ideas which always remain in the realm of the mind (Popov, 1966, p.4). Popov, however, adds that, since principles are a conclusion on how the objective should be utilised, they are in this respect a combination of the objective and subjective (ibid.)

[9] Metodologicheskie problemy, p.333; cf. Tyushkevich, 1975, p.21.

[10] Popov, 1964, pp.125-6; Grudinin, 1971, pp.309 ff.; Metodologicheskie problemy, pp.334-6; Zamorsky, 1975, p.19.

[11] Popov, 1966a, pp.2-3; Grudinin, 1971, pp.304-9.

[12] Savkin, pp.1 ff.

[13] Nauchno-tekhnicheskii progress, p.137.

[14] The initial assumption underlying the military doctrines of the chief Western powers and many studies of military art seems to be that of the unchanging character of principles, despite the changes in all conditions of fighting and all factors which influence war. This is implied in very general statements about war - for instance, concerning the unchangeable internal logic of combat, and also in detailed reasoning on the subsisting validity of particular principles in present conditions.

Contrary views are also expressed. Criticism of the assumption about the 'eternal' character of principles has been implied in: (1) criticism of the validity of particular principles; (2) criticism of the too general wording of the principles which indicates their universal validity but only as general ideas without any operational utility; (3) comments about the changing wording and content of particular principles; and (4) comments concerning the need to change the principles under the conditions of the nuclear missile age. The main criticism, which underlies all others, is that principles are closely linked with the conditions of fighting, and any radical change in conditions must be followed by a radical change in principles.

However, most scholars who criticise the existing set of principles do not question the very idea of immutable guides to combat, but only a certain concrete set. They often present their own system as 'almost immutable laws of conduct, independent of time or place or weapons, equally applicable to the platoon commander and the field marshal . . .'

Some scholars take here a compromising position. André Beaufre who describes principles of strategy as rules thought to be laws of general application and lasting validity, considers the existing rules to be doubtful under the radically new conditions. He states: 'Nevertheless, if rules could be evolved they would form a fixed point around which strategic thinking could revolve and only the method of application of the rules could be subject to the evolutionary process'. In other words, up to this point strategy has radically changed in step with the revolution in the material conditions of fighting, but from now on to an indefinite time in the future the development of strategy will proceed in an evolutionary manner, and the principles themselves would not change, only their application.

It can be concluded that, while in the official doctrine principles are still treated as immutable truths, in the conviction of many scholars this can only be attributed to the most general versions of them - as one-word maxims which like the ten amendments are applied elastically according to the conditions of each concrete situation.

[15] Savkin, pp.152-5. Morozov, 1974, writes about the 'socio-political principles of military development, including the principle of the Party leadership over the army, and the principle of internationalism in defence of the socialist countries'; the emergence of the socialist system, and of the armies of the new socialist type, have given rise to the above new principles (p.4).

[16] Grechko, 1975, Ch.8.

[17] Grudinin, 1971, pp.304-7.

[18] V. Kruchinin writes: 'The basic assumptions i.e. the principles of military strategy - represent the concise expression of important views on the preparation for, and conduct of, armed struggle' (Izmeneniya printsipov sovetskoi voennoi strategii, *Voennaya Mysl'*, 1962:6).

[19] O sovetskoi voennoi nauke, pp.324-28; Voennaya strategiya, 1968, pp.20-24; Kruchinin, 1962; I. Zavyalov, Skorost', vremiya, i prostranstvo v sovremennoi voine, Voenizdat, Moscow, 1965; his 'O vidakh i formakh voennykh deistvii,' *Voennaya Mysl'*, 1965:1; N.F. Miroshnichenko, 'Izmeneniya v soderzhanii i kharaktere sovremennogo boya', *Voennyi Vestnik*, October 1966; Savkin, pp.167 ff.

[20] O sovetskoi voennoi nauke, p.324. The authors write that Jomini presented 4 principles, Leer 12, Fuller 7. The contemporary American theorists list 9 principles.

[21] Savkin, Printsipy voennogo iskusstva v rabotakh sovetskikh avtorov, 1917-1920, in: 1972, Ch.I.

[22] Voennaya Strategiya, pp.20-24; Savkin, Ch.3; Tyushkevich, 1968; L.

Vorobjov, 'Choice of Direction of Main Blow', *S.M.R.*, 1970:3; Popov, 1966. In Western studies, the question of utility of the traditional sets of principles of military art in the nuclear missile age has generated a fierce debate. In this, I detect three, or even four (including the thesis of the undesirability of any principles) main positions.

One position regards the traditional set of principles as still valid (indeed, this implies that they are eternally valid), and the task of the theorists, military writers and commanders is to discover and demonstrate how these principles should be applied in all conceivable kinds of war and military operations: in a possible nuclear total war, in a limited war, conventional war, counter-guerilla warfare and psychological warfare.

Some scholars contend that all 'new principles', occasionally proposed for inclusion in the traditional set as meeting the requirements of the new epoch in warfare, should be treated as mere methods of application of the existing principles. The other proposal is to treat the existing set of principles only as a framework, and to give to them a wholly new interpretation, according to the revolutionary new conditions of warfare. The third view is that the traditional sets of principles are incompatible with modern conditions of fighting and it is necessary to work out a new set.

There is, of course, also the view that any established, and thus inevitably rigid, set of principles of warfare or military art is undesirable, not only because no such set can be elaborated in a satisfactory way, but also because in modern combat the commander must have, and should have, the full possibility of acting according to the conditions and his own assessment of them and of the methods that must applied.

[23] Zavyalov, 1970, writes: '... the emergence of nuclear missiles has revealed the material basis of the principle of simultaneous destruction of the enemy throughout the entire depth of his combat and operational deployment as well as destruction of the most important military-economic targets deep in the rear of belligerent states'.

[24] Zavyalov, 1970, enumerates the following 'common' principles: 'the principle of simultaneous action against the entire depth of the enemy's operational formation; the principle of key objectives and bold actions full of initiative; the principle of the creation, use, and renewal of reserves and the ability to transfer the main strike from one axis to another and to carry out manoeuvres with men and equipment; the conduct of combat operations cut off from the main forces, on separate, isolated axes, and with a break in coordinated actions and control; and several other principles'.

Here, as we see, certain new principles appear, or the traditional ones appear in a modified form.

[25] Voennaya strategiya, pp.20-4; Savkin, Ch.3.

[26] This principle has developed from the principle which was dominant in the first half of the XIXth century — namely: 'Keep your forces concentrated', and which, with improvements in the means of transportation and communica-

tion, was transformed into the principle: 'Move separately, but fight together' (Popov, 1966, p.4).

[27] 1971, p.304. The authors of 'Metodologicheskie problemy' discuss several new principles of military art: the principle of first priority detection and annihilation of the enemy's nuclear capability; the principle of forestalling the delivery of nuclear attacks on the enemy in the'course of war; the principle of 'dispersed concentration'; the principle of the concentration of basic efforts on principal direction by means of manoeuvres with missile trajectory, and the like (Ch.XIV.2).

[28] pp.325-6.

[29] Grechko, 1975, Ch.8. The list is common to all principles concerning direction, command and control, since their essence is identical, although the spheres in which they are manifested are different.

[30] Ibid.

[31] Skirdo, 1970, pp.101-21.

[32] On the other hand, in some studies only principles which relate directly to the military commanders, are emphasised: the sole responsibility and collectivism, centralisation, initiative and independence, foresight and constant knowledge of the situation, firmness and flexibility of control, continuity, concealment, high proficiency and others. (Nauchno-tekhnicheskii progress Ch.VI.2). These are very similar to many principles of military art. They are also said to have the same function: to bring the phenomena and processes in the field of military affairs into conformity with the requirements of the objective laws of war and the current situation. Thus they tell the commanders how to organise fighting on the basis of laws and assessment of the conditions of combat.

[33] Zemskov, 1972.

[34] This principle is complemented by: 'a determination of the decisive theatre of military operations and of the identity of the principal enemy and, consequently, a selection of the key factor in war; and a concentration of the main forces and weapons for defeating the principal enemy' (ibid.).

[35] This is also presented in the following way: the commander must combine military science with the art of fighting. Only the knowledge of the modern science and technique makes possible to fight successfully, however the commander makes use of such elements as intuition, risks (which he considers justified), and other factors associated with military art. Science is more affected by objective laws than art, and their interaction may be in some sense regarded as an interaction between the objective and subjective. Cf. Zemskov, 1972; Grechko's article entitled 'Science and the Art of Victory' ('Nauka i iskusstvo pobezhdat'), Pravda, 19.2.1975.

[36] Grudinin, 1960, p.127; Krupnov, 1963, p.91.

[37] Vazhentsev, 1969; 'The principles of military science are objective. They arise from practice and are confirmed by it' (O sovetskoi voennoi nauke, 1964, p.324).

[38] Savkin, pp.122-3, 278-9. Cf. note [8] in this chapter.

[39] The history of wars brings evidence to the assertion that such principles of effective warfare cannot be regarded as laws. For instance, the concentration of efforts on the decisive axis at the decisive time in itself did not decide the outcome of particular battles or operations; it always depended on the kind and strength of the enemy's counteraction (not to mention a possible defeat on other axes from which means and forces were removed). 'The presence of numerous exceptions to the action of the "law" of concentration does not provide a basis to call this thesis a law possessing inevitability and stability of operation' (Savkin, p.84).

[40] One can, however, stop at this point and conclude that laws of the effectiveness of armed struggle determine only the way people will act in typical situations. It is highly probable that in situations that are similar in important respects men would act in similar ways because they know the laws of war and principles of effective fighting, and they aim at victory; in our formula on war, the knowledge of laws and principles and the aims are the repetitive conditions, or circumstances (C), while the manner of action would here be regarded as the outcome (E).

The commander is expected to behave in a determined way (his actions are expected to fit a certain pattern) because of the operation of objective laws which the commander knows, principles of effective action which he would observe, and aims which always consist in the pursuit of victory. (One can say that the 'because' here derives its force from laws, principles and aims.) These would not be laws of the effectiveness of armed struggle, however. If we insist that the result of fighting, and not the way it is done, is the outcome (E), then the probability of an expected one, as presented in the text, is undetermined.

Part III

Comments

7   Comments on the concept of laws of war

The search for laws

The Soviet concept of laws of war can be seen from two angles. From the onto-logical viewpoint, Soviet theory categorically assumes that laws of war do exist; this basic initial proposition has here been presented and reviewed; the assessment of its truth, however, goes beyond the scope of this study.

In the epistemological framework, the Soviet basic concept of a scientific law reflected in its definition is comparable with the traditional and current non-Soviet definition of a universal deterministic law asserting uniform causal ties and relationships between phenomena.[1] However, in presenting particular laws and groups of laws Soviet scholars have replaced, in many cases, the universal necessity of the recurrence of these ties and relationships by their probability, and 'causes' by 'determining influence', without changing the concept and definition of the law of war.

The aim of this chapter is to assess the character of the laws of war formulated by Soviet science in relation to these - initial and modified - concepts. I shall also occasionally try to assess the validity of the statements on laws, by confronting them with obvious logical tests and empirical evidence.

The methods

What has been the method applied by Soviet theoreticians in their search for these laws? I should like to investigate here whether and to what degree Soviet practice corresponds to the methodological literature and occasional statements on the methods which should be applied.[2]

In the methodological writings, two main methods of searching for laws of war are prescribed. The first is the logical-analytical one. It consists in deriving laws of war from philosophical or sociological laws, and also from laws in other disciplines (economics, psychology, etc.).

The second method, the historical one, consists in the first phase in recon-structing the past (wars and events preceding them) on the basis of documents and other evidence, then collating and comparing similar conditions preceding and accompanying similar processes and phenomena of war (or different conditions which determined a different course of events). Logical inductive analysis follows, aiming at finding out the general, common and essential elements in similar phenomena, which can serve as a basis for discovering recurring essential features and ties. The discovery of causal relationships, and the formulation of laws and regularities may result from such analysis.[3]

A complementary - empirical - procedure also seems to be prescribed: researchers should aim at the scientific description of a contemporary phenomenon (phenomena) by accumulating facts about it, its properties, and its causal and other relationships with other phenomena. Then they should analyse the accumulated facts, discover essential features of the phenomenon, propose generalisations about its properties and relationships and hypothesise laws concerning its causation, relationships and development.

The direct observation of a contemporary phenomenon (phenomena) under the natural conditions of its occurrence (for instance, the observation of a war which has occurred in our time), can be combined with an analysis of processes organised just for such observation (war-games, manoeuvres). Here, in other words, one can investigate a substitute subject, a model, instead of the original subject which is less accessible or even completely inaccessible (e.g. nuclear war).

One can also construct models of military operations in a possible future war based on these investigations and using various logical-mathematical methods.[4] Such a procedure gains importance just from the difficulty of providing sufficient empirical material for making generalisations concerning a future war.[5]

All the above methods of a deductive and inductive character can hardly be separated in practice; they complement one another in a search for laws based on the general dialectical materialistic methodology, as Soviet scholars see it.

The Soviet way of searching for laws is not confined, however, to the logical, historical and empirical procedures. Soviet military theory is not a pure science. It is conceived of and constructed as a system of ideas designed to serve the current political and military doctrine and policy; in the Soviet view, that military theory ought to be in accord with the fundamentals of the Marxist-Leninist ideology and with the political and military doctrine based on the scientific analysis of reality, can only contribute to the fulfilment of its scientific functions. This is called in Soviet science 'the partisan approach' to the scientific research.[6]

In the traditional and contemporary non-Soviet approach, the subordination of a scientific research policy, or even the necessity to organise the research in accord with the political doctrine, is regarded as a factor limiting the cognitive potentialities of the science, although not necessarily nullifying them. In the Soviet view it must not be the case. It depends on the character of the doctrine: if this is progressive, it can but encourage a thorough scientific research. Progressive forces must base their struggle on a deep understanding of reality if they want to win. Progressive cause needs truth, it must be based on the knowledge of the actual ties and relationships, and their development.

In more detail, Soviet military theory is assigned the task of justifying the current doctrine, and secure the preparation for future wars by its cognitive and ideological values. To perform the strictly military function researchers ought to analyse the experience of the past wars and the contemporary development of armament and military art, and to present conclusions and predictions which will be useful for the current doctrine and policy. In accomplishing the ideological, and in particular the propagandist function, they ought to present the past wars waged by the Soviet Union and the future ones as politically just, serving progress, and militarily sound. Laws which are regarded as a very important component of the system of ideas are included in the mechanism of accomplishing both functions. In particular, they should help to explain past victories by the just cause of wars and the superiority of Soviet armed forces, and consequently to strengthen belief in future ones.

In all sciences, scholars when formulating theory, consciously or unconsciously take as premises some set of philosophical ideas and values and all agree that these values are bound to have effects on the scientist's findings. Some of these effects may be desirable, others not. There may also be external influences which limit the scientific freedom and objectivity of the researcher: if he is employed or subsidised by the politico-military establishment, as frequently happens in the military field, the governing doctrines cannot fail to affect his research, its focus and even his findings, since these should be in accord with the needs of policy. In such a case, scholars usually try to claim that this influence is only marginal in their effort.[7]

Each ideology, however, has its customs. Soviet scholars state that in their search for laws of war they not only consciously apply the Marxist-Leninist philosophical and methodological ideas but also consciously proceed from the Soviet long-range and current political and military doctrines. Moreover, Soviet military theory should not only be based on both the governing philosophy and doctrine, but be tested by checking against them. Cases where a scholar questions the official policy (which happens frequently in the United States) are unknown.

(The analysis of this problem goes beyond the scope of this study, however. It is based, as we see, on several premises: (a) that social progress needs a true knowledge of reality; (b) that it proceeds towards socialism; (c) that it is embodied in the policy of the Soviet Union; (d) that each scientific idea, including ideas on war, and laws of war, must be true if it springs from the political and military doctrine of the Soviet Union, or at least is in accordance with it. The latter premise is in fact replaced by the tacit assumption that scientific ideas, including laws, are true if they correspond to the current Soviet policy.

Note that in the first post-war decade, when the nuclear rearmament of the Soviet armed forces was a future matter, all philosophy of war was based on past experience and did not correspond to the changed nature of war. This was expressed, inter alia, by the thesis on the five permanently acting factors that determine the course and outcome of war, treated as the basic law of war, with its depreciation of the importance of surprise, and implicit neglection of nuclear weapons. Such examples may be multiplied.

The very necessity to be in accordance with the current political and military prescriptions, as we see, has prompted scholars to formulate ideas that do not accord with the actual development of military affairs.)

149

The underlying methodology

Regardless of which of the above briefly-sketched methods of formulating a certain group of laws or a single law have been given priority, one common general methodology is considered to underlie all of them - the materialistic-dialectical one. This is said to consist in the application of the following scientific apparatus:[8]

> The main propositions of philosophical materialism: this means that the causes, features and relationships of war are regarded by the researchers as objective and cognisable and rooted in the material life of society;
>
> Laws of materialistic dialectics: these express the internal division of war as a whole and of its phenomena and processes into so-called opposites, simultaneously united and mutually conflicting as driving forces of the development of war; and they present the transition of quantitative changes into qualitative ones and the dialectical negation of negation as the forms of this development;
>
> The dialectical interaction of the so-called twin categories: of the content and form, general and individual, necessary and fortuitous, and others, which constitute rules governing the essential ties and relationships between phenomena;
>
> The main principles of dialectical logic: of universal connections and mutual conditionality of factors and processes; of the objective approach based on the proposition of the objective existence of nature and society;[9] of the concrete-historical assessment based on the proposition that all things, phenomena and processes are in a state of continuous movement and development; and finally the principle of partisanship.

The practice

Let us see how this general methodology and particular methods have been used in the formulation of specific categories and groups of laws.

To begin with the *general laws of war*, these constitute, to a significant extent, an application of (or logical conclusions from) the propositions and laws formulated by dialectical and historical materialsm or, in more detail, by the Marxist-Leninist philosophy, sociology, economy, theory of history, and theory of policy. They have been formulated mainly by the procedure of a logical conceptualisation via non-empirical and deductive reasoning on the basis of the philosophical propositions and more general laws; history has then been ransacked for examples that might confirm the formulated laws.

To take the philosophical propositions first, the whole Soviet concept of general laws of war, and especially of laws of the genesis of war and of the dependence of the character of war on policy, is based on the premise that war is a form of class political struggle rooted in the economic contradictions of the so-called antagonistic society, and caused by the policy of the exploiting classes. General laws of war express the dependence of all social activities on the economic basis and political superstructure, and the conduct and outcome of war depend on the correlation of class forces.[10]

Thereby the material sources of war have been recognised as the primary ones, having an objective character; they operate independently of the will of people, can and should be cognised, and people should take an active attitude toward their operation, either paving the way for them, or creating conditions which paralyse their action.

In other words, the general laws of war as scientific formulae reflect the main propositions of philosophical materialism: the priority of matter over thought, the objective character of the external world, and the cognisability of the world; they have been directly derived from the application of philosophy to social change and development i.e. from historical materialism.

While propositions of philosophical and historical materialism are directly reflected in the formulae of the general laws of war, laws of materialist dialectics are said to be implied in them. Soviet scholars illustrate the explanation and interpretation of the laws of war by them.[11]

The law of unity and conflict of opposites, which is regarded as the kernel of dialectics, since it is said to explain the internal sources of development of objects, phenomena and processes, is the main law used to illustrate the laws of the origin of wars. War is the ultimate form of resolving the contradictions between the opposing class forces within particular societies and within the international system. The struggle between the two antagonistic camps is presented as the main contemporary form of this contradiction, rooted in the internal class antagonism and manifested on the international scale. War between these camps would be an attempt to resolve the contradiction. Other conceivable types of war are rooted in the great contradictions of our epoch.[12]

Thus both fundamentals of the law in question - that all objects and phenomena are characterised by inherent opposites (class society by its antagonistic classes, international system by its two camps), and that the two opposites interact and conflict - are used to illustrate and explain the laws of the origin of wars.

The other two laws of dialectics have rarely been directly applied in the interpretation, explanation or, at the very least, illustration of the general laws of war, even in studies and articles devoted particularly to this problem. It can only be hypothesised that the outbreak of war is meant as a leap-like interruption of the continuous course of peaceful political intercourse, and in this sense a manifestation of the law of transition from quantity to quality. Even more difficult is to guess how Soviet scholars would interpret the application of the law of negation of negation, although there is no reason why such an interpretation should not be provided. War, with its aim of crushing the enemy's will, 'negating' the existing situation-set of conditions and creating a new one, provides many opportunities for the application or illustration of this law.[13]

The above deductive procedure consisting in deriving the general laws of war from philosophical and sociological laws, has at times been complemented by formulating more specific laws to 'fill out' the more general laws with more concrete content, thus increasing their precision. For instance, the law of the dependence of the course and outcome of war on the global correlation of forces has occasionally been complemented by laws stating particular dependences which could be regarded as components of the primary or summary law.

The historical method of seeking the general laws of war should also be mentioned. Through the analysis of the wars of our epoch, and especially of the two world wars and all fighting waged by the Soviet Union, generalisations have been made concerning the dependence of the origin of wars and the character and conduct of war on policy, and of its course and outcome on the correlation of forces.

The generalisations, connected with the correlation of forces more than others, seem to constitute conclusions from the analysis and observation of wars of our epoch (which resembles the empirical method), and they directly reflect the assumptions of Soviet political and military doctrine, in which the necessity to create a favourable correlation of forces plays a dominant role. All general laws of war are in accord with this doctrine, and, on the other hand, in the doctrinal expositions these laws are frequently presented in the form of general propositions.

The method of searching for the *laws of military art* comes closer to that of the general laws of war than to the search for the other laws of armed struggle (which is evidence of the confusion with the basic division of the set of laws — see Chap. 8). It would be a mixture of the logical-analytical method and historical analysis, if not for the fact that Soviet scholars have inherited the basic law in this group - the law of the dependence of the development of military art on the material basis - from Engels; and all analyses start with his formula.

It should be noted that just this group is the favourite object to be illustrated by the laws of dialectics (reviewed in Chap. 5), and especially by the law of the unity and conflict of opposites and of negation of negation. The scholars try to demonstrate the development of military art as a kind of dialectical cycle based on the latter law; describing the history of military art they often mention that it proceeds according to the laws of dialectics.[14] The difficulties with a direct application of other laws e.g. the law of the transition from quantity to quality, have compelled scholars to make many deviations from the classical interpretation of it (Chap. 5). Laws of the dependence of military art applied in particular wars on external factors, which as a group are only emerging not only derive from, and correspond to, the respective laws of war (although at another level of the action of these factors) and are an application of the basic law of the development of military art, but also are ocasionally divided into separate and more specific laws, the latter stating the dependence of military art applied in individual wars on the policy and political aims of these wars, on the economy, on the techno-scientific and techno-military conditions, and on the correlation of the fighting forces involved.

To turn to the *laws of the effectiveness of armed struggle*, the procedure of formulating them has apparently been different from that in the above-mentioned groups. They are largely generalisations of war experience and conclusions from the contemporary development of military affairs (primarily techno-military progress). In many cases they may be treated as reformulated principles of military art.

In other words, these laws can be regarded as established through inductive generalisation by the use of the two supporting empirical techniques. However some scholars stress that like all other laws, they reflect the propositions of philosophical materialism; and they all assume that the material basis of each military operation exerts the decisive influence on its course and outcome.

One can also demonstrate, they say, that the laws of dialectics are valid here. As mentioned above, the two fighting parties, their intentions and actions embody the two opposites in armed struggle.[15] Fighting is characterised by two opposite forms of action, namely attack (offensive) and defence, which are connected. One form is transformed into the other depending on changes in the situation and neither of them exists without the opposite one. Another important contradiction is that between the necessity to concentrate the maximum of forces on the direction of the main effort, and to disperse[16] them in order to protect them against a nuclear attack. One group of contradictions arises from the psychological conditions of fighting: contradictory negative and positive tendencies: losses, fatigue and fear being instances of the former, fighting spirit, discipline and hatred being examples of the latter.[17]

Mention should be made of the application of the dialectical twin-categories and principles of dialectical logic. As for the dialectical interaction between twin-categories, this has been mainly applied in the reasoning on the features of laws of war (Chap. 2), but not in the formulation of particular laws. The principles of dialectical logic are presented on each occasion as premises of investigation, although without demonstration of any more detailed procedure.[18]

These principles operate in Soviet theory as standing presumptions which do not need evidence in particular cases; conversely to be defeated they could require contrary evidence in a particular case. Parenthetically, since the opponent is not allowed to participate in the discussion, the evidence that he does not observe these principles is an argument for his faulty position.

Testing the laws

In the scientific procedure, one formulates a law after testing the hypothesis on the given tie or relationship to see whether it is well confirmed by the relevant evidence available (and - ideally - no refuting facts have been found) and whether it is logically connected with more general and more specific laws.

Soviet scholars present laws of war as resulting from the deductive, logical-analytical philosophical and sociological investigation, and also historical and logical analysis of past and present experience, and tested by the current practice. Practice is the key term in the interpretation of testing; the main assumption of Soviet methodology is that only practice can answer the question of the validity of any law (or hypothesis); if our action gives results predicted on the basis of the given law, the latter is valid. If the results deviate from the prediction, either other factors have affected the change (for instance, the action of other laws, or fortuitous events) or else our knowledge has been incomplete, and the formula of the scientific law ought to be changed.[19] Because of the qualitative and probabilistic character of most of the laws of war it has naturally been very difficult for Soviet scientists to test them by means of these methodological guidelines.

As noted in Chap. 4, the statements on probabilistic hypotheses, called laws by Soviet scholars, do not allow us to establish what value of the initial conditions may - roughly speaking - cause wars, nor what are the probability values stated by the hypotheses. To take the laws of the origin of war, we do not know what extent and what specific content the conflict between the opposing social forces has to assume, and what the politico-military situation has to become to bring about war. We do not know what extent the unevenness of the development of capitalist countries has to reach, how intensive the aggressiveness of the exploiting classes has to become, what amount of discontent of the exploited classes is needed to bring about war. And without such criteria, we cannot measure and cannot test. In any particular case, we can only hypothesise that since certain kinds of initial conditions have been followed by a war, the latter was caused by the former, according to the probability hypothesis in question; in other words, the outbreak of an individual war can be here treated as a confirmation of a hypothesised law.

Even more difficult is to test the laws of the dependence of the character, course and outcome of war on external factors which concern the causation of entire continuous processes, influenced by the continuous operation of an aggregate of factors. All variables in this causation with its many component dependences are hardly measurable (even hardly identifiable at each time and place), thus hardly testable.

Let us exemplify these difficulties by a law of war (or armed struggle) of the most frequent kind in the Soviet set, namely a law which holds that a certain factor (variable) or a complex of factors (variables) exerts the decisive influence on the course and outcome of war (armed struggle). In support of such a statement, one should adduce evidence that:

1 the asserted influence of this factor (variable), or the complex of factors which is hypothesised as the determining one, really takes place and correlates with the respective course of war (armed struggle) and its outcome;

2 it affects the course and outcome of war in the way asserted in the statement; in particular, other factors do not affect war to a greater extent i.e. variations in war produced by variations in all other factors are small in relation to variations produced by the given factor or complex of factors;

3 there are logical and empirical reasons for extrapolating the evidence -

if it has up to this point confirmed the statement - to encompass all wars of the given type (including probable future cases); and, if the law is regarded as operating in all wars in all epochs, to include other types of war.

But the fulfilment of these conditions is fraught with problems. To begin with, the causation of military events by social factors is usually indirect. The influence of the economic potential on the course and outcome of war (or armed struggle) is for example exerted through many intermediate factors: through political actions, for instance, pressures exerted partly by economic forces. An economic blockade may support military operations; the morale of the population and armed forces is always influenced by the economic situation, and so on.

Moreover, since many other potentials and factors operate at the same time, it is difficult to prove that just the economic potential has been the determining or even one of the determining factors, and that there is no room left for the influence of other factors.

War has a specific character which does not make things easier. More than other social activities it consists of a continuous clash of action and counteraction, and it proceeds through the continuous interaction of many laws. The operation of the law in question can be paralysed by that of others, since the opposing parties try to create favourable conditions for laws which work for them and against the enemy.

However, it is a matter of doubt whether even the fulfilment of all the above-mentioned conditions finally confirms the hypothesis under discussion and allows it the status of law. It is asserted in such a general form that it would have to be filled out by definite laws specifying the kinds of military actions and their course and outcome which regularly follow specific changes in the factor (variable) or factors (variables) in question; these laws would perhaps be more amenable to empirical tests which could finally confirm the law.

The other main difficulty is that the laws of war cannot be tested either by an experiment (which would mean artificially to unleash war in order to test the laws) or by thorough observation (which would mean an objective and even dispassionate inquiry simultaneously into all details of the conduct of war and fighting);[20] the main way of testing laws - especially the general laws of war and the most general laws of armed struggle - is to analyse past wars. Critics doubt whether such 'testing' should be recognised as sufficient for confirmation of the laws in question.[21]

The Soviet concept of laws of war, however, implies that Soviet scholars regard such objections as inconclusive. They would probably answer that one should take as the first premise of testing that the laws of war are a direct reflection and application of the laws of social development, and also that they have been brought into accord with the realities of the given epoch (the principal contradictions and the development of the politico-military situation); thus one should first test their logical compatibility with the more general laws and secondly demonstrate their compatibility with some contemporary evidence i.e. with certain politico-military events the course and outcome of which can be explained by the asserted laws. On the other hand, a quantitative investigation is obviously not required, they would argue, to explain the mechanism of social activity, social political struggle and, finally, war. These are not amenable to quantitative measurement. On the contrary, it can only mislead by drawing attention to secondary indices, and diverting it from the determining characteristics.

Thus it is sufficient to provide evidence that if certain conditions are fulfilled, the general course of political events preceding war, the course of war and armed struggle as a whole, and of particular operations and battles, will probably be similar to those predicted or assumed. And such necessary conditions will be (probably largely) fulfilled, since they result from the lawful development of class society. To Soviet scholars, it is not necessary to point out the probability values involved in the wording of the laws; these can be presented quite roughly and the explanation of the mechanism of the events can be reduced to a general description of how laws and initial conditions can explain the main direction and course of events.

Finally, to return to testing by practice, Soviet scholars present the argument of the 'usability' of the laws. If the application of the given law has served the attainment of some definite results e.g. if it has contributed to victory in a military operation or increased the effectiveness of the armed forces in the peacetime, it may provide confirmation of the validity of the law. Effectiveness in action is the criterion and the ultimate test verifying cognised laws. To put it another way, if the given law serves the implementation of the political and military doctrines of the Soviet Union and Soviet military policy, then it is valid.[22]

It would seem that the main techniques used by Soviet scholars for testing many of the laws of war, especially the general laws, serve not so much the testing *sensu stricto* as the confirmation of laws which are assumed to be valid *ex origine* since they have been formulated on the basis of the Marxist-Leninist philosophy and in accord with the political and military doctrines. The fact that most general laws of war are derived from the main propositions of historical materialism prejudges the result of testing them against these propositions; and since the terms of the laws are always adapted to the requirements of the current political and military doctrines, they will always correspond to them.

The procedure of 'confirming' laws by demonstrating their compatibility with laws of social development, of which the interpretation is the core of a philosophy i.e. dialectical and historical materialism, is a risky one. It assumes that this philosophy is the only true reflection of world history; and the only scientific interpretation of the world, society, and man. Those who do not share this view cannot accept that laws of war can be tested, substantiated and confirmed by such a procedure.

It is easy to provide historical facts which confirm any such law. Facts can often be variously interpreted, and since the causal ties of war (or armed struggle) with external factors, as well as their internal relationships, are numer-

156

ous, complex and multidimensional, and since particular factors affecting war and armed struggle often act indirectly and are intermixed with other factors, it is the interpretation of the facts and relationships that determines whether a certain fact can be presented as supporting or refuting the law. In other words, while the laws in question e.g. laws of the dependence of war (or armed struggle) on external factors, are difficult to *test*, they are easy to *illustrate*. One can always find out a coincidence of a certain course and outcome of war, or military operation, with a respective alignment of forces or factors and contend that the correspondence between the conditions and the course of fighting confirms the law in question.

The above brief attempt to describe the way in which Soviet scholars test most of the laws of war is based on the Soviet way of presenting and discussing these laws. As an example of the inevitable difficulty of testing such general, qualitative and probabilistic laws, one may mention the impossibility of testing many of them in an empirical way; and of producing the initial conditions necessary for observing the development of war and thereby testing hypotheses about laws, as this would mean the unleashing of war for the sake of experiments and tests. Moreover, this would have to be a war appropriate for testing the most important laws i.e. a war between systems.

What remains, therefore, is the possibility of analysing the very few past wars that bear some resemblance to the hypothetical war between systems and using them to illustrate the law-like statements. Critics will doubt whether such tests are sufficient to confirm the hypotheses.

The above comments do not apply to certain laws of the effectiveness of armed struggle, the validity of which can be tested by manoeuvres and wargames. Some Soviet scholars generalise the value of such tests and contend that all laws of war presented by Soviet military theory have been tested.[23] However, the laws of the effectiveness of armed struggle are far from being the most typical items in the Soviet set of laws of war.

The character of laws

The way in which Soviet scholars test the statements which they call laws of war, seems to confirm the preliminary suggestions about their character made in this study (Chaps. 4, 5 and 6). A summary of these may be introduced by a brief comment on the Soviet view of the laws. Soviet researchers apparently are not troubled by the difference between the definition of a law of war and their own conclusions about the probabilistic (or probabilistic-statistical) character of most laws.

On the one hand they formulate most laws of war as if they represented uniform and universally valid links and relationships and make no definite reference to a lapse of time or conditions limiting the scope of the class of phenomena which they cover.[24] Soviet theorists, while asserting the principle of the changeability of laws, much prefer to leave the wording intact and change only the interpretation. They also prefer to state the various manifestations of the law in various types of war, particular instances of war or even particular events of war rather than to formulate specific laws for specific types and instances of war or specific kinds of military operations. They make no reference to the conditions of the validity of laws which would limit their universality.

On the other hand, Soviet scholars note that many events of war do not follow the rigid prescriptions of the universal laws, that the deviation from a model course of events are numerous, that the action of the laws and their impact are different in different wars, at different times and places; and that even the general course of events, in some cases, cannot be predicted with full certainty. Some scholars state that the knowledge of the laws of war is 'relative' and limited to concrete historical conditions, and that only some elements of the laws concerning future wars can be cognised. Others even propose that a new concept of law is needed which will bring together the orthodox one and all the modifications made when it is examined in the light of new conditions.[25] Thus some kind of probabilistic or probabilistic-statistical law is seen by many as more appropriate for many ties and relationships of war.

The scientific status

It would be very difficult to give the same assessment to all these different statements which Soviet military theorists call laws; scientifically, they differ greatly from one another.

Some of them resemble *universal laws*; they represent statements at a very high level of generality, such as the proposition that policy decisively influences war or that the correlation of forces determines victory.

Some scholars would perhaps consider such statements trivial truths connected with the very essence of war, which do not need any codification and elevation to laws. Besides, they are tacitly taken for granted and applied in any investigation. Calling them laws does not add explanatory value to the theory of war.

However, on this at least two comments can be made. As regards, for instance, the dependence of war on policy, not everyone accepts that war is fought for political aims. Numerous theorists assume war to be a non-political, or at least not a wholly political, phenomenon; among those who consider it political, many think that while being a continuation of policy, or fought for political aims, war is nevertheless governed by its own laws which begin to operate with the first fight; the influence of policy then becomes secondary.

Moreover, as a trivial truth, the conceptions of war and policy should have the same meaning in all approaches or interpretations. The opposite is true, however, and the Soviet view of policy as expressing relations between classes, class states, and nations led by classes, as reflecting first and foremost the economic interests of classes, and relating all kinds of policy to internal policy, differs greatly from many traditional and contemporary approaches. The treatment of war as a form of class struggle or its reflection is a corollary. And this is a quite different approach from, for instance, 'trivial truths' about the relation between war and policy stemming from Clausewitzian tradition and reflected in many doctrines and theories.

The same comments may be made on the laws of the correlation of forces. The Soviet concept of these forces, their class essence and structure, with emphasis on the value of the socio-economic and political system, attributes to them a quality far from the usual one. This allows for a very different assessment of the dynamics of the correlation and its impact, which is far from trivial.

Other laws of war, such as the most general laws of the genesis of war, are to the same - if not a higher - degree the reflection of a specific philosophy of politics and war. Thus, while the scientific status of these laws of war, as presented by Soviet researchers, can be questioned for not fitting what is regarded as a law in other approaches, these law-like statements represent without doubt a specific view of war, its essence and dynamics, that is definitely different from the traditional one.[26]

Some statements called laws constitute hypotheses that resemble *descriptive generalisations*, political assessments of the contemporary situation from the point of view of Soviet ideology, doctrine and policy. Laws of the genesis of particular types of war may provide an example: that all contemporary wars fit into the design of imperialism i.e. that the main current of policy followed by wars in our epoch springs from the struggle of imperialism against socialism.

Laws of a third kind denote causal ties between war and certain external factors, having the character of *very general dependences*, for instance, the law of the dependence of the course and outcome of war on the economic potential, or scientific potential, and the like.

The two latter kinds of statements concern a probabilistic course of events. They assume non-identical initial conditions and a non-predetermined course and outcome of events. It may happen that in some cases the event in question will not occur at all. For instance, it may be true that imperialism generates war; however, the manner of generation differs in different cases - places and times - and it may happen that even in a typical situation war will not break out.

Probabilistic hypotheses are made concerning the course of military operations which can also be treated as principles of military art; most of the so-called internal laws of armed struggle can be included here.

Statements are also made concerning laws governing techno-military procedures which are similar to the *natural deterministic laws* about uniform ties and dependences, since they concern actions which are subsumed to physical, chemical, mechanical and other laws and regularities. They play a secondary role in war as a social activity, but may profoundly influence the course of military operations.

Summing up, most above-mentioned statements about laws may be regarded as probability laws or hypotheses. The occurrence and the supposed course and outcome of war can be regarded as probable (or highly probable) in view of the initial conditions and these probability hypotheses.

Two comments are possible concerning the assessment of most laws of war as probabilistic. Firstly, it would seem that the Soviet *concept* of laws of war *implies* that these are probability laws; *they must be such since they operate through human action.* Such laws cannot determine the genesis, course and outcome of war, and its phenomena and processes, with the force of inevitable necessity, without allowing for exceptions, extenuations and deviations. We cannot assert that, because of certain initial conditions, the genesis, or course, or outcome of war, or its phenomena, must be what we expect.

We can only expect that because such initial conditions frequently cause a certain course of events (which in this sense may be called typical) it is likely that in each case under investigation such a relationship will occur. There are factors which can cause deviations from the typical and expected, and they are mainly connected with the fact that human activity cannot be fatalistically predetermined. A conceptual relation exists between the probabilistic character of laws of war and the nature of human activity. This relation somewhat diminishes the predictability of the events of war, but it is not without merits.

Statements called laws give some insight into the causes of war, factors influencing its course and outcome, its internal dynamics, although not to such an extent as natural laws; on the other hand, since we do not commit ourselves to the existence of universal deterministic laws operating with the force of necessity, it makes appeal to the conscious human activity which is necessary for the operation of probability laws of war, and which can prevent their action if it would proceed against our interests. The predictive component of such concept is a stimulant to action in that it promises success, victory or prevention of war.

The second comment concerns another aspect of the impact of human action on the probabilistic character of laws of war, namely the interpretation of the expression 'determines' in the wording of many laws. We read that the genesis of war and its phenomena and processes are determined by certain factors or that, in the same way, certain factors decisively influence these phenomena. In Soviet philosophy, this is regarded as a kind of causation. However, the formulae of laws do not indicate the degree of the dependence (or of the impact). They do not assert whether the factor in question is the only one influencing phenomena of war, or whether its action is sufficient to produce the occurrence and the given course of the phenomena. It would be perhaps advisable to include in the wording of such a law the qualifying term 'usually'. It even happens that the expression 'determines' or 'decisively influences' is replaced simply by 'influences'.

Indeed, it is frequently difficult to establish more precisely the degree of impact. One should take into account that there are many variables in this equation:

1 Laws of war create the favourable or unfavourable conditions under which men act; the way in which they will utilise the favourable conditions

and counter the unfavourable is not predetermined (see above).

2 Individual laws act within the larger framework of the operation of an aggregate of laws, therefore the probability of the outcome which would be determined by the given law if it acts separately should be assessed in this larger framework.

3 There is always a wide *ceteris paribus* clause to be read into the laws of war.

4 While some laws operate as directly determining the course of events, others act indirectly, inter alia, through more specific laws. For instance, the war-generating role of the exploiting social system is indirect, the system influences the outbreak of concrete wars through the concrete contradiction and concrete policy (e.g. the contradiction between the imperialist countries and the underdeveloped ones and conflicts over specific issues). Any evaluation of the degree to which the more general laws determine the outbreak and course of concrete wars should take into consideration the probability of the operation of the more specific laws.

5 Causal ties and relationships constituting the essence of the probabilistic laws of war exist in a broader framework of the interaction between phenomena. It would be desirable in the assessment of the degree of determination of the phenomena of war by causal laws not to disregard the other ties and relationships.

All these circumstances affecting the degree of the causal impact naturally make the assessment of its magnitude difficult. However, Soviet scholars who discuss these laws are not troubled by such difficulties. In qualitative laws of this kind, they say, the very fact of the influence - whether it determines or significantly affects or simply affects the events and phenomena of war - is regarded as relevant to explaining the essence and dynamics of war.

Laws in explanation

The above diversified picture of the scientific status of the Soviet statements on the ties and relationships of war should be complemented by an assessment of their value as tools of explanation and prediction. This is because the formulation of laws is not an end in itself but should serve practical purposes. Firstly, it should explain the past and present; secondly, it should help to predict future; and thirdly, contribute to further development of the theory of war.

'To explain' means many things and the content of this procedure has been the subject of many protracted controversies.[27] In the Soviet presentation it is tacitly assumed that this term does not need interpretation: laws of war explain the direct and indirect causes of the origin and dynamics of war-events i.e. of factors which generate war and influence its course and outcome.

These laws mean however little without the theory which they represent: i.e.

historical materialism. Only the theory itself allows us to arrive at the probable story behind the appearances. When a law is invoked for the purpose of explaining a war it is the whole theory which is involved. Only if we know the theory will reference to the law itself provide an explanation. For instance, the law of the determining effect of policy on the character of war connects the terms policy and war which carry profound theoretical load - the socio-political doctrine of war as instrument of policy. This law represents the scientific expression of the whole doctrine, a transformed theoretical proposition which has always been applied in the analysis of past and present wars; therefore the law as such can add little to the explanation of the given relationship.

Nor do such laws allow us to dispense with a thorough investigation of the whole factual material. For instance, in the investigation of the main causes of a specific war, the application of a law stating the type of such causes with regard to the given type of war cannot replace the search for the specific causes of this individual case of war. The law merely reminds us that often the cause has been found to be that surmised, and therefore it proves worthwhile to have been on the lookout for it as a likely cause of the given war. Even if it is confirmed that it played a vital role in the actual causation of the given war, one should treat the factor in question as the sufficient condition, only *ceteris paribus*. However, since one never knows whether it really was *ceteris paribus* in the given case, one has to investigate other possible causes. In other words, the law in question does not point out the main cause definitely and unequivocally.

Thus the knowledge of these laws may here serve as a guideline to the organisation of the investigative and explanatory work, and may help to focus research on the most important, necessary and recurrent ties and dependences. Similar guidelines, however, have also been applied before. Soviet military theorists have always applied the propositions of historical materialism, and focused on ascertaining the class-political roots and causes of wars, on seeking the influence of economic and other social factors on war, on stressing the subordinate role of warfare in relation to policy, and so on. These guidelines, however, were not related to laws. For instance, the principle that the development of military art is rooted in the development of the material basis and not in the free creative activity of great commanders was observed independently of whether it was at times called law, or not. The chief monographs dealing with the history of military art discussed successful combat techniques without reference to what are now called laws of the effectiveness of armed struggle.

Laws as an instrument of prediction

Predicting future wars In Soviet theory, individuals and social groups act in accordance with their interests. Social laws operate through such action. The full awareness of one's interests and the knowledge of laws contributes to more effective action, and permits planning and foresight considering its course and outcome. With regard to war, these general assumptions can be applied to the prediction of the outbreak of war, its general course, evolution and outcome and to the planning and conduct of individual military operations.

In the past, Soviet scholars applied the laws of historical materialism to an analytical description and explanation of past wars rather than to predicting wars of the future; and when they attempted prediction they were not successful.

In the inter-war period, contrary to predictions based on the theory of the inevitability of war, no war broke out for a long time between the Soviet state and the states involved in the 'capitalist encirclement', and when war did come its outbreak and development were quite different from the predictions of Soviet scholars and politicians. The Soviet Union first remained outside the war, and was then involved in it at a time unexpected and unpredicted by the Soviet leadership. Nor was the course of hostilities similar to the expected one. On the contrary, the course of armed struggle and the changes in the political situation were far from the predicted ones, and Soviet armed forces were compelled to use unforeseen methods of fighting. Only the fact that the socialist state finally became not only a participant in the war, but also one of the victors, could be presented as being in accord with laws of history and war as defined by Soviet theorists.

In spite of this lack of success in prediction, Soviet scholars do not give up. Unlike many Western scholars, who deny the possibility of predicting the outbreak and course of future wars, they continue - as always - to assert that general laws of war and of armed struggle (re-formulated according to the conditions of the nuclear age) allow them to predict the origin and conduct of future wars, their development and outcome.

One typical statement may well illustrate their attitude of conviction: 'On the basis of the international military-political situation, the overall distribution of forces in the world, the consequences of the techno-scientific revolution and the military preparation of the aggressive imperialist circles Soviet military science can predict the possible nature of a future war, the methods by which it will be waged, and the roles to be played by the different services and branches of the armed forces'.[28]

This means that: (1) the knowledge of the laws of social development and general laws of war enables the Soviet political and military leaders to predict the development of the political-military situation, including conflicts and crises which may lead to wars, and to assess the possibility of a future war, and the way and time it will break out;[29] (2) the knowledge of the laws of the development of military art is of help in predicting the development of the techno-military basis of war and of military art; and (3) the knowledge of the internal laws of military struggle and the principles of military art, based on laws, reflected in military doctrine, regulations, manuals and other documents of guidance will enable the commanders to plan and successfully conduct military operations.[30]

In some studies, to analyse the situation on the battlefield correctly, to draw proper conclusions, and to take right decisions means to predict and to act according to the prediction.[31] Prediction constitutes, in other words, one of the main declared reasons for seeking and presenting the laws of war and their mechanisms. A knowledge of these laws is said to be the primary requisite for taking decisions, even if there must be many links in the chain from laws to decisions, the main one being a correct assessment of the actual situation.

It would appear, however, that the derivation of decisions from the knowledge of laws and the mechanisms is more an abstract ideal, a model or a lip service to theory than an actual procedure. This applies not only to decisions taken on the battlefield, but also to the big decisions on starting a war and waging it. Politicians take into account, implicitly or explicitly, general ideological assumptions, Marxist-Leninist propositions concerning the world, society, politics, and war, as well as ideas about the contemporary world and assessments of the politico-military situation; but they pay little attention to laws of war. And even the above-mentioned ideological and political assumptions and propositions in the process of assessing by the leaders the situation and taking decision are regarded as commonsense guidelines rather than laws.

When a commander analyses and assesses a situation, what he considers are not so much the laws, or even the principles of military art, as the military manuals, regulations, orders from the higher levels of command and other documents for guidance, which in some degree reflect laws and principles, but even more reflect an evaluation of the general and particular situation.

However, it should be noted that in spite of declarations about the full predictability of events, Soviet scholars sometimes make reservations which somewhat weaken this general assumption. They say, for instance, that since the course and outcome of war as a whole is determined by probabilistic laws, a given outcome can only be expected but cannot be predicted with full certainty.

(It may happen that one and the same scholar at the same time asserts both the predictability and the unpredictability of armed struggle:

'The probabilistic-statistical laws, which determine the course and outcome of war as a whole, determine the concrete military operations in their decisive aspect (v reshayushchem), allowing sufficient room for the action of various tendencies. Otherwise, the outcome of the armed struggle would be prejudged. One of the parties, after counting and estimating its forces, and seeing that the enemy is superior, would accept defeat.

... They (the statistical-probabilistic laws and law-tendencies) determine unequivocally the main direction and main outcome of war (and armed struggle)'.[32]

It appears that the outcome of war and armed struggle is at the same time determined, prejudged — and is not).

The second reservation is even more far-reaching. It is stated that laws of armed struggle are different from both natural and social laws; they concern an extremely antagonistic process, a constant attempt to destroy the enemy forces and preserve one's own, for the attainment of directly opposed military-political goals and under conditions of a continuously changing correlation of forces.[33] (Against this it may be argued that opposite political goals are not only charac-

164

teristic of war and armed struggle but are inherent in the whole process of class struggle, which is said to be governed by social laws.)

One consequence is that prediction here is more difficult than in the case of either natural or social laws proper. The other consequence is conceptual: the basic assumption that laws of armed struggle like the general laws of war are social laws is changed here. (Here, it may be asked, if the general laws of war, and laws of armed struggle, are of different character - social and non-social respectively - how can they be combined into one set, or system, of laws?)

The third reservation is a corollary. It is stated that phenomena of war as other particular events and phenomena of historical processes cannot be predicted with full certainty. Only the main direction of the historical evolution and its final results, which are connected with laws, with the repetitiveness of events and with stable features of development can be foreseen. This is because only the main causes of the process connected with the laws of historical materialism introduce the element of necessity; the secondary causes involve fortuity (see Ch.2). Social phenomena cannot be repetitive in all details since identical conditions never recur. This may be related to war as well.

In particular, the following factors diminish the predictability of events in war, and especially in armed struggle:

1 Armed struggle is affected by the action of many external and internal factors, only a few of which can to some degree be foreseen.

2 Many laws interact.

3 The human factor can paralyse the action of some laws and create conditions favourable for the action of others.

4 The enemy counteracts at every point and at every time.

5 Many accidental events influence the course of fighting.

Consequently, even if one's own actions can be planned and therefore to some extent be predicted, the enemy actions introduce an element of unpredictability. Even if one can deal with some factors, others can be elusive; one can calculate the effects of one's own action in the operation of some laws but not in others. In a particular military operation, for instance, the initial correlation of forces does not predetermine the outcome, since it may change - even many times - during the fighting.

Thus Soviet scholars accept that the outcome of single events in war - particular military operations - cannot be prejudged and thus predicted with full certainty. Consequently, war as a whole, and armed struggle as a whole, must retain their individual features: no two wars are identical, even under similar circumstances.

Soviet theory implies, however, that one can foresee the main possible alternative courses of events; one can and should foresee not only the main line of historical necessity but also the effects of other causal chains which could affect the main course of events. Such predictions would help to create conditions favouring positive impacts and eliminating negative ones. Thus one can foresee alternative possible courses of the development of war and of particular military operations, if one knows the laws and can properly analyse the course of war and the military situation.

Scientific prediction of the development of armaments

Although often discussed jointly with other problems of scientific prediction (see above), a quite different problem is the scientific prediction in the development of armament.

If one accepts that the process of basing the development of armaments on the development of science and technology should be called scientific prediction, one can agree with Soviet scholars that such prediction and forecasting play an important and constantly increasing role in the development of weapons and combat equipment and that military science looks (or should look) ahead and develops plans based on designers' ideas for creating more advanced armaments.[34]

However, while it is a fact that Soviet science and technology have nowadays created foundations for the development of armaments based on long-range forecasts, and while the ties of military development with the general techno-scientific development are obvious, the way in which knowledge of the laws of war makes possible such scientific prediction has not been demonstrated. It will be recalled that in spite of knowledge of the laws of war, the Soviet leadership wrongly assessed the prospects of the development of many kinds of weapons on the eve of World War II, and also came second to the United States in the creation of nuclear arms. Thus is seems that the task of discovering the way in which the relation between knowledge of laws of war and scientific prediction in this field should be transformed into an effective political procedure has not been fulfilled.

Use of laws in development of the theory of war

One problem which has hardly been considered by Soviet researchers is the theory-generating role of laws of war. Occasionally, it has been said that laws are not only an outcome of the theoretical development but also an instrument of further theorising, but the idea has not been worked out.

Paradoxically enough, the hitherto presented body of laws may serve more as an incentive to further research than as a tool for it. If this is so, it is because of the very general way in which many of the formulae are expressed and the inde-terminate degree of probability which they state. The knowledge of laws gives only a general understanding of the factors relevant to the origin, course and outcome of war; it should be complemented by an explanation of the mechanism of the laws.

All the difficulties enumerated above concerning the interaction of laws, the indirect way in which many laws affect war and the influence of laws other than causal may be regarded as appropriate items for scientific study. The exploration of some of these problems may lead to the formulation of specific laws which can complement the more general ones (see Chap. 8).

To sum up, it is difficult to present any general assessment of the utility of the laws of war in Soviet research and practice, because of the diversity of their current scientific status and functions. The difficulty also arises partly because the whole theory is only in *statu nascendi*,[35] and although the laws have been regarded as relatively stable, it is generally considered that they must be adapted to the nuclear missile age.

Laws must be changed

A most important consideration influencing not only the predictability of events in future wars but also affecting the whole shape of the existing set of laws is that in spite of many efforts at reform and adaptation to the conditions of the nuclear missile age, these laws still look backwards, and are far from being completed. While some scholars state that the hitherto operating laws will also 'in principle' operate in a nuclear missile war, others assert that the revolution in military affairs makes it necessary to introduce fundamental changes into the content and formulation of laws of war, especially those of armed struggle, and to discover quite new laws. Still others take an intermediate position and, assuming that the traditional laws of war will operate in future wars, maintain that the future, probably new forms of their manifestation should be investigated to discover the mechanism of their action under changed conditions.

It seems that none of these postulates has been realised; no new laws have been proposed,[36] no essential changes in the traditional formulae presented, and the task of investigating the new mechanism of laws of war in a future war remains only a postulate. Scholars see numerous difficulties in accomplishing all these changes.[37]

However, changes *are* necessary.

To begin with the laws of the origin of war, the traditional formulae about the four traditional types of war have not undergone any essential changes. The renunciation of the doctrine of the inevitability of war has been reflected only in comments on the diminished possibility that imperialism will initiate or cause particular types of war.

However, the conditions under which regularities in the incidence of wars which have been elevated to laws occur, have profoundly changed. For instance, although one can accept the thesis that countries develop unevenly, the way in which they do so is quite different from that prevailing in the beginning of this century. At that time sudden leaps in the development of individual countries generated sharp contradictions and led to world wars. The law of the genesis of inter-imperialist wars, formulated on the basis of the contemporary analysis by Lenin, must now be replaced by a new one, reflecting new objective

167

relationships between the development of Western powers and the diminished probability of wars between them.

Similarly, the increasing state intervention in many Western countries which aims at reducing anarchy and spontaneity in economic affairs (although it does not seem to resolve the principal social contradictions) makes the crises and outbreak of internal revolutionary violence of the traditional type less likely. On the other hand, other conflicts generated by 'rising expectation' in the underdeveloped countries and many other causes may lead to internal violence of a different type. The traditional law concerning the origin of revolutionary wars, or civil wars, should be changed, or replaced by a set of laws concerning internal development in societies differing in the level of socio-political and economic development.

Laws of the relationship between politics and war should also be re-examined. It seems to me that while politics will always influence the character of warfare, more specific assertions (whether law-like or not) must be formulated separately for particular types of war, especially with regard to a thermonuclear war between systems (see Chap. 8). Obviously, the thesis often formulated by Soviet scholars that nuclear war 'although not an instrument of politics' will be its continuation (or rather result) introduces a new quality to the standard formula, since it is precisely the use of armed violence for attaining political aims that is the essence of war.

Laws concerning factors that influence the course and outcome of war were formulated with regard to a prolonged war of the traditional type. Soviet theory that is oriented to nuclear war needs new laws, appropriate to a relatively short war with quickly-developing military operations. With regard to such a war the primacy of the economic factor in the correlation of forces should perhaps be replaced by the primacy of the military power available for use in the very beginning of a war. Even if the wording of the law (laws) of the correlation of forces generally remains unchanged (since in the final analysis economic power determines available military power), it should be formulated separately and variously with regard to the course of war as a whole and to particular levels of military operations. In individual battles and operations - especially those involving the use of nuclear weapons - the 'forces in being' will play the determining part.

With regard to the laws of the conduct of armed struggle, and especially the laws of its effectiveness, a radical re-examination seems to be necessary. The whole complex of these laws in Soviet theory concerns a thermonuclear war between systems; its main premise is that the Soviet forces will win such a war, and they should cognise the laws operating in it in order to win. On this premise, most scholars try to adapt the traditional laws. Some, however, seek new laws, and this seems wiser: the quite new quality of a thermonuclear warfare would be governed by quite new laws.

One can, however, question the very doctrinal premises asserting the certainty of Soviet victory in a thermonuclear war. Many agree that the term 'victory' loses its meaning with regard to such a war, and these sceptics have also included Soviet politicans and theorists.

One can also question the applicability of the term 'law' with regard to a phenomenon unique in history: even if a thermonuclear war between systems breaks out, and even if some countries survive it, it certainly will not be repeated. Can we speak of a 'law' without 'repeatability' of the ties and dependences which it asserts? Thus, either laws of other wars also operate in a thermonuclear war, even if in a modified form, or there will be no laws in the meaning of the term adopted in Soviet theory.

The reasons for laws

A brief listing

One can only guess why Soviet scholars present so many different statements termed laws, why they insist on providing laws to account for each regularity in the origin and conduct of war, why they insist on a common classification and integration of them into one set, or system, and why they constantly widen the scope of this system.

One reason can be that the presentation of laws of war, according to the Soviet general assessment of the role of laws, is considered by Soviet scholars as turning the study of war into a science. They now seek a unified military theory that would encompass the whole realm of military affairs: (1) the theory of war as a socio-political phenomenon, combined with the theory of armed forces in the so-called teaching on war and army; (2) the theory of the conduct of armed struggle (military science) and (3) the theory and programme of preparing for a future war (military doctrine). In all these areas theory is constantly expanding. Its volume grows, and new fields covering the connections of war with other social phenomena are constantly included. At the same time, military theory differentiates, individual branches of the knowledge of war, and aspects of war and of the prevention of war are separated into relatively independent fields. As a corollary, constantly new law-like regularities are being discovered and new law-like statements advanced. The expansion is directed outside and inside, new groups of laws appear, but also more specific laws which fill out the existing, more general law-like statements. And with each newly formulated law the military writers remind the reader that the system of laws of war is an indispensable part of such united and all-encompassing theory.[38]

Soviet military leaders and scholars repeatedly stress that without laws there is no science, no military doctrine based on science, and no effective leadership of armed forces in times of peace and war. 'Successful leadership in the development of social phenomena - and consequently also war - first of all assumes thorough understanding and skilful use of those laws which govern the development of these phenomena'.[39] In other words, it is repeatedly stressed that the formu-

169

lation of laws is not a scientific end in itself. The highest uses of laws are practical uses, in promoting and accomplishing practical activity on an ever higher level.

It is stated that the formulation of laws helps the leaders to predict the development of the politico-military situation (including the development of the techno-material basis of the conduct of war), the outbreak of a possible war and its course and outcome i.e. contribute to the development of military doctrine; it also furthers the implementation of current military policy by giving a theoretical superstructure to the main tasks of preparation for future wars, to the formulation of them and focusing the efforts of the economy, armed forces and the population in general on the crucial items.

To a much greater extent, however, it would seem laws are used as justification of policy which has already been carried out, especially justification of the continuous increase in military power. If such an increase is presented as following objective laws, it must be regarded as necessary and just. To take a simple example, laws such as that of the correlation of forces, of the role of armament, of the significance of surprise in nuclear war, etc., are presented as a justification of economic and military efforts, and of a high degree of readiness for starting military operations at any point of time.

Laws of war are also regarded by Soviet scholars as a means of ideological and political struggle. They are formulated in a way which can be exploited for propaganda because they state the inevitable victory of socialism and the military superiority of socialist states. They serve as a tool for criticising Western ideology, and military doctrine and policy.

Finally, in this short list of hypothesised reasons, laws of war may be of some use in educating and training armed forces. They impart what Soviet leadership considers to be military knowledge in the highly condensed form of a few propositions, and the art of fighting comprised in a small number of statements about the rational methods of acting. Both may serve as kinds of commandments or guidelines in schooling and training.

A concrete example

Before summing up this section, the law of the correlation of forces will be presented as an example of a law that is used to justify long-term policy. The qualitative character of this law and the correlative character of the factors which it deals with serve to justify any continuous military build-up.

Even if one considers only the military components of the correlation of forces, each method of measuring it has serious shortcomings.[40] The main difficulty encountered lies in the asymmetries between force structures and in the equation of dissimilar units. As regards strategic weapons in particular, while some comparisons can be made concerning the numbers of these, the above-mentioned asymmetries, together with the difficulty of comparing the quality of the leadership, the organisation and training of forces, the state of morale, both of the population and armed forces, the abilities of economic systems to meet the needs for these extremely costly and sophisticated weapons, diminish the value of any comparison.

In the conventional component, apart from the difficulties of measuring the quantitative indices and quality, there are always uncertainties in making an estimate of ready conventional strength which would be available in an international crisis and, even more important, which would be available at the point of conflict.

The dependence of the effectiveness of conventional armed forces on time, space, location, climate, terrain, etc. also varies in different armies, which makes the comparison of their strength more difficult. In short, force availability and geographical influence must be taken into account.

Moreover, there are difficulties in estimating the correlation resulting from the lack of an accurate estimate of what both sides really have at their disposal. There is insufficient confidence in the ability to acquire reliable data on the numbers and performance of the strategic weapons, defensive systems, shorter range defensive systems, and on the weapons which the other side develops or deploys. And one can know even less about the other side's doctrine and objectives regarding the design and development of weapons and forces.

Moreover, in the Soviet view, the correlation of forces means much more than that of military power. It encompasses the aggregate national (or coalitionary) power made up of political, economic, scientific-technical, military and spiritual components as well as military power proper and is based on the character and quality of the socio-economic and political system. And these are intangible values to a much greater degree than the military components.

Thus the assessed correlation can be regarded as a rough approximation derived from a very arbitrary assessment of particular components, and the relative value of each component is also different at different historical points of time.

The correlation of forces is considered to be dynamic, which means that both strengths subject to comparison - and their relationship also - are constantly changing. Although the Soviet side is presented as continuously progressing, and the capitalist side as decaying and disintegrating, the change concerns more their relative than absolute strength; the latter can grow on both sides. Thus the supposed or asserted constant growth of the power of the adversary can always be used to justify further increases in one's own forces.

Finally, the law assumes that only a favourable correlation of forces in relation to the adversary i.e. superiority over him, permits victory in a possible war.

The notion of superiority, however, is even more elusive and enables every leadership to make an even more subjective evaluation of 'what is enough'. To estimate 'what is more' is nearly impossible, and the right (claimed by the leaders) to evaluate 'how much more' constitutes a mandate for an endless build-up of armaments and of the levels of armed forces.

The conclusion to be drawn from all these considerations seems obvious. The law of the dependence of the course and outcome of war on the correlation of forces may be used to justify a continuously high level of military competition and unremitting military preparations. It may be used to justify the assumption of the doctrine and military policy that no lasting constraints on unilateral military planning are acceptable.

Such uses of this law confirm the doubt whether usefulness, in the sense of justification of the Soviet political and military doctrine, can be applied as a criterion for judging the scientific status of a statement, even in the Soviet conceptual framework. For instance, the law of the correlation of forces (although not presented as a law) may serve equally well the political and military doctrines of the United States, justify its military build-up, which, according to the same criteria, is indicative of its unscientific character. This shows the danger of presenting doctrine as one of the sources of truth for scientific research.

Concluding comments on the working formula (equation) of war

In Chap. 2 it was suggested that for the purpose of analysing the Soviet way of explaining the events and processes of war a working formula is useful. This formula connects laws (L), conditions or circumstances (C), human actions in war (A), and events and processes of war (E), which are being decisively affected by L, C, and A. A preliminary interpretation of these variables has also been advanced.

From the presentation of the Soviet concept and set of laws it can be concluded that the set of variables and the interpretation of them require some complementation.

1 To take the latter first, one additional factor has been introduced into the Soviet presentation of laws and the way in which they operate, and this factor includes the systemic conditions which characterise the socio-economic and political system. These constitute what may be called the basic conditional factor, since they are always presented as a highly creative and motivating force which permeates all factors and dependences in war i.e. all the component parts of our working formula.

They are embodied in the political and military leaderships which realise the fundamental long-range aims of societies and their current politico-military doctrines. These aims and doctrines are rooted in the character of the system and express its nature. Thus the system is here used to denote not a high abstraction but rather the given society with its concrete structure, its leadership and its policy. This system is said to determine largely the initial conditions of any war, and the military power with which the belligerent starts the war, the character of the politico-military coalition which wages it, its political aims and so on. The system largely determines the actions of individuals, of the population, of the armed forces, of particular officers and soldiers, their feelings, emotions, decisions and activities.

The character of the system, moreover, is said to determine the degree of knowledge of the objective laws of war, the way in which the laws of military theory are formulated and, most important, the degree to which these laws can be utilised, forced to act in favour of a belligerent, or paralysed if they operate to his disadvantage. For instance, in the Soviet view the law of the increasing role of the popular masses in war can best be cognised by the science developed in a socialist state. It can be expressed in a more direct and exact formula, and best exploited by socialist leaders and armies.

Thus in the simplified formula which illustrates the Soviet interpretation of the mechanism of causal laws of war, the set of factors which decisively affect the incidence, the course and the outcome of war may be complemented by the systemic factor (S), or the basic conditional factor, which has a direct bearing on all other components of the formula.

The introduction of this factor to the explanation of the action of causal laws in war may be in line with Western ideas about the role of the political system in the causation of war and waging of war. However, the notion of system, which, in the Soviet interpretation, means one of the five basic socio-economic formations (structures) in human history and is nowadays applied to illustrate the contradiction between the two antagonistic systems, capitalist and socialist, is so basically different from any Western concept in this subject that it can be regarded as a new term in the formula.

Thus, although the impact of the socio-economic and political system on war does not enter the picture as *deus ex machina* nor as a new force unknown to the traditional Western theories of war, Soviet scholars vest it with special importance. While in the West, the inclusion of the systemic factor is regarded as the taking into account of trivial truths, which need no such attention *expressis verbis*, in the Soviet presentation these conditions have gained scientific status and are used for the sake of argument, for the specific explanation of the past and for supporting Soviet assertions concerning the future.

Moreover, many laws of war are formulated in such a way that by application of the systemic factor they appear to confirm assertions about the inevitable victory of the socialist state and its army.

The law of the decisive impact of the moral-political potential on the course and outcome of war, combined with the assumption that only the socialist system, and the just aims for which its army always fights, can produce a high moral-political condition, may serve as an example. All other conditions being equal, the socialist system is said to achieve the best utilisation of the above-mentioned potential i.e. the most effective transformation of the theoretical possibilities into real factors.

2 In the light of the Soviet presentation, the interpretation of the whole set of factors should be re-assessed, as regards what it includes, and what it does not. Firstly, the meaning of the conditions C can now be explained in more detail. The factor of correlation of forces has appeared as its core. This decisively affects the course of military operations, and even before hostilities begin, it decides the way in which war will be conducted. It is a highly dynamic factor, a

variable in the proper sense, which changes with each human action in war and, since it influences the whole course of war, it supersedes the concept of 'initial conditions' in the classical causal explanation.

While the importance of the correlation of forces in C is evident from the Soviet presentation as a whole, another crucial component of C has been omitted. This is the vulnerability of the nation and its armed forces to the destructive force of the enemy. In any assessment of forces - whether economic, techno-scientific or military - and consequently in any assessment of the correlation of forces of warring sides, account need only be taken of the part of them which can really be used and which can survive enemy attacks. Vulnerability appears as the negative item in the sum of components of military power. In the history of warfare, belligerents have always aimed at diminishing their vulnerability, either by interposition or by dispersion. In a nuclear war, the pre-emptive strike would probably be the decisive method.

Soviet scholars have not taken into account this important aspect of the correlation of forces in their discussion of laws of war. In particular, they have not formulated any laws concerning 'survivability' in war (see Chap. 8), which is a new aspect of the problem of vulnerability in the nuclear age.

Secondly, while correlation of forces - the core of C - is a correlative magnitude *ex definitione* and a dynamic one, and while actions A are both correlative and dynamic since they mean actions against the enemy and counteractions to his actions, laws L (although *ex definitione* constant) also take various forms and act in different ways for the opposing sides, and also in different situations even for the same side. Since the warring sides use them in different ways, their impact is also a correlative magnitude.

To sum up, the formula in question should express the correlative and dynamic character of all factors which affect the occurrence, course and outcome of war.

Concluding comments on the concept of laws

The Soviet concept of the objective laws of war and their scientific formulae may be viewed in three epistemological perspectives. Three general assumptions are available as alternative points of departure for its assessment.

1 One can accept that Soviet statements called laws of war fit the most general concept of a law as a recurring tie or relationship between things, phenomena or processes. The question whether the ties or relationships expressed by laws of war in the Soviet concept are necessarily, or only probably, recurring may be left open and considered variously in relation to different groups of laws.

2 One can regard these statements as basic propositions on the essence and conduct of war and as the core of the general theory of war, covering the

essence of all war-phenomena.

3 One may regard the statements called laws as descriptive generalisations and guidelines based on experience and common sense and underlying the successful preparation for, and waging of, war.

This is not a purely hypothetical set of alternatives, indeed, Soviet scholars in various studies present statements with the same content in all three above-mentioned variants.

For instance, the assertion that the possibility of achieving quick results - not only direct operational but also strategic successes - is a distinctive feature of nuclear war is presented in some descriptive studies as a kind of guideline statement;[41] in doctrinal expositions it is treated as one of the main propositions concerning the essence of a possible future war;[42] and in many theoretical studies it is classified with the new internal laws of armed struggle.[43] (Expressed in similar terms, it is also regarded as a new principle of military art).

(In the Western methodological framework, all such statements can be considered from various angles with regard to what is called in the Soviet set different categories and groups of laws; some of these are general truths, other probabilistic hypotheses with an unclear degree of probability, and still others principles for successful action in war).

Independently however of the scientific status of such assertions which may be partly explained by the different perspectives in which the given feature or relationship of war is seen and presented, they reflect the Soviet views of war. As mentioned in Chap. 1, an analysis of these assertions can give some insight into the content of Soviet military theory, which is one aim of this study. However, the organisation and analysis of such assertions presented as laws is here viewed as the primary aim. Therefore my main concern has been to present the Soviet concept of its own philosophical and terminological framework: I have tried to see the laws of war as Soviet researchers do when attempting to construct a unified military theory with an underlying system of notions, categories and laws.

Notes

[1] Carl G. Hempel, 'The Function of General Laws in History', *The Journal of Philosophy* 39, 1942, pp.35-48.

[2] Metodologicheskie problemy, Ch.II. The authors of 'Problems of War and Peace', 1972, write about the 'fusion' of both approaches, the historical and logical, with the primacy of the former: 'Only a historical approach to the analysis of wars relying on dialectically fluent and flexible concepts can adequately reflect the different objective content of wars, their qualitative variety' (pp.57-8). Grigorenko et al., however, assert that the logical and historical approaches differ from each other. The historical method consists in the analysis of events with their full content, including contingencies and deviations from laws and regulari-

ties, while the logical method means considering events in their generalised form, as necessary law-like ties, and excluding everything fortuitous and non-typical (pp.67 ff.). Cf. I.A. Vazhentsev, Marks i voennaya istoriya, Moscow 1969; Voina, Istoriya, Ideologiya, 1974, Ch.Ch.1, 2, 3, 7; Zhilin, 1966, 1975a, b; Marksistsko-leninskaya methodologiya voennoi istorii, 1973, 1976; Sushko, 1964a M. Sidorov, 'Marksistsko-leninskayà metodologiya voennoi istorii', *Voenno- Istoricheskii Zhurnal*, 1973:10; Tyushkevich, 1974; 'Voennaya istoriya i sovremennost', *V.I.Zh.*, 1974:3; Cf. Schaff, 1955; Dmitriev 1973; Metodologiya voenno-nauchnogo poznaniya, 1977; 'Istoricheskii i logicheskii metody' in: Sovetskaya Voennaya Entsiklopediya, vol. 3, pp.623-24.

[3] This is considered possible, since for the formulation of laws it is enough that several situations examined resemble each other in relevant respects; an exact repetition of events is not required, because only the essential ties and relationships should recur. 'Exactly the same' is a notion which has no meaning for any actual research for the laws of war. For the sake of explanation of the nature and essence of war it is necessary to identify universals which are represented in laws and not particulars.

[4] I.I. Anureyev, A.E. Tatarchenko, Primenenie matematicheskikh metodov v voennom dele, Voenizdat, Moscow 1967; V. Vaneev, Voina i avtomatizatsiya, Izd. DOSAAF, Moscow 1962; M.N. Goncharenko, Kibernetika v voennom dele, Izd DOSAAF, Moscow 1963; Sushko, 1964a; V.A. Bokarev, Kibernetika i voennoe delo, Voenizdat, Moscow 1969; V.V. Druzhinin, D.S. Kontorov, Idea, Algoritm, Reshenie, Voenizdat, Moscow 1972; Cf. Metodologicheskie problemy voennoi teorii i praktiki, 1969, and Zakharov, 1967. Cf. Galkin, 1975, pp.56 ff; Metodologiya voenno-nauchnogo poznaniya, 1977. Mathematical methods are nowadays widely used in the management of troops - this is the main theme of: Anureyev, Tatarchenko, 1967; some authors emphasise their importance from the angle of the 'struggle for time', which is becoming a decisive factor in modern warfare (N. Smirnov, N. Bazanov, 'Mathematical Methods in Warfare', *Soviet Military Review*, 1968-9); 'modelling many of the processes of armed struggle at sea . . . has become an important means of developing and refining practice . . . models, which use mathematical methods and Methods in Warfare', *Soviet Military Review*, 1968:9); 'modelling many of the physical modelling of combat action by revealing quantitative relationships among different rules and conditions for using physical models' (Gorshkov, 1975); 'scientific prediction under contemporary conditions is impossible without understanding and employing the latest achievements of science and technology, particularly mathematical research methods and computers. Mathematical methods bring good results not only in the field of assessing the expected effectiveness of weapons and equipment but also in military art - in assessing the possibilities of troop groupings, in finding the optimal variants for their operations, and in organising the control of troops. These methods make it possible to look into the future with great certainty and facilitate understanding of the quantitative grounds for scientific predictions. For instance, the reproduction of the

model of a battle on a computer makes it possible to count the number of variants and choose the best, optimum variant' (Zav'yalov, 1972).

[5] Galkin, 1975, pp.57-9; Cf. Metodologiya voenno-nauchnogo poznaniya, 1977; Cf. the criticism of the preoccupation with mathematical-statistical methods in Western science, Appendix I.5.

[6] Grigorenko, et al., 1959, pp.26 ff.; O sovetskoi voennoi nauke, 1964, p.75; Sushko, 1964a; Korotkov, 1965; Metodologicheskie problemy, Ch.I; Metodologiya voenno-nauchnogo poznaniya, 1977. Grechko combines three basic requirements of Marxist-Leninist methodology: 'Party principle in science, objectivity in examining any phenomenon, and comprehensiveness of scientific cognition' (1975, Ch.10), and states that thanks to this 'Soviet military science opens up the real world of the phenomena of war and its laws and patterns. It does not need the distortion of objective processes of social life and military affairs. The inseparable ties between the partisan approach and the scientific character of cognition is most often illustrated by the assertion that only the working class is interested in the cognition of objective laws underlying the role of wars in history, since the historical development must bring about the victory of this class. (Cf. Gerechte und ungerechte Kriege, Deutscher Militärverlag, Berlin 1970, p.16, in which scholars who repeat similar Soviet statements contend that such a criterion is simultaneously partisan and deeply scientific.

Milovidov adds to the principle of the partisan approach the requirement of discovering in each phenomenon its political and class essence. This especially relates to war, which 'is, according to Lenin, wholly (naskvoz') policy' (1974, pp.15-6).

In 'Filofskoe nasledie' the partisan approach is described as follows: 'In the first place Soviet military science is distinguished by open and consistent partisanship, which is vividly manifested in a class approach to solution of all problems of war. The partisanship of Soviet military science is defined by the military policy of the Soviet state as elaborated by the Communist Party ... The class character of military theory of the socialist state is not in contradiction to its objective truthfulness but on the contrary serves as a condition for attaining a high degree of scientific content, for it corresponds to the interests of the principal revolutionary forces of the present day, the tasks and aims of their struggle against imperialism and reaction' (pp.137-8).

[7] Soviet military scholars frequently mention one of the main assumptions of Soviet philosophy i.e. that each science is ideologically oriented and, as part of the social superstructure, serves class interests. Every scholar's outlook on life and his life-work is influenced by the culture of his nation and by the interests, views and customs of his social environment (social group, strata, class). The research he accomplishes, its direction, and even the findings, reflect these interests and this ideology, whether he is aware of it or not. The pressure of other ideologies, the cognition of the laws of social development and other circumstances may change the ideological determination of individual scholars, but this does not invalidate the general rule.

[8] Metodologicheskie problemy, Ch.1; Rybkin, 1975; Metodologiya voenno-nauchnogo poznaniya, 1977.

[9] The principle of objectivism is said to allow for two simultaneous interpretations: in the first, it means the approach to nature and society, and the things and phenomena that belong to them, as objectively existing. In the second, it means the scientific approach, examining nature and society as they are without subjective and wilful distortions. In other words, this principle may be interpreted as simultaneously ontological and epistemological.

[10] Soviet scholars consider that the application of philosophical materialism to the analysis of war is what distinguishes the Soviet approach from the Clausewitzian one, based on philosophical idealism. 'The Marxist-Leninist theory of war and politics is based on the principles of dialectical materialism on elucidation of the material, economic factors that underlie and determine politics, and on analysis of their class nature' (Problems of War and Peace, 1972, p.81).

[11] Grigorenko, et al., 1959, Ch.II; Krupnov 1963; Grudinin 1971.

[12] 'The types of war in our time are determined by the main lines taken by the social struggle . . . A classification of wars takes into account the main contradictions or the aspects of those contradictions that are responsible for the military conflicts, and also the social forces clashing in the armed struggle' (Marxism-Leninism on War and Army, 1972, pp.69-70).

[13] Ogarkov quotes certain examples of the negation of negation, taken from the development of military art (1978, pp.119-20). Cf. note 53 in Ch.5.

[14] Krupnov, 1963, one of the main themes, esp. in Chs. III-V. Grigorenko et al. write that, according to materialistic dialectics, movement follows not a closed ring but an ascending spiral (1959, p.57), and military events are to be regarded from this angle. Savkin points out that the laws of materialistic dialectics do not operate apart from laws of war, but in inseparable connection with them. 'Moreover, inasmuch as the laws of dialectics and laws of armed struggle concern the very same ties and relationships and the very same processes, the laws of dialectics are not manifested independently and directly, but operate through the laws of war and armed struggle, and are particular laws with regard to them' (1972, p.71).

[15] Grudinin, 1971. Savkin writes that the law of unity and struggle of opposites acts in war through all its laws and, in particular, through the law of the correlation of strictly military forces of the warring sides. 'Here the enemies themselves act as opposites in the development of military affairs'. The struggle between enemies for attaining superiority in forces and for winning victory is expressed, in particular, in a competition to create a more sophisticated weapon and to accumulate it; in a drive for greatest destruction of enemy forces and preservation of friendly forces in the course of military operations; in rivalry in development of military art, military training, and skill of troops, etc.' (p.71). Cf. Rybkin, 1975, p.16.

[16] Grudinin, ibid.; Savkin, ibid. C. Safronov writes: 'The interaction of

opposites and their conflict can be observed in warfare too. While there are wars they will all be characterised by two main forms of action, namely attack (offensive) and defence. They are interconnected and one form is transformed into the other depending on the changes in situation'; a description of the 'struggle' and interaction follows (1977:6, p.29). He also describes other contradictions, such as that between the strength of the force and the quantity of equipment on the one hand, and the scope of their employment on the other hand, or between concentration and dispersal of forces (pp.29-30).

[17] 'Each military unit fighting against the enemy reveals negative tendencies (losses, fatigue, and natural sense of fear, interruption of communications, etc.), which are opposed by positive tendencies (hatred for the enemy, fighting spirit, discipline, rehabilitation of the forces, etc.)'. (Rybkin, 1975, p.16).

[18] Rybkin asserts that in the analysis of the character of war the principles of dialectical logic appear as the following specific principles: to discover the objective actual causes and aims of the given war; to analyse international policy in conjunction with the internal one; to take into account the ties and relationships between classes and states; to take into account the development of policy during a given war; and to consider the influence of the consequences of the war on the assessment of its character (1973a, p.14).

[19] This approach should be distinguished from the so-called pragmatic philosophical position. While in Marxism-Leninism, the effectiveness of human action is a criterion with whose help it is possible to verify the knowledge of objective laws independent of human mind, in the pragmatic approach practical usefulness is an instrument of establishing or defining the truth. *It does not verify the truth, it creates this truth.* The two contrasting concepts are discussed by Leszek Kolakowski in 'Karl Marx and the Classical Definition of Truth', *Marxism and Beyond*, Paladin, London 1971, pp.59 ff. Note, however, that the above difference concerns the scientific laws. Another difference must be recognised with regard to the very existence of the objective laws which Marxism-Leninism asserts; pragmatism takes a position close to agnosticism.

[20] Grigorenko et al., write that since wars, and especially the big ones, are a rare phenomenon, the development of military art cannot be furthered through direct contact of the researcher with the phenomenon studied (pp.9 ff.). Savkin writes that our knowledge of laws of armed struggle is relative, because of the limited value of operations by officers and troops in staff exercises and manoeuvres, which are conducted without a real enemy and include other conditional elements (p.65). Tyushkevich states: 'It is well known that the advanced and elaborated military theories can really be verified only in a big war against a strong enemy' (1975, p.19). Scientific leadership of the armed forces is unthinkable without a profound mastery of military theory. Today every military leader must know the laws of war, of armed struggle; he must know the ways and means of defeating the enemy in the shortest possible time and the laws governing the development of the art of war' (M. Cherednichenko, 'Concerning a Scientific Approach to Leading Troops' (Book Review), *Soviet Military Review*, 1967:2.

[21] Many other objections have been made and some may be worth listing. (1) Since the conditions under which military events occur will never be exactly the same, no uniform ties can be hypothesised, tested and confirmed. (2) Even probabilistic universal hypotheses cannot be tested because of the very limited number of cases which can be analysed with a sufficient degree of accuracy. (3) The most general hypotheses about war represent general ideas which are not amenable to any empirical test and therefore can serve neither as laws or hypotheses nor as propositions to which all phenomena of war can be subsumed, nor as valid propositions on them.

[22] One may wonder, however, how to assess laws of which the knowledge and utilisation results in the growth of the effectiveness of the capitalist armed forces. If practice confirms theory, these laws are valid, but if, on the other hand, they serve the reactionary cause, they cannot reflect the mechanism of social development i.e. they cannot be valid.

[23] The essence of the processes of war, naturally, is best seen in the course of war itself. 'Does this mean that in peacetime its cognition is impossible? Not at all. The newest means and methods of analysis, including mathematical ones and modern exercises and manoeuvres, allow us to cognise the essence and laws of the phenomena of a nuclear missile war with a sufficient degree of reliability' (Grudinin, 1971, p.180). Here one may observe that this is a risky enterprise. For instance, 'the first law of war' as presented in a comprehensive study on military art holds that the course and outcome of a war waged with the unlimited employment of all means of conflict (i.e. nuclear weapons) depends primarily on the correlation of available, strictly military forces of the combatants at the beginning of war, especially in nuclear weapons and means of delivery (Savkin, pp.89 ff.). Obviously, in such a war the possession of more or less capability to destroy and kill cannot be of decisive importance for its outcome, since there is no difference whether one can destroy the opponent three or five times. It is the strategy applied for using the military force in concrete situations - as part of the strategy of conducting this concrete war as a whole - which will determine its course and outcome.

[24] Savkin writes: '. . . universality of a law consists in the fact that all phenomena are decisively subordinated to it in the field in which it acts (p.55). However, afterwards he distinguishes between the *universal* laws of the material world' (e.g. laws of materialistic dialectics) which act in all spheres of being and awareness, *general* laws with a broad sphere of action (as the laws of conservation of energy), and *particular* laws, specific for individual sciences (p.57). As we see, the degree of universality results in different terms, universal being only attributed to the most general laws.

[25] Savkin, Ch.2.

[26] Soviet scholars do not, naturally, regard these general laws as trivial truths. On the contrary, the ties and relationships which they assert are said to be neglected or deliberately omitted in Western theories. The law of the dependence of war on policy is a case in point: Western theorists are charged with

either concealing or distorting the political content of war (cf. Grechko, 1975, p.276).

[27] For a review of analysis of this discussion, see: Arthur C. Danto, Analytical Philosophy of History, Cambridge University Press, Cambridge 1968; William Dray, Laws and Explanation in History, Oxford University Press, Oxford 1957; Carl G. Hempel, Aspects of Scientific Explanation and Other Essays in the Philosophy of Science, The Free Press, New York 1968; Karl Popper, The Poverty of Historicism, Beacon Press, Boston 1957.

[28] Zavyalov, 1972, pp.2-3. It is implied in this, and other, Soviet statements on the predictability of events on the basis of laws that if laws are not directly applicable for prediction, they may be used for this aim through propositions, assessments, principles of military art which these laws underlie.

[29] 'Military science can and must give sound forecasts of the beginning and development of possible critical situations, likely variants of the unleashing of war by the imperialists against the USSR and other socialist and peace-loving countries' (Gareyev, 1976, p.17).

[30] Galkin points out two kinds of prediction: that of the character, course and methods of conduct of a future war by using the present military technique and taking into account the actual correlation of forces; and the prediction of the development tendencies of these components or factors (1975, p.56).

[31] Zavyalov, ibid.

[32] Tyushkevich, 1975, pp.240-1.

[33] Savkin, 1972, p.56. The assessment of the laws of armed struggle as a special kind of law is implied in the concept of military science. Since this science is said to deal with war as a social phenomenon, it belongs to the social sciences. On the other hand, since it also investigates the natural-technical processes and phenomena of war, it is closely linked with the natural and technical sciences (Garejev, 1977).

[34] Zavyalov, ibid.

[35] It should be noted that the discussion of the problem of laws has always been a component part of the process of clarifying the scope and structure of military theory. For instance, when at the time of the great doctrinal debate, 1953-1955, the subject of military science as distinct from the teaching on war and army was discussed, the problem of the existence of specific laws of armed struggle, which should be analysed by military science and be included in its defining characteristics, was in focus. The investigation of the problem of laws *eo ipso* contributed to the development of military theory as a whole.

[36] There are exceptions, however. Savkin's 'first law of war' may serve as an example of a new law (pp.280 ff.).

[37] Galkin points out some of these difficulties: the uncertainty concerning the actual forces and potentialities of the adversaries, the heterogeneity of the components of military power and the constant qualitative and quantitative change of the material basis of war (1975).

[38] With regard to military science, it is stated: 'Understanding of the laws of

armed struggle and formulation of the principles of military art are the chief factors which separate Soviet military science and Soviet military art into relatively independent branches of knowledge and define their practical value in the field of organisation and conduct of armed defence of our Motherland' (Savkin, 1972, p.52).

[39] Zemskov, 1972.

[40] Cf. Thomas W. Wolfe, Soviet Military Capabilities and Intentions in Europe, The Rand Corporation, Santa Monica, California, 1974 (p.5188); Maxwell D. Taylor, 'The United States — A Military Power Second to None?', *International Security*, Summer 1976; Richard G. Head, 'Technology and the Military Balance', *Foreign Affairs*, April 1978.

[41] Nauchno-tekhnicheskii progress, p.5.

[42] Voennaya strategiya, 1968.

[43] Cf. Ch. 5.

8 Comments on the system of laws

Soviet military theory has reduced the investigation of the laws that operate in war to two categories: concerning (a) the genesis and conduct of war as a whole and (b) the fighting proper. These two categories constitute the first level of the set or system of laws of war, its first logical division. On the second level they are subdivided into groups of laws, which in turn, on the third level, consist of subgroups or particular laws. Certain more specific laws may constitute a fourth level. This construction, of my own devising, seems to come closest to the criteria implied (but apparently not discussed) in Soviet studies.

The system seemingly adopted by Soviet scholars (and analysed in this perspective in my study) is close to the type of classification often called 'artificial', since it is based on the logical, or analytical division.

Another system based on the types of war (with each group of laws concerning one type of war) would resemble the so-called natural classification corresponding to the empirically-given phenomena. However, while the latter could better serve the analytical description of the particular types of war, the standard division suggested here seems to correspond better to the task of analysing the nature of war as a whole and the features common to all or several types of it.

(This brief mention of the hypothetical alternatives in the concept of the system assumes that the Soviet concept of a system of laws of war is purely epistemological. Although Soviet scholars insistently argue for the existence of objective laws, they never discuss the problem of the existence of their system, but confine themselves to statements like 'war is governed by a system of laws'. It is an interesting question whether if it is assumed that laws exist objectively, must then the system? If it does, there can be only one true system of scientific laws reflecting the objective one.)

In assessing the set of laws of war, which Soviet scholars view as a comprehensive and coherent system, I shall first try to answer the following questions and then draw conclusions with regard to the state of the system and its value.

The questions are:

1. Is the distinction between the categories clear and is it observed in the Soviet study of war?

2. The same question concerning the distinction between groups.

3. The same question concerning the distinction between laws of war and principles of military art.

4. Does the set of laws encompass all aspects and processes of war and all types of war?

In other words, my main concern in the assessment will be with the *consistency* and *completeness* of the set of law, which is regarded by Soviet scholars as a scientific system.

The two categories: confusion in the concept

Although the usually-adopted approach in the organisation of the set of laws of war is to make a basic division into two categories, this is not the only approach proposed by Soviet scholars (see Ch.3), and even its conceptual presentation includes a good deal of confusion.

The scope: are general laws of war to be included?

The first kind of uncertainty is connected with the unfinished discussion on the scope of military theory. Some scholars contend that the analysis of war as a socio-political phenomenon should be associated with historical materialism and other sciences — e.g., economics, and technology. As a corollary, the so-called general laws of war should be left to those sciences, while military theory should deal only with laws of armed struggle which would distinguish it from all other sciences.[1]

The clarification of this problem is not furthered by scholars who associate the study of the most general problems of war, including laws of its genesis, and of its relationship with policy, simultaneously to historical materialism and to the so-called teaching on war and army, considering the latter to be part of military theory, or a link between historical materialism and military science.[2]

The distinction

While the above lack of clarity concerns the inclusion of what is usually regarded as one of the main categories of laws of war in the system of these laws, another conceptual confusion relates to the distinction between the two categories, general laws of war and laws of armed struggle. It is generally recognised that the former concern war as a whole, and the latter armed struggle as its part,[3] but many scholars present them as closely connected and enmeshed with each other.[4] Some write that general laws of war are also laws of armed struggle, since they affect the course and outcome of fighting; and on the other hand laws of armed struggle are said to be also general laws of war, since fighting is the core of war.[5] In a variant of this approach, general laws of war are said to act through the laws of war.[6]

A typical statement may be quoted: 'The laws of war (here, apparently, the general laws of war — JL) and armed struggle closely interact, intertwine and enmesh. Therefore, a division of them into systems or groups bears an arbitrary or relative character . . . By virtue of this, laws of war are, in a certain sense, also laws of armed struggle, since they not only determine the course and outcome of war as a whole, but also have a direct and indirect influence on the development of military operations. On the other hand, laws of armed struggle are, in one degree or another, also laws of war, the more so as armed struggle comprises the main content of war'.[7]

One should also note that, in fact, there are no commonly-agreed standard definitions of laws of war, general laws of war and laws of armed struggle as distinct from each other.

These conceptual confusions are not without practical consequences. Because of the lack of final agreement on the question of the scope of military theory, for instance, the set of laws of war has been reduced, in some presentations, to the laws of war as armed struggle. This occurs not only in such books as the 'classical' *Voennaya strategiya*, which can be explained by the fact that it deals in the first place with military science, but also in textbooks covering the whole of military theory, including the teaching on war and army, as in Kozlov's handbook for commanders, in which all laws are presented in the course of the description of military science and obviously included in that subject.[8]

The fact that in discussions of concept the difference between the two categories turns out to be relative adds to the confusion: both categories of laws of war are often presented jointly. This is done in different ways.

1 Either particular laws are discussed simultaneously as belonging to general laws of war and to laws of armed struggle; this is done, for instance, in a collective work on the methodology of military affairs, as regards the law of the dependence of the course and outcome of fighting on external factors.[9]

2 Or particular laws which belong to different categories are jointly discussed. This may be exemplified by the joint discussion concerning the impact on the direction of war of two laws: the law of the determining influence of the political goal on the conduct of war (i.e. a general law of war), and the law of the determining influence exerted by forces and means on the methods and forms of armed struggle (which is a law of armed struggle).[10]

3 Finally, both categories of laws have at times been described as constituting a single category, and even they have been given a common denomination.[11]

The borderline groups

A different but also significant practical consequence of the lack of a definite conceptual distinction between the two categories is that whole groups of laws are quite differently placed by different scholars in the general structure of military theory: they are considered as belonging to the general laws of war, or else to the laws of armed struggle, or simultaneously to both categories. The laws of the dependence of the course and outcome of war on the correlation of forces (Chap. 4) and laws of the dependence of military art (Chap. 5) illustrate this point.

Let us briefly consider the above confusion.

The place in military theory of the *laws of the dependence of the course and outcome of war on the correlation of forces* has been traditionally a very controversial subject; and disagreements remain even today.

In the period 1945-1953 the study of factors influencing war was included in military science and this situation was criticised in the years of 'the great debate' after Stalin's death, as an unnecessary extension of military science diverting attention from principal problems of the conduct of armed struggle.[12] In consequence, it was transferred under the heading of the teaching on war and army where it still remains. However, the problem is not finally resolved. The Minister of Defence writes that military science only 'takes into account' the social, economic and ideological factors, while the study of them is said to be outside its scope.[13]

Others continue, however, to include the investigation of these problems in military science. For instance, according to the 'classical' work on military science,[14] and to the officer's handbook,[15] military science 'concerns generally the means and capabilities of armed struggle and the conditions and regularities involved. It deals with the economic, moral and strictly military factors which influence the character, course and outcome of armed struggle and determine the general directions in which economic, moral and military capabilities must be studied and used in order to defeat the enemy.'[16]

While, in these alternative approaches, laws in this group are considered the subject either of the teaching on war and army or of military science, a third view includes them in both disciplines. For instance, the law of the dependence of war as a whole on the correlation of the whole of forces of warring sides, and the law of the dependence of armed struggle on the correlation of the armed forces, constitute here one law applied to two spheres of action - a broader one and a narrower one. 'Therefore the general laws of war are included not only in Marxist-Leninist studies concerning war and army but also in the sphere of Soviet military science'.[17]

While apparently logical, such a position necessarily leads to the repetition of the same ideas and descriptions in works devoted to the two different disciplines. Even in one and the same study, the same dependences are discussed in chapters dealing with either of the two disciplines and even the terminology is similar since in both cases the statements are called laws of the dependence of the course and outcome of war. Consequently, boundaries are becoming unclear between these disciplines which seem to deal with the same subject.

The other group with an unclear place in the body of laws consists of the *laws of the dependence of military art*. Although classified by many scholars with the laws of armed struggle, these laws are also sometimes included among the general laws of war e.g. in general discussions about the socio-political analysis of war as a whole.

In one variant, it is assumed that the general laws of war which view war and military affairs in the class-political perspective include the dependence of all their aspects, among them military art, on the economic basis and socio-political superstructure.[18] In another version, the influence of military technology and man on military art is included among the propositions of historical materialism, said to underlie the teaching on war and army, and consequently the general laws of war.[19]

Indeed, all systems have a border-area where it is unclear whether certain items belong to one sub-set or another, whether they possess or not the definitive characteristics of those sub-sets more or less markedly i.e. whether they exhibit certain features to a sufficient degree. But as we see in the system of laws of war under review not merely single borderline cases but whole groups of laws have such an unclear citizenship, and this necessarily diminishes the consistency of the whole system.

The groups: lack of criteria

Regardless of the different ways in which groups of laws have been formed and the varying scientific status of the laws within them (Chap. 7), one should note the lack of any clear criteria for the division of the set of laws into such groups. Although each group has a name, which in some way defines its content, neither a general principle for dividing the whole set, nor criteria for distinguishing the groups from each other have been formulated.

Confusion about the distinction

In Soviet writings on war, the lack of a clear conceptual distinction between the two levels of war, the characteristics, dynamics and conduct of war as a whole and the specific features of armed struggle as its main front, reflected in the above-mentioned unclear distinction between the two categories of laws of war, has resulted not only in inconsistencies in the classification of certain groups in one category or other but also in a similarity in the concept and wording of laws in groups belonging to different categories. For instance, the law of the dependence of armed struggle on policy, in the version presented by various scholars, is hardly distinguishable from the corresponding law stating the dependence of war as a whole on policy.

Although some similarity must here be expected, since laws of armed struggle correspond to the respective general laws of war which state the same kind of links or relationships, this should not lead - as it does - to confusion. In extreme cases, laws belonging to different categories are formulated as joint laws: the expression 'the dependence of war and armed struggle . . .' has sometimes been used.

Tendency to combine adjacent groups

The other consequence is that the two neighbouring groups of laws - namely, laws of the course and outcome of war and laws of military art - which in the standard set belong to the two different groups (and categories), are formulated in very similar terms; and this similarity leads to proposals which either place both kinds of laws in one group, or - in extreme approaches - combine them in one law.

This confusion is understandable. The dependent variables in the two groups of laws, 'the course and outcome of war' and 'the methods of armed struggle' have much in common. The methods are an inherent part of the picture i.e. the course of war; and it is also difficult to separate the process of fighting from its outcome. The outcome of fighting is sometimes directly touched on in the wording of the respective law of military art. In one such version there occurs the expression 'Methods of armed struggle *and its results*' (my italics),[20] and in another, armaments are said to influence decisively *military art*, and people - soldiers - influence decisively the attainment of *victory*.[21]

The important common element in both of the dependent variables is their relationship with policy and the political system. Especially in a time of revolutionary political change, both military art and the course and outcome of any war depend - according to both laws - on these revolutionary changes.

As regards the determinants in the wordings of both groups of laws, in some presentations the correlation of forces, or capabilities, determining the course and outcome of war consists of similar components as the material and spiritual basis, expressed in the law of military art i.e. of economic, techno-scientific, moral-political and other potentialities.[22] In some recent versions, military art is said to depend directly on the level of development of the productive forces i.e. on the economic potential[23] and on political relations between states and classes within states (the political factor).[24]

. All these similarities would perhaps make the separation into two groups of laws, and their assignment to different categories and different theoretical disciplines seem artificial. This has resulted in two kinds of changes being proposed: in the classification of the two groups of laws, and in their wording. In a more moderate change, *all* 'laws of dependences' are classified with the general laws of war; for instance, in one proposal, the law of the dependence of military art on the quality and quantity of weapons, and a similar law of the dependence on the quality and abilities of the soldiers (including the commanding personnel), are put together with the law of the dependence of the course and outcome of war on the correlation of forces.[25]

In an extreme proposition, both kinds of laws are combined in one group, or even in a single law. Both dependent variables are united as also are both determinants; the ability of a country to fight and win, and the development of military art, are presented as jointly dependent on the complex of economic, political, moral, and strictly military potentials. The combined law is referred to the 'classics', which are cited as stating that war, military art and military affairs as a whole depend on the entirety of social development i.e. of the economic and political structure of society. Marx and Engels asserted that the system of production and the economic and political structure of society are crucial for the development of the military structure, military science and art and for the course and outcome of war. Lenin regarded economic factors as decisively affecting the military potential (consequently the course and outcome of war) and the military art that goes with it.[26]

In conclusion, the above deviations from the standard classification cannot fail to strengthen the impression that the whole so-called system of laws is far from being clear and consistent.

188

Laws and principles: different or similar?

It is also worth while to consider the distinction between laws of armed struggle and principles of military art, which is one of the methodological premises of the Soviet set, or system, of laws of war. Since the phrasings of many corresponding laws and principles are very similar, Soviet scholars emphasised the difference between the two analytical constructions and attempted to provide evidence in support of it. However, there are reasons to doubt that they have succeeded.

The definition of principles emphasises that they differ from laws but fails to explain the difference clearly (see Chap. 6). One view is that principles are only a reflection of corresponding laws, another is that they complement laws by the subjective element (human activity) and a third view is that they include both the objective and subjective side of purposeful human behaviour, and therefore have a wider scope than laws.

In another attempt, the origin of principles from laws has been emphasised. In traditional military theory, principles emerged before the cognition of the objective laws, and frequently without them at all. Soviet scholars say that this empirical way of establishing principles is unsound from the scientific point of view, since principles should emerge on the basis of cognition of the objective laws; otherwise they will be only partially true guidelines. Before the emergence of Marxist teaching, they say, a truly scientific way of establishing principles was impossible.[27]

According to Soviet scholars, the Marxist-Leninist methodology is the only one that permits the formulation of principles of military art based on science, and Soviet theory has used this opportunity.

Two objections may be made to this argument. Firstly, since laws exist objectively *per definitione*, people are always affected by laws, whether they succeed in expressing them as scientific laws or not. It is therefore conceivable that traditional principles could be based on people's experience of objective reality, even though they do not articulate the knowledge they gain from experience as 'laws'.

Secondly, even if the derivation of principles from objective laws could be considered more scientific, Soviet scholars have not demonstrated how they accomplish the task which their Western colleagues are said not to be able to do; they have not explained how they formulate principles on the basis of cognised laws.

Let us briefly recall how the successive sets of principles (see Ch.6) in Soviet military theory were established. The first set of principles was based on the experience of the civil war of 1918-1920. The principles which had been applied in the war were afterwards 'codified' and no connection with any laws was then mentioned. They were changed before the outbreak of World War II on the basis of the new armaments and manoeuvres, and in this case also no laws were utilised - at any rate none have been mentioned in any study or manual.

Similarly, during the war against Germany, when principles of military art were further developed and new content was added, this was done on the basis of the improved methods of fighting. No laws have been mentioned when this development and change has been described.[28]

In the nuclear missile age, a new set of principles concerning a possible future war has been formulated, based either on experience (e.g. the principle of surprise) or on hypotheses concerning a future war. These were grounded on the properties of nuclear weapons and missiles, and no laws have been mentioned in the process of conceptualisation of the principles. Besides, most of these principles are a simple adaptation of the traditional ones to the conditions of the nuclear missile age.

Thus instead of the postulated way of formulating new principles: from the new conditions (primarily armaments) to a changed manifestation of laws, and from laws to principles, the changes in principles have resulted directly from the development of technology and armaments.

Moreover, it can be hypothesised that, contrary to the methodological assumption, certain laws of armed struggle have been formulated on the basis of principles previously applied and proved correct. The so-called law of the concentration of forces on the main axis is an example. In some fields of military theory new principles have recently been formulated and, on the basis of these, lawlike statements will perhaps be made in the future: the principles of the conduct (or strategic-military conduct) of war constitute an example.

It would, perhaps, be more appropriate to treat principles not as a direct application of laws but as patterns of the thought and behaviour of commanders which are in common use and can be profitably applied for utilising the past experience and, if it is summarised in the form of laws, for utilising the latter for choosing what laws are to be given favourable conditions to act, and what laws are to be obstructed; and also how to change conditions to pave the way for more favourable laws. Thus instead of attributing the emergence of principles directly to the cognition of the laws, the former could be considered as embodying the historical experience of utilising the knowledge of war, independently of whether this knowledge includes cognised laws or not.

To put it another way, principles could be treated as repetitive patterns of military behaviour with which commanders, on the basis of experience, respond to military situations that are recognised as in some sense typical (identical with many previous situations) in order to save time and unnecessary effort, and to obviate the thorough examination of each individual situation and the search for the most appropriate course of action. In such an approach, the knowledge of laws - where they exist - can be valuable, but it is not conceptually connected with the principles.

However, the adoption as a theoretical assumption of such possible conceptual relationships between laws and principles which would perhaps better fit the actual mechanism of commanders' actions, is but wishful thinking, since Soviet scholars have obviously decided to link the two concepts, attributing to the scientific laws the principle-generating function. It is doubtful that they have succeeded in this attempt.

Note that the Soviet contention that principles of military art are not valid or cannot be fully effective if they are not based on the cognised laws, has not been demonstrated. No convincing examples of 'non-valid', or 'non-effective' contemporary 'bourgeois' principles have been quoted; on the contrary, while the philosophical and ideological premises of Western military art are, in Soviet writings, constantly assessed as basically wrong, it is admitted that Western science has correctly solved many *practical* problems of military art, including principles of warfare.[29]

Lack of a general theory

The lack of clarity in the conceptual framework of the Soviet theory of laws of war - in the distinction between the main categories, subordinate groups, and laws and principles - apparently can be viewed as resulting from the lack of a general theory of laws of war.

Each science, discipline or field of research, it would seem, aims at creating a general theory which precisely establishes the main concepts, and the structure of main propositions and theorems in a complete and consistent system. This constitutes a summary of the hitherto gained knowledge and at the same time a framework and incentive to further research.

The general theory of laws of war should deal with the methodology of research, should aim at establishing methods of analysis and discovery of links and relationships of war, and of determining the scientific status of certain statements - whether they should be regarded as laws, propositions, descriptive statements or something else. It should establish the relationships between laws of varying degrees of generality, and the links between them and the non-law-like statements, and it should resolve problems of the manifestation and impact of laws.

General theory should also establish the relationships between laws of war and laws in other fields of social activity; the place of causal laws in the aggregate of all recurring and essential relationships of war; the place of individual laws in the aggregate action of laws, and so on.

One specific problem that may arise in the theory of laws of war, is the interaction between the laws of war as a socio-political phenomenon and its laws as armed struggle. Is the primacy of policy reflected in the primacy of the general laws of war? Does it not occur that the logic of fighting comes to dominate political considerations and the laws of armed struggle becomes predominant? Problems of this kind constitute a higher stage in the development of the theory of laws, and if Soviet scholars will turn the theory of laws of war into a discipline of science, they must go beyond the stage of creating a set of laws.

Here the establishment of a complex of precise terms seems to be indispensable. However, apart from the lack of agreed definitions for laws of war, general laws of war and laws of armed struggle, the following other deficiencies in terminology may be noted:

1 No standard terminology for the groups of laws is presented.

2 No standard wording of the main laws exists. For instance, the determinant in the laws stating the dependence of war on policy is represented by various terms: policy (politics) as a general notion, political system, economic-political basis, class-political relations, political superstructure, the political content of war, etc.

3 No standard set of factors affecting the course and outcome of war and armed struggle has been established. Indeed, there is no agreement even concerning the term: factors, potentials, forces, or possibilities.

4 The action of laws has been described in various terms: laws operate (act), manifest themselves or simply exist; their action can be paralysed, neutralised, etc.; they determine, influence, have force, etc. While some nuances are inevitable and even necessary, they may also express divergent interpretations of the 'behaviour' of laws by different researchers. Others may use different terms because they do not attach importance to such differences.

5 Finally, no set of principles in standard terms has been presented.

Lacunae

The Soviet concept of war and laws of war implies that all inherent (i.e. recurring) features, ties and relationships of war essential to its character, mode of conduct, course and final outcome are to be regarded as laws. This is tantamount to the general assumption that phenomena and processes of war are governed by laws. Thus the elements crucial to the concept of war are the necessary recurrence of a feature, tie or relationship and its profound impact on war, expressed by the adjective 'essential' (see Ch.2).

To be complete, a system of scientific laws of war should include the whole of the essential recurring external and internal links and relationships of war. However, the problem also has other dimensions.

A system should explain the nature and dynamics of war; it should also give rise to other generalisations and interpretations (or include them as complementary statements) which explain the way laws manifest themselves and operate. Laws of war are, as a rule, presented as formulae concerning war in general, without specification of its types and typical individual instances; they state some general features of the character, conduct and course of war, without specifying how they operate in concrete types of war, its individual instances, its main phases, typical situations and so on.

The complementing generalisations that are lacking may be of two kinds. They may constitute specific laws, if they fulfil the two crucial characteristics of a law i.e. if they recur in each phenomenon of the class in question (each instance of the given type of war, each typical situation, each action of a certain component part of armed forces), and if they exert a profound impact on its character, course and outcome. They may also constitute other generalisations, statements about important features of the process or phenomenon, regularities in its course, mechanism of the operation of laws, and the like.

Thus to assess the completeness of the system of laws one should consider (a) the lacunae in the hitherto presented set of laws of general character, i.e. operating in all wars (at least, in wars of our epoch); (b) the gaps in the set of specific laws, which concern particular types of war and the processes and phenomena of war; (c) other kinds of generalisations connected with the manifestation of laws and their mechanism.

I shall however arrange the brief review of the lucunae in the system not according to the kinds of statements that are lacking since this would entail an arbitrary decision concerning which kind is appropriate to any generalisation that is lacking, but according to the problems which have not been sufficiently conceptualised in the form of certain laws or other kinds of generalisation. Three such questions will be reviewed: (a) whether the system of laws (and other generalisations) encompasses all essential phases of war, its origin, development and termination, all its fronts, and also changes in its social character; (b) whether it includes all types of war; and (c) whether all aspects of warfare and all typical situations are taken into account.

Phases, fronts, direction of war

To be complete, a system of the scientific laws of war and complementary generalisations should include all main phases of war: its genesis and outbreak, its conduct and development and its termination.

As regards the genesis and outbreak of hostilities, only some more general laws have been presented, relating more to the roots of war than to its immediate causes. These are the laws about the impact of the contradictions inherent in the socio-economic class system, and the main contradictions of our times, and the political struggle which reflects them, on the origin of war.

There is a lack of laws, however, which express the essence of the concrete policies which transform the possibility of the occurrence of wars into reality. Such laws would deal not only with typical kinds of contradictions which may lead to wars (see the section of the types of war) but also with regularities in the development of the war-generating international and internal conflicts over concrete contradictory interests, tendencies and issues.

No law or generalisation concerning the mechanism of the outbreak of war, for instance, dealing with factors which operate for or against decision on war have been advanced. Although some recent studies have been devoted to the analysis of crises as the crucial stage of international conflicts, whose development decisively operates either for or against the outbreak of war,[30] such problems as the decision-making process and crisis management have not been conceptually worked out, and as usual, the Western 'preoccupation' with them has been criticised.

No laws, of course, have been formulated. If they had been they would presumably concentrate on the long-range factors that are said to affect the escalation of crises into wars. In Soviet teaching, the emphasis in the description of any international situation is on the world-wide struggle of the two opposing systems and the dynamics of the correlation of world forces. In this, the interaction of long-range factors, such as the nature and policy of imperialism, and on the other hand the nature of the forces of peace and progress (read: socialism) and their policies is regarded as deciding the escalation or de-escalation of the intensity of struggle, and in particular of crises.

This brings us to another big problem which is conspicuous by its absence in the group of laws which concern the genesis of war, namely the laws of the prevention of war. Two alternative ways of resolving conflicts and crises - war and peaceful resolution- should be in some way conceptually connected. In the West this has been emphasised, and the theory of deterrence has not only complemented the traditional scope of problems connected with the outbreak and conduct of war, but sometimes replaced it. In this field various 'principles', and even 'laws' have been presented. (The preoccupation with deterrence has been sharply criticised by many scholars and not only in the USSR.). In contradistinction, in Soviet theory, in spite of the inclusion of the 'theory of peace' in the description of the tasks of the so-called teaching on war and army, and in spite of the formulation of the main principles of the doctrine of peaceful coexistence, the problems of coexistence and prevention of war have not yet been included in military theory, and even less 'codified' in the form of laws.

(The idea of laws operating on behalf of the non-occurrence of an event may seem strange; however, in social activities both the occurrence of the action of social forces, and the prevention of it, is an outcome and continuation of the preceding activity. If such activity recurs, i.e. proceeds similarly in similar conditions and leads to similar results - for instance, to the avoidance of a war - it may be regarded as following certain laws. Certain regular, or typical, factors facilitating the prevention of war should actively pursue this aim; they should be stronger than the forces pushing towards war; they should act rationally and effectively; internal contradictions in the war-camp also may help to prevent war.

It is therefore conceivable that, in the terms of the Soviet conceptual framework, there exist certain regularities in the war-preventing process which can constitute premises for the search for the respective laws.)

Moreover, since the origin of war is affected both by the factors operating on behalf of its outbreak and by those hindering it, and since such interaction decides the actual outbreak of individual wars (and many typical developments in such a process may recently be observed), certain law-like regularities or other characteristic features of the development of war-generating crises, if detected, would probably express the interplay of the 'war-generating' and 'war-preventing' laws.

To turn to the main phase of war, the actual hostilities, the conduct of war is also reflected only in some very general laws stating the impact of the complex of factors (potentials), or individual ones, on the course and outcome of war. They do not assert anything about the mechanism of such an impact. Moreover, the fact that some of these factors play a more important role and others a less important one, and that their relative impact has changed through the ages (and may change even during a particular war with its transition from one phase to another one) has not been reflected either in the wording of the respective laws or in any complementary generalisations.

The main problem, that of the direction of war i.e. of the strategy of war as a whole, of the mechanism of accomplishing strategy and of its dependence on various internal and external factors, has not been expressed in any law-like statements or other generalisations.

Nor have there been law-like statements concerning the interaction between various levels of strategy - primarily between the military and state strategy, the latter also including modes of waging war at the political, economic, and ideological levels. While the interactions between military operations on various levels - as regards strategy, operational techniques and tactics - have been expressed in the so-called internal laws of armed struggle, no corresponding internal laws of war have been given their proper weight.

Until Stalin's death, there was a dearth of studies devoted to the theoretical problems of the strategy of war as a whole (called in the West 'grand strategy'). The fact that, in the Soviet Union, state strategy was always determined by the narrowest leadership, and decisively influenced by one person, was perhaps the cause. In the sixties and seventies several memoirs have been published describing the process of working out grand strategy but not attempting to make conceptual generalisations or to discover regularities.

This important problem has however been touched on in the so-called principles of the conduct of war (or strategic-military conduct of war) or, in a variant, of the political direction of war, as mentioned in Chap. 6. The number of presentations of various sets of such principles is increasing and it cannot be excluded that some of these principles will in the future be presented as laws. This would confirm the suggestion that some of the statements presented in Soviet military theory as laws of war are merely transformed principles.

The next 'absent' group of laws concerns the development of the general course of war. No laws or other generalisations mention the escalation (and de-escalation) of war, nor the rules that govern the transition of war from one phase to another. It seems that just in such transitional periods certain laws manifest themselves most significantly: radical changes can result only from the influence of certain important external or internal factors and relationships. Nor have any laws dealing with the termination of war, the factors which influence termination and the mechanism involved yet entered the picture.

One of the most striking instances of 'gaps' in this category is the lack of any laws concerning the war-survival activity, which will be one of the crucial features of any future war. Today, the belligerents have one more principal military aim than in any previous war i.e. with the defeat of enemy forces and destruction of its ability to continue war, the aim of ensuring the survival of their own country, of its material basis and its population. The war-survival capabilities have a double role in war: to win and to survive.

Moreover, since in the Soviet doctrine the ability to win a war is tantamount to the ability to prevent it (by deterring the enemy from starting it), the war-survival capabilities are of decisive importance also for peaceful coexistence.

These three purposes of war-survival activities - deterrence of war, and, if that fails, victory and preservation of the nation - involve the important role of war-survival capabilities in the conceptual framework of military theory. However, while war-survival measures have acquired a central place in Soviet strategic thinking[31] and constitute a major element in its military preparedness, the problem, unlike others of the same order and importance, has not been reflected in conceptual considerations and generalisations and in law-like statements. If laws are formulated, they will supposedly be included both in a future group of laws concerning preparedness for war and in the laws of the conduct of war as a whole. It seems to me that generalisations concerning war-survival activity should also be included in the wording, interpretation or description of the mechanism of all laws connected with the correlation of forces, as an important component of that correlation.

To give some examples, a law-like statement or other generalisation is conceivable about the basic requirements for war-survival. These requirements would be a combination of population-survival measures with key-industry survival measures, plus a combination of civil defence with the offensive operations of armed forces.[32]

It can also be hypothesised that some law-like statements (generalisations) will express the connection between war-survival capabilities and the capability to wage war after the enemy's destructive strikes (the so-called 'broken back' war).

One of the main developments in the military picture and political content is a radical change in the political character of war. This is a real possibility. For instance, a war in defence of independence may change into an aggressive war for the seizure of territories. Soviet theoretical and historical studies quote such examples (the Napoleonic wars being one of them).[33]

An additional problem is that concerning the transformation of one war into another one of a different type, with partly different protagonists. A frequently-quoted example is the transformation of the Russian participation in the First World War into the revolutionary civil war against capitalism.

None of these developments and transformations, like the above-mentioned processes of transition of war from one phase into another, has been expressed in the form of law-like statements or other generalisations, although some scholars have mentioned the laws of the development of war as one of the main kinds of war.[34] Up to now it has been more a postulate than an actual group in the existing classifications.

Are all types of war included?

Only laws of the genesis of war can be systematisied according to the particular types of war, although there are gaps also in this group. Other laws do not usually specify what types of war, or which individual cases of war they concern and how they manifest themselves in these types and cases, let alone the conditions under which they are valid. No additional statements have been made concerning the mechanism of their operation. In other words, the formulae on laws or their interpretations usually do not indicate how to apply them to particular types of war. Either they are considered as applicable to all wars, or only to some types of war which, however, are not specified. It can be hypothesised that, in principle, these laws concern interstate wars fought by the Soviet Union, and to apply them to other types would necessitate the introduction of additional statements. There is no indication whether laws of the particular types of war (if they exist and operate) are special cases of the general laws or a modification (variant) of them; or whether they have to be formulated as quite new laws. It may be recalled that Lenin said that each type of war has its own specific laws.

The problem deserves attention since the operation of certain general laws in particular types of war may be significantly different. For instance, the law which holds that politics determines the character of warfare, and in particular its basic strategy, does not indicate how it does this in a civil war, national-liberation war or war of a mixed type. In these different types, however, political factors cause wars that differ as regards duration, intensity, geographical scope, the weapons used, and so on. The differences are especially great now since, as mentioned before, the changes in the relations between politics and warfare resulting from the new political structure in the world and from nuclear missile armaments are different for different types of war.

Another example is the law which holds that imperialism is the main root of modern wars. This law was traditionally complemented by a more specific law stating that wars originate in uneven development of particular capitalist countries. Here there has been a profound change. When these two laws were formulated ('discovered') they were related only to the genesis of wars for an imperialist redivision of the world (as exemplified by the genesis of World War I). In our times they do not lead to such wars (because inter alia there is no leap-like development of certain countries which is felt as a threat by others). These changes also are not indicated in the wording of the two laws, nor has their application to other types of war been mentioned.

Approaching this problem from a somewhat different angle, consider the lack of generalisations concerning the impact of the techno-military revolution and social changes in the structure of the contemporary world on the war between systems, on armed interventions in the Third World, on national-liberation wars, on civil wars. The impact has been different in each of the above cases. The changes mentioned diminish the probability of a global intersystemic war but they may result in more local wars with varying political contents.

197

Similarly, there are no generalisations expressing the various impacts of the political factor on the effectiveness of armed struggle in a global nuclear exchange, or in an armed local intervention, or in a guerilla civil war. No less diversified is the pattern of the impact on a particular type of war of the economic potential, of the international situation and other factors influencing war.

To digress, it may be asked whether, in order to facilitate the diversification of laws of war according to types of war, the classification of the latter should not be extended e.g. to include wars of mixed type with two components: internal war and foreign intervention. It may also be doubted whether revolutionary war and counter-revolutionary war, although they involve the same protagonists, constitute one type of war, if the dominating political aims in both are different. The same can be said concerning the pair of 'corresponding' wars: for national liberation, and for regaining control of a former colony.[35] A special problem is constituted by other wars, such as those in the Afro-Asian underdeveloped countries, which will be discussed below. Laws and complementary generalisations concerning such new types of war are up to now *terra incognita*.

As regards the principles of military art, the main concern of Soviet scholars is with principles relating to a nuclear missile war between systems; the lack of a set of principles for other types of war, for instance, for a non-nuclear interstate war, for guerilla civil war,[36] and others, either as an application of the general principles or as a significant modification of them, also constitutes a gap in the hitherto presented system.

Finally, it should be noted that both in the set of laws and that of principles local wars are ignored, although the probability of them is now considered significant. Soviet scholars stress the so-called globalisation of local wars i.e. their tendency to escalate by including more and more countries belonging to the opposite systems and thus to produce a significant impact on world affairs. This is described as a new feature of the contemporary epoch.[37]

To conclude this section, the general (perhaps too general) character of many laws of war up till now presented in Soviet teaching may perhaps be explained, if only partly, by the fact that among the three different levels of generalisation corresponding to the three 'natures' of war (the general nature of war, the nature of its particular types, and of individual wars - see Chap. 4, p. 61), Soviet scholars hitherto have focused on the highest level. Laws on this level may give insight into the most general features of war, its dynamics and role in social life; however they are hardly applicable to the analysis of particular types and instances of war. Here the problem of 'filling out' or complementing laws enters the picture.

The problem of 'filling out' the laws

The lacunae discussed in the two previous sections give a partial answer to the question of the completeness of the set of laws: the groups lack specific laws or other kinds of generalisations which would 'fill out', or complement, the generally-formulated 'primary' laws by applying them to the particular types of war and its phases. The way in which the laws manifest themselves in particular types and phases of war as well as the mechanism of their operation have not been given due attention.

Another kind of lacuna can also be pointed out: there is a lack of specific laws or other generalisations which would express the way in which the general laws operate with regard to the particular levels and aspects of fighting, in various situations and places. It would be useful to confront the experience accumulated with regard to a certain law, with the lack of conceptualisation of this experience in specific laws, or rules governing the mechanism of that law.

With regard, for instance, to the law of the dependence of the development of military art on the material and spiritual bases of war, while the wording of the law itself does not reveal how military art changes, the history of wars has indicated characteristic features of the development.[38] To summarise the main ones:

1 The development has not proceeded evenly; periods of continuous development have been interrupted by revolutionary changes and also by periods of stagnation and decline.

2 Nor has the process of changing forms and methods of armed struggle under the influence of a new material base - in particular weapons - evolved in an automatic way. It has always taken time to analyse the new weapons and discover the best ways to use them; some capabilities which they created at first remained latent and could be discovered and harnessed only by thorough analyses, experiments, manoeuvres and - if there was a war - by battle experience.

In other words, the new and old armaments have coexisted for some time and likewise the new and old methods of fighting; attempts have been made to adapt the new armaments to the old military art, as well as a part of the old armaments to the new methods.

3 Particular component parts of armaments have changed differently: as a rule the means of destruction, on which the effectiveness of the whole system of armament depends, have changed first, and the two other components of the system, the means of delivery and the means of control, have followed this change.

4 Different levels of military art have changed differently. In the past, tactics changed first, changes in the methods of conducting operations followed, and strategy changed last. This sequence of changes occurred at a time when the new weapons were being introduced predominantly to the tactical units and used in close combat, while operational and strategical successes were obtained from the tactical victories. In contrast, the present changes at all three levels of military art occur simultaneously, and since the new means of armed struggle enable the command to carry out independent strategic missions, the strategic form of armed struggle now changes first.[39]

5 Military art is now developing along two main lines, one of them involving the use of nuclear weapons and the other that of conventional weapons.

Although these are interconnected - since in a hypothetical nuclear war both conventional and nuclear weapons will be used, and even 'pure' conventional operations will be carried out under a constant threat of the use of nuclear weapons - the fact of these two lines makes the mechanism of the global change more complex.

6 The development proceeds along two different lines, one being the gradual improvement of existing types of armament, the other the creation of qualitatively new weapons which radically change all potentialities of armaments. Under the impact of these different kinds of changes in the material bases the mechanism of the changes in military art was different: continuous in the first case, leap-like in the second.

7 The material basis of the changes in military art is different in different countries. While previously it had not exerted a decisive influence on the changes in military art (which anyway was gradually becoming similar in nearly all countries), the modern revolutionary changes connected with the nuclear missile armament are very far from becoming universal, and have affected only the armies of the most developed countries and partially those of their allies. They have not affected decisively the art by which wars of the last decades have been fought.

8 In different periods of history and in different countries, various additional factors have to be included which affect the actual influence of the changes in the material and spiritual basis on military art. For instance, the higher the level of military theory, the quicker can new methods be introduced and applied. The abilities of the commanding personnel and the moral-political qualities of the troops have a similar influence. On the other hand, the changes may be impeded by the counteraction of conservative forces (e.g. in the military establishment) who are interested in preserving the old armaments and old methods of fighting.[40]

The above brief list of characteristic features of the development of military art, which is given without comment, has not been reflected in specific laws that would complement (and fill out) the primary or basic law of the determination of the development of military art.

Such specific laws could relate the operation of the basic law to the different components of the determinant variable (for instance, in order to specify the different impacts of armaments and of personnel), and the dependent one (different kinds of change at different levels of military art); they could relate it to different kinds of military operations (nuclear and conventional war, offensive and defensive operations) and to different periods and countries (for instance, to the developed and undeveloped countries and to the capitalist and socialist systems). They could also express the impact of different stimulating and impeding factors on the size and rate of changes. Moreover, the law could be made specific in relation to the varying scope of the concept of military art, ranging from the narrower one, confined to the art of fighting *sensu stricto*, to the broader including the organisation of armed forces, the systems of command and control, of training and education, logistics, etc.; the way in which the changes occur, their scope and rates are apparently different with regard to different interpretations of the basic concept of military art.

Law-like statements concerning all these manifestations and mechanisms of the basic law of military art are possible. Some scholars even state that many laws of armed struggle operate on the basis of the law just mentioned.[41]

This basic law exemplifies problems which concern all laws of war. If we proceed from the Soviet concept, specific laws or other generalisations concerning the manifestation of laws and the mechanism of their operation are conceivable in all groups. For instance, since general laws of war operate with aggregate notions in both the determinant and dependent parts of the statements on laws (politics, correlation of forces, course of armed struggle) specific laws may be formulated when considering separate components of these notions.

All the above considerations concerning specific laws take as their point of departure the assumption that recurring ties and relationships constitute laws. They also assume that these are essential in so far as they exert a decisive impact on the course of fighting. Since however the term 'essential' is far from clear (see Chap. 2), objections may be raised to the 'fragmentation' of laws, for instance, by dividing the aggregate factors that influence war, by lowering the level of fighting which is expressed by laws, by narrowing the sphere of the action of laws, and so on.

Thus it may be contended that the division of the aggregate factors that influence war may mean to separate the inseparable and to distort the real picture of the relationship; for instance, policy that leads to a war (or 'the political content of a war') must perhaps be treated as an inseparable unity of the deep systemic contradictions that act permanently, of the tendencies specific to a certain place and time and of the immediate conflicts about issues and policies. Neither issues nor policies have a separate influence and an independent impact on the outbreak and course of war.[42]

Another comment is that the excessive narrowing of the sphere of action of laws may lead to the substitution of the essential links and relationships characterising armed struggle as a whole for particular regularities characteristic of individual features of armed struggle or forms of military operations (such as offensive operations and artillery or infantry operations) or principles of rational action (see Ch.6).[43]

Finally, the search for more specific laws may lead to the substitution of the laws proper for various explanatory statements. A continuum of such statements may emerge, 'laws' of different levels may represent ranges in this continuum from descriptive statements through bi- or more correlational statements to general explanations which merit the status of laws.

Attempts to fill the 'gaps'

Regarding the Soviet response to the need for more generalisations to fill the lacunae, one can observe a current trend in Soviet literature to present new laws that complement the more general ones; some examples have been quoted.[44]

It happens that researchers present such specific laws calling them, however, 'regularities' ('zakonomernosti'). They write that the laws of war manifest themselves in regularities which have a profound impact on the course of fighting.[45]

The law of the dependence of military art on the material basis of war, for instance, manifests itself in several regularities e.g. connected with the use of side-arms in previous centuries, and connected with the use of fire-arms as well as with the use of aircraft, tanks, artillery and the like. Offensive operations have their regularities as also does defence. There are regularities proper to each level of warfare: strategic, operational and tactical. There are different regularities proper to war as a whole, and to the action of particular kinds of units. And there are regularities connected with the specific features of fighting, such as 'the use of the most effective means, and the most decisive methods and forms of armed struggle'.[46]

Naturally, the authors mean here laws *sensu stricto*, since they frequently use the term 'regularity' interchangeably with 'law', and the term regularity is applied to links and relationships which other scholars call laws.[47]

Wars in the Afro-Asian underdeveloped countries

Up to this point, I have applied the criterion of the completeness of the system of laws - the inclusion of all aspects and processes of war, all its stages, all types - to the Soviet concept of war with its apparatus: policy, which is the continuation of war; change of methods from peaceful to military; fighting by organised entities of the armed forces; with state, class and nation as the protagonists, class being for crucial factor, always on or behind the scene; and political instrumentality deciding the assessment of war in the given system of values and beliefs. The four main types of war presented in the Soviet typologies include apparently the most typical traditional instances of war in this concept.

However, in the last two or three centuries, wars have occurred which differ conceptually from this framework. In many areas outside the so-called Occidental World, and especially in the underdeveloped countries of Asia and Africa, wars were accepted as normal incidents, and on some territories as a continuous procedure of both internal and international life, sanctioned by the systems of values and beliefs as a course of action, which in some places became a way of life. Wars were frequently fought not for clearly-defined political goals, but - internally - as an organic part of the inner order, a way of sustaining and disrupting the existing internal structure and - externally - with a religious or purely ethnic motivation.[48]

Many of these areas are still only on the way to a modern class-structured state in which war can be conceptually conceived according to the classic 'policy/war' formula.[49]

The variety of kinds of warfare in these areas adds to these conceptual difficulties, and laws concerning such wars have not yet been presented. Even the frequent interstate wars in the Third World, which fit the classical 'policy/war' formula, have not acquired a fixed place in the standard typology.[50]

The system needs re-examination

If the presentation of the Soviet concept of laws of war and of the system of these laws, has shown nothing else, it has surely indicated the need for the re-examination of it. But what should be revised first - assuming that the laws of war reflect the cognition of reality in the light of some more general theory of society and on the basis of analysis of the contemporary development? Apparently, the re-examination of the theory of society and the re-assessment of the situation in the contemporary world must come first. The necessity to re-examine the concept of laws of war, to change their content and to fill in lacunae in the system indicate that there is also a delay in the development of their socio-political premises and assumptions.

It seems that the Soviet theory of society has not been adapted to the realities of our epoch, although the fact that it is a new period in history, with new laws and characteristics, has been emphasised in all Soviet sciences. A new political doctrine has emerged - that of peaceful coexistence between states - but it has not been coherently combined with the theory of a constant and growing ideological and economic struggle between systems; the ideas of a peaceful coexistence between systems, and even between all states, have not been coherently combined with the principle of the growth of the internal struggle of popular masses for better conditions of life in the class societies. And without such a transformation, the theory of war, and laws of its origin and conduct, cannot be re-examined and adapted to the new conditions. The traditional formulae should be adapted to the diminished possibility of wars between systems and between great powers, and to the diversified gamut of probable wars on a more limited scale, international, internal, mixed, and perhaps also new unorthodox types - all of them with a changed politico-military character.

If the laws of war presented by Soviet theory are to serve not only the justification of the current Soviet military policy, but also contribute to the development of a true science of war, they will have to go beyond the preoccupation with a thermonuclear war between systems (which could invalidate not only much of the hitherto-developed theory of war, but also some principal ideas of the Soviet theory of social development): they should be adapted - at least in their doctrinal, non-classified form - to the realities of this world of ours.

The need for changes discussed in Ch.7, and the lacunae which have been discussed in the present chapter are partly caused by the fact that until the underlying philosophy of society is adapted to the new conditions, more general laws cannot be changed or renounced, nor can they be complemented by laws concerning particular specific conflicts and situations; they cannot include new problems arising from the new reality, such as the prevention of an impending war or the termination of a current one. Derived from a unique philosophy and model of society, and from specific interpretation of contemporary history, they can be adapted to the actual world only if and when the interpretation of the new reality corresponds to this.

Some proposals

If we leave open the question as to what aspects of war are essentially iterative enough to permit generalisations, and whether these generalisations should be considered and termed laws, or lawful regularities, or universal hypotheses, or probabilistic hypotheses, or propositions, or simply descriptive statements, one can conceive of an even more complete, and at the same time more coherent system of statements, expressing the main features and relationships of war, which would cover all main problems of the theory of war from its genesis up to its termination, and even the social consequences.

Up to this point I have tried to look at the system in question as related to the Soviet conceptual framework, i.e. as a set of laws, and to suggest which 'gaps' in it could be filled. Now I should like very briefly to suggest a construction, or rather a scheme, encompassing links and relationships of war which should be included in a system of the main propositions on war, regardless of whether they should or should not have the status of laws. Two structural modifications that might be effected *vis-à-vis* the Soviet set of laws of war are here proposed.

The structure of the system of propositions would correspond to the two aspects of the nature of war: as a socio-political phenomenon, and as armed struggle.

Thus the basic division would apparently liken that used by Soviet scholars, however with one essential difference: propositions concerning armed struggle would be confined to the effectiveness of armed struggle and, in this connection, to its internal ties and relationships; thus all relationships of armed struggle with social factors, including the dependences of military art on the material and spiritual basis, would be classified with the characteristic of war as a socio-political phenomenon. Accordingly, the two compartments of the set of propositions could be termed 'socio-political propositions on war' and 'military propositions on war'.

I should like to see the set of the propositions on war as a socio-political phenomenon enlarged.

It seems to me that to confine the investigation of the socio-political framework of war to its genesis and conduct is to reduce its social role. War is fought in order to change the socio-political situation and bring about political and social transformations. Without the assessment of the consequences of war, the presentation is necessarily incomplete. And this is part of a broader problem: the formulation of propositions concerning the role of war as a cause of a subsequent change in the state of society would contribute to working out the problem of the place and role of war in social development.

Thus a more complete range of problems connected with the socio-political essence of war would include the genesis (with its opposite: the prevention), the conduct (including the termination) and the consequences of war.

With the above modifications, with the addition of propositions suggested in the course of this analysis (lacunae) and with some rearrangement, the main item of the system of propositions on war could encompass the following ties and relationships of war:

I The socio-political characteristics of war

1 Origin of war
   The roots and sources of wars, and of types of war in the particular socio-economic formations, and especially in our epoch
   The immediate causes of wars and the mechanisms which start them
   The prevention of wars

2 Character of war
   The dependence of the political and military character of war (in the first place, of its strategy) on policy
   The dependence of policy on the course of warfare
   The dependence of military art on the material and spiritual basis

3 Conduct of war
   The dependence of the course and outcome of war on policy
   The dependence of the course and outcome of war on the correlation of the complexes of the social potentials (economic, techno-scientific, moral-political and military)
   The interrelation between political and military strategy
   The escalation and de-escalation of war
   The termination of war
   Survivability in war
   Internal ties and relationships of war

4 Socio-political consequences of war
   The political consequences
   The socio-economic consequences

II Military characteristics of war

1 Dependences of the effectiveness of armed struggle on external conditions
   The dependence on the political content of war
   The dependence on the technico-military basis of war

The dependence on the state of military art
The dependence on the effectiveness of the conduct of war as a whole

2 *Internal ties and relationships of armed struggle*
  Ties and relationships between the levels of military art
  Ties and relationships between the meahs and the methods
  The interaction of the subjective and objective in armed struggle
  Ties and relationships between various methods of military operations
  Ties and relationships between the action of the component parts of armed forces.

Conclusions on the assessment of the system

I have tried to put together from many more or less consistent expositions an account of the Soviet set, or system, of laws of war, or rather to suggest what it might look like. As we have seen it has many shortcomings and inconsistencies:

(a) No agreed criteria for the structure of the system have been put forward - in particular, no criteria for its division into groups;
(b) No clear distinction exists between categories and laws and groups of laws;
(c) No clear distinction is observed between laws of armed struggle and principles of military art;
(d) The system is not complete: it contains many 'gaps', whether we look at it from the perspective of aspects, stages, or types of war.

To sum up, much as Soviet scholars would like to create a coherent and complete system, they have not succeeded in doing so and there has been no such system to date.

Since Soviet scientists consider the formulation of laws as the aim and main achievement, the lacunae in what is regarded as a system of laws of war could mean 'gaps' in the whole theory.

Such a conclusion, however, would be hasty. The lack of law-like statements may testify to the insufficient cognition of a problem; but it can also happen that some important conclusions have been drawn and propositions formulated which have not been termed laws, although similar statements concerning other problems have been allowed such status.

Indirect evidence that Soviet scholars recognise the need to complement the existing set by new laws, including the specific ones, is provided by the fact that not only are new laws constantly mentioned, but new statements also are presented which, according to the Soviet concept of laws of war, should acquire the status of a law.

New links and relationships are pointed out as inherent in the nature of war.

For instance, in the category of the general laws of war, some proposals of this kind concern the dependence of the character of a given war, or type of war, on the character of the historical era. This dependence is termed 'inevitable link', objective historical interrelationship', etc., which may mean both the ineluctable character of such relationship and its recurrence in each case of war. The relationship is also said to have methodological importance; an analysis of it 'enabled Lenin to discover a number of new types of wars that occur under conditions of imperialism'.[51].

Soviet scholars often use the term 'regularity' ('zakonomernost') to describe processes and phenomena of war, and to indicate that there exist recurring ties and other relationships between them and external factors, or certain internal recurring interactions which are governed by laws; here the term 'regularity' is used not as equivalent to 'law', as is often done in Soviet writings, but as an indication that the given process, phenomenon or field of activity is governed by laws.[52] For instance, the growing influence of the socialist states on the development of international relations, or the change of the correlation of world forces in favour of socialism is often termed a 'regularity of our epoch'.[53] It is not excluded that certain laws will be presented as underlying this regularity, as well as having an impact on the prevention of war.

In another example, on the basis of the analysis of past experience, and of the development of military technology, it is asserted that the increasing role of the initial period of war is a historical regularity connected with the development of methods of combat.[54] According to one interpretation of the concept of 'regularity', such an assertion should mean that here one or more laws are at work. Such laws have not been presented, however. Perhaps they will be in future. To sum up, the analysis of new aspects of war, expressing conclusions about newly discovered ties and other relationships and regularities in their occurrence, will probably lead to further expansion of the set of laws.

A reverse trend is conceivable i.e. towards dismantling certain law-like formulae and depriving them of the status of a law, or even towards a general replacement of statements about laws by propositions or other kind of generalisations. However, such a trend seems improbable, since the emphasis on social life and development being subject to laws is one of the characteristic features of all Soviet research in the social sciences. On the other hand, since neither the whole system of laws of war has been agreed on by all scholars, nor particular statements about laws have been accepted by all, there remains the possibility that some scholars will place their analysis and findings in a different scientific setting.

3 If the notion of a law of war seems strange to us, and if we consider that Soviet theory has not succeeded in justifying the use of this term in relation to several or all links and relationships of war, or if it has raised many doubts and questions with regard to their necessary recurrence in each war, then we can replace it by the notion of 'proposition' or some weaker term, such as 'guideline statement'

Cf. Ch. 7, p.174).

While the use of such different terms means a significant methodological difference, it does not affect the Soviet views of aspects, ties, or relationships of war, nor does it significantly change our assessment of their scientific validity. To be valid, not only a law but each proposition or descriptive statement must be verified according to scientific procedure: tested, and logically and empirically substantiated.

It seems to me that the set of laws of war presented in Soviet studies, complemented by the regularities which indicate the existence of other laws, and also by several propositions and descriptive statements, which may or may not become laws with the further development of the Soviet theory of war, gives us - independently of the actual scientific status attached to them by Soviet scholars, and independently of our own assessment of their scientific value - not only a view of Soviet methodology in the analysis of military affairs, and not only a list of aspects, links and relationships of war which Soviet theorists regard as essential for the understanding of war and which they deal with, but also a picture of Soviet views of war, its socio-political roots, and role as instrument of politics, of the relationship between war and other social phenomena, and of the internal ties and dynamics of war.

The above-mentioned set of laws allows us to complement our knowledge of the basic premises of Soviet military doctrine. Consider, for instance, the lack of laws (and any other generalisations) concerning the prevention of war: this results from the Soviet resistance to drawing distinctions between the concepts of deterring war and winning it, and programming the forces separately for both.

The extreme emphasis in the wording and interpretation of the general laws of war on the dependence of war on class policy and on the dynamic correlation of class forces (with the comment that this favours the Soviet Union) implies an emphasis also on taking full advantage of the political offensive in time of crises and wars, as well as of all social, national and political conflicts in the enemy camp.

Most of the laws point to the preoccupation of Soviet doctrine with the intersystemic nuclear global war. The emphasis on the decisive aims of such a war underlines the general premises that no limitations in arms and means could be observed, that any intersystemic war would inevitably take the form of a total thermonuclear war. All the changes in the formulation of laws which emphasise the forces in being, and the law-generating statements on the primary importance of the initial period of war, surprise and consequently preparedness for a war, indicate the above-mentioned preoccupation with a nuclear war and the primacy of offensive strategy.

Finally, the concern with making the theory of war a science, and with its laws in particular, points to the preoccupation of the Soviet military with the detailed planning of a nuclear war, their resistance to ideas of a possible spontaneous course of war, its possible escaping the control of policy and its destructive impact on the social order. Such ideas contradict the essence of the ideological premises of Soviet preparations for war.

Summing up, the hitherto-presented (suggested) set or system of laws of war, in spite of its essential deficiencies, both conceptual and structural, may be regarded, on the one hand, as an attempt to construct a coherent set of propositions on the main links and relationships of war; as an expression of the age-long discussion on the nature of war it seems valuable. On the other hand a review of this system of laws may be of use to researchers on the problems of war and peace, since it reflects the contemporary state of the Soviet theory and doctrine of war. Inconsistencies and lacunae may here mean problems on the scientific agenda which perhaps deserve to be dealt with.

Notes

[1] O sovetskoi voennoi nauke, Ch.V; Popov, 1964, Ch.II; Voennaya strategiya.

[2] Marxism-Leninism on War and Army, p.300.

[3] There are, however, expositions in which laws of war as a whole are distinguished from laws of armed struggle, without a clear indication that these should be treated as two separate categories of laws. For instance, in the Sovetskaya Voennaya Entsiklopediya it is stated: 'Laws of war manifest themselves variously depending on the scale and character of war. There are laws whose sphere of action encompasses the whole of war as one process; other laws manifest themselves in military actions on the strategic level, or only on the operational and tactical levels' (vol. 3, Moscow 1977, p.377).

[4] Savkin, 1972, p.87. Another scholar writes that the difference between the two categories of laws is relative and that they are interrelated and interwoven (Zemskov, 1972, p.15).

[5] Various expressions are used here: (general) laws of war are, 'in varying degrees' laws of armed struggle, or 'at the same time' (Zemskov, 1972, p.15) 'as well as' (Zavizion, 1973); 'to a greater or lesser degree' (Azovtsev, 1971, p.26). Therefore 'the general laws of war fall within the scope of both Marxist-Leninist teaching on war and army and of Soviet military science' (Zavizion, 1973, pp.27-8).

[6] Zavizion, 1973, p.27. In another study, laws of the dependence of the course and outcome of war on the complex of potentialities of warring sides are included in the general laws of war, but are said to fall within the scope of military science studies (Zakharov, 1967, p.47).

[7] Savkin, p.87.

[8] Kozlov, Ch.III, pp.97 ff. The first Deputy Minister of Defence writes that 'Soviet military science is to be regarded as a system of theoretical knowledge of the laws of war *and* armed struggle' (italics added) (Kulikov, 1973). In the fifth

volume of the Soviet Great Encyclopaedia, military science is defined as dealing with 'laws of war', and similarly in the second volume of the Soviet Military Encyclopaedia (1976) it is defined as 'the system of knowledge of the character of *laws of war*, the preparation of armed forces and the country for war, and ways of conducting war' (p.208).

[9] Metodologicheskie problemy, part II.

[10] Zemskov, 1972, pp.15-6.

[11] The term is either 'laws of armed struggle', or 'laws of war' (at times 'general laws of war') or 'laws of war *and* armed struggle'. In the first collection of articles on military affairs in the post-Stalinist era, only one category was presented, namely *laws governing armed struggle* (G.A. Fedorov 'Dialekticheskii materializm i sovetskaya voennaya nauka', after: Marksizm-leninizm o wojnie, wojsku i sztuce wojennej, Wyd. MON, Warsaw 1955). Examples were quoted from a group of laws, now termed 'internal laws of armed struggle'. Similarly, in the first three editions of the collective work on war and the army, regarded for years as a kind of officers' manual, all laws of war and armed struggle, including laws of the origin of war, were placed in a single category called 'laws of armed struggle'. In another context they were described more broadly as 'laws which determine the origin, course and outcome of wars' (Marksizm-Leninizm o voine i armii, 1st ed. 1957, 2nd ed. 1961, 3rd ed. 1963, Voenizdat, Moscow, cf. Ch.Six.4 'Kharakter zakonov vooruzhennoi bor'by'). In the fourth edition, 1968, which gave a more detailed classification of the laws in both categories they are called 'laws of war and military operations' and are included, apparently, in the sphere of military science.

In another variant, the term 'laws of war and armed struggle' is treated as the common one for all laws (S.N. Kozlov, 'Voennaya doktrina i voennaya nauka' in: Problemy revolutsii v voennom dele, Voenizdat, Moscow 1965, p.57).

Some scholars, who treat all laws as constituting one category, use different terms for it interchangeably — Voennaya strategiya, for instance, mentions 'regularities of methods of conducting war', 'regularities of armed combat', and 'laws of armed combat' (3rd ed., pp.14, 16-18, 20). There are also studies in which the traditional term 'laws of war and armed struggle' is preserved, although two different categories are specified.

It seems to me that in individual cases the use of a single term for all laws, or the assignment of all of them to one discipline, results more from the choice of the subject of study than from a conscious obliteration of the differences and boundaries between the laws or disciplines. Studies devoted to military science tend to include all laws in its scope, as also do studies on the teaching on war and army [cf. Zavyalov, 1967 ('laws and regularities of war'), Skirdo, 1970 ('general laws of war' as applied to both categories), pp.96 ff.]. It should also be noted that there is some confusion regarding the terms used for the two categories. General laws of war are also called 'laws of war as a whole' (Marxism-Leninism on War and Army, p.311, Metodologicheskie problemy, p.320), or simply 'laws of war', which is identical with the term given to the whole body of laws (Popov, 1964).

[12] O sovetskoi voennoi nauke, 1964.

[13] Grechko, 1971, p.43. Cf. his 1974, 1975.

[14] O sovestskoi voennoi nauke, pp.233 ff.

[15] Kozlov, 1971, Ch.III.

[16] O sovetskoi voennoi nauke, ibid.; Kozlov, ibid. In another description the analysis of the laws that express the ties of armed struggle with the political, economic, ideological and other factors, have been directly included in the scope of military science (Zavizion, 1973, p.12). One study specifies two important laws - the law of the dependence of the course and outcome of war on the character of the political aims, and the law of the dependence of the course and outcome of armed struggle on the correlation of the potentialities of warring sides - as the main laws of *war as armed struggle*, studied by military science (Azovtsev, 1971, pp.28-9).
Finally, in a collective methodological work on military affairs, one chapter is devoted to the problems of the dependence of war on the correlation of forces, and another chapter includes the law of the dependence of war on this correlation within the scope of military science (Metodologicheskie problemy, Ch.XIII, Ch.XIV.1). The latter law is assessed as being simultaneously law of war and law of armed struggle. However, since it expresses the course of military operations it should come under military science.

[17] Zavizion, 1973, pp.27-8. In a similar assumption, the group of laws expressing the dependence of the course and outcome of war on the correlation of economic, scientific-technical, moral and strictly military forces of the warring sides is said to be studied by the Marxist-Leninist teaching on war and army, and also by Soviet military science. These laws constitute a point of departure and a general theoretical basis of Soviet military science (Marxism-Leninism on War and Army, 1972, p.310).

[18] Dmitriev, 1975, p.12.

[19] Milovidov, 1974, p.13.

[20] Morozov, Tyushkevich, 1967.

[21] Istoriya voin i voennogo iskusstva, 1970, p.552.

[22] Kulikov, 1973, writes that the economic, moral-political and other factors exert a direct influence on the development of strategy.

[23] Skirdo, 1970, p.97. Similarly, V.V. Larionov writes that the primary sources of the revolution in military art are to be sought in the development of production ('Novye sredstva bor'by i strategiya' in: Problemy revolutsii v voennom dele, 1965, p.125).

[24] N.A. Lomov, 'Novoe oruzhie i kharakter deistvii vooruzhennykh sil', in: Problemy revolutsii v voennom dele, 1965, p.116; Strokov, 1966, Ch.XVII.

[25] For instance, Morozov and Tuyshkevich, 1967, include all the laws mentioned in the class of laws determining the outcome of war. Skirdo, 1970, includes them in a single uniform group of laws of war. Cf. Zakharov, 1967, who also combines all laws of dependence in one group, but seems to assign the study of them to military science.

[26] Azovtsev, 1971, pp.40-5.

[27] Savkin, 1972, 'Science was in no position to discover these latter (principles - JL) before the appearance of Marxist teaching. The path along which the essence of a phenomenon and laws of its development are first deeply perceived and then principles are formulated has unquestionable advantages' (p.7).

[28] Grechko, 1975; Kulikov, 1976; Ogarkov, 1977; Nauchno-tekhnicheskii progress 'Combat readiness', in Ch.V.4; Tyushkevich, 1978. 'The Air Defence Forces of the USSR live by the law of constant readiness for combat' (A. Polyakov, 'By the Laws of Combat Readiness', *Soviet Military Review*, 1978:4, p.1.

[29] For instance, Milshtein, Slobodenko, 1961.

[30] Mezhdunarodnye konflikty, 1972, esp. Ch.1. Western powers ('imperialism') are said to apply conflicts, crises and local wars as main methods of the contemporary anticommunist struggle, partly because intersystemic wars have become too dangerous for them. However, crises and local wars are always pregnant with the outbreak of a world war, and the analysis of the factors favouring or hindering such an outbreak is of great importance.

[31] In the Soviet view, since nuclear strikes may cause immense destruction, 'the problem of defending the population and the material resources of our country and its industrial-political and strategic centres from the effects of nuclear weapons has become one of the chief concerns of modern warfare' (Yegorov, Sklyakov, Alabin, 1970, p.5). This problem has been analysed in: Leon Goure, War Survival in Soviet Strategy, with a foreword by Foy D. Kohler, Center for Advanced International Studies, Univ. of Miami, 1976). One of Goure's main conclusions is that the Soviet leadership believes that its largest and most comprehensive war-survival programme gives the Soviet Union a distinct advantage and improves its chances of not only surviving but even winning an eventual nuclear war.

[32] More detailed statements might concern the combination of particular military measures, such as massive anti-aircraft defence and pre-emptive first counterforce strike, or civilian measures like the training of populations in civil defence and in coping with the consequences of enemy strikes.

[33] The change of the character of World War II is another frequently quoted example. In Soviet presentation, this war began as an imperialistic, aggressive unjust war from both sides; as the extremely antihuman intentions of the German militarists were displayed more and more distinctly, the war of the anti-German bloc began to acquire an objectively progressive character and the process of basic change of the nature of war was completed from the moment of the forced entry into it of the Soviet Union (cf. G.A. Deborin, O kharaktere vtoroi mirovoi voiny, Voenizdat 1960, esp. pp.117-138; Kulish, Vtoroi front, Voenizdat, Moscow 1960; Sekistov, 1970; Bochkarev, 1965).

[34] Tyushkevich, 1975.

[35] Soviet researchers, however, try to overcome this difficulty by the argument that Marxism-Leninism sees in each war 'two wars', and separately assesses the war waged by each of the adversaries (Dmitriev, 1975, p.14). Some

scholars divide all wars into just and unjust, and then subdivide these categories into types. Each war is thus included in two types, depending on which party's participation is taken as the point of departure (Bochkarev, 1965). In some East-German publications a quite new concept of a 'type of war' has been put forward: while the definition has remained that types of war include instances of war having a similar socio-political essence, the latter is related separately to either of the opposing sides. Thus each war is classified with two corresponding types, one characterised by the socio-political aims pursued by one side, the other by the aims of its adversary. For instance, war between the bourgeoisie and the working class belongs to the unjust reactionary counter-revolutionary wars of the bourgoisie against the working class, and at the same time to the just revolutionary wars of liberation waged by the proletariat against the bourgeoisie (Rau et al., Gerechte und ungerechte Kriege, pp.42, 45-6). In some publications, in the description of the types of war only one warring side is characterised (Filosofskoe nasledie, Ch.II.1).

[36] Certain features of civil wars are sometimes pointed out: the specific means by which military operations are waged; the rapid change of the methods and forms of armed struggle in keeping with the concrete situation; the offensive, active character of military operations by the revolutionary forces. The latter is called 'the main strategic principle' (Marxism-Leninism on War and Army, pp.82-3). Perhaps in the future a complete set of principles of civil wars will be proposed. Cf. Khmara, 1964.

[37] Mezhdunarodnye konflikty, Chs. I, III; Dshordshadse, 1976.

[38] Krupnov, 1963; Shtemenko, 1963; O sovetskoi voennoi nauke, 1964; Pukhovskii, 1965; Penzin, 1967; Derevyanko, 1967; Zavyalov, 1971; Savkin, 1972; Lototskii, 1973; Nauchno-tekhnicheskii progress; Voennaya strategiya, 1968; Bondarenko, 1966; Problemy revolutsii v voennom dele, 1965.

[39] Sbytov, 1965; Pukhovskii, 1965, pp.33-35; Shtemenko, 1963; Savkin, 1972. 'The situation is different now when the powerful and far-reaching means of armed combat, used in a mass quantity, are able in the shortest time to carry out strategic missions on a scale which could only be dreamed by military leaders of the past . . . there is reason to assert that in the strategic forms and methods of combat these changes occur even sooner than in tactics and operational art . . .' (Nauchno-tekhnicheskii progress, p.133).

[40] This could be observed at least twice in the history of the Soviet armed forces. After the October Revolution and civil war, while some military and political circles emphasised the value of the experience acquired by the revolutionary troops and contended that the whole pre-revolutionary military art should be rejected, others asserted that any new military art should be based on the old one. In the second case, after World War II, in the face of the nuclear revolution, military leaders and politicians who contended that the experience of the past should be the basis of future military art delayed the victory of the new nuclear missile doctrine.

[41] Sushko, 1964c; O sovetskoi voennoi nauke; Cf. Chap. 8, p.192, and notes

46, 47.

[42] Cf. Mezhdunarodnye konflikty, p.41.

[43] Cf. Savkin, pp.84-5. 'The sphere of action of laws of armed struggle is armed struggle itself, and not just its individual parts.' There are reasons to doubt whether such limitation should here be applied however.

[44] In another example, Sbytov writes of 'appearance of a new law in a nuclear war which lies in the fact that war will be accompanied by massive extermination of people and massive destruction of resources' (1965, p.90).

[45] 'Laws of armed struggle concretely manifest themselves in various particular regularities which emerge in the processes of the development of military affairs' (O sovetskoi voennoi nauke, p.317).

[46] O sovetskoi voennoi nauke, pp.316 ff.

[47] A corollary problem is whether it would be justified to describe as 'regularities' with a law-like status each specific manifestation of a more general law in particular types or phases of a war, in specific typical situations, in relation to particular kinds of military operations or levels of warfare.

This seems, in the first place, to depend on the recurrence of the tie or relationship which is a manifestation of the more general law. If there is a number of similar cases - a class or sub-class of events - in which the law manifests itself in a similar way, one can accept that in the Soviet conceptual framework this is a regularity in the sense of a specific law. It would be difficult, however, to apply this term to unique phenomena. For instance, the specific forms taken by certain laws of war during the October Revolution were unique. In other civil wars fighting took the form of a protracted war with a low level of intensity (China).

While the very fact of the dependence of the character of armed violence on policy may be treated as a manifestation of the respective law, the specific form which it took constitutes no regularity since it is hardly conceivable that it will recur in future. Thus the main criterion for establishing whether a feature of a war, or of a phase, type or aspect of it, can be regarded as a regularity or a specific law is the same as for all laws: its necessary recurrence. While I have focused my reasoning on these features, others should not be left out of account: the recurrent tie should be essential, it should belong to the determining characteristics of the war, or of phases, types, etc. of it.

The general conclusion is that, even in the Soviet conceptual framework, care should be taken not to use the term 'law' too freely in relation to particular ties and relationships of the phenomena and processes of war.

[48] For instance, according to some findings, warfare was endemic in all regions of sub-Saharan Africa; it was regarded as a way of life; it assured the continuous identity of groups but inhibited the evolution of a reliable political structure on a stable territory. Internal violent clashes were also customary and constituted the ordinary progress of the contest for power. In the Middle East, the religious motivation ('holy war') was prevalent. In India anarchy was endemic and warfare was not only normal but continuous. In Southeast Asia, in pre-nineteenth-centuries, the acceptance of rebellion, subversion, war and the

threat of war was a normal part of everyday life. After: Adda N. Bozeman, 'War and Clash of Ideas', *Orbis*, Spring 1976.

[49] Therefore also the changes in the interpretation of the war/politics formula - for instance, the diminished political instrumentality of war - cannot be applied to most wars in the non-Occidental world.

It seems, however, that Bozeman, 1976, over-emphasises the differences between the 'Occidental' and 'extra-Occidental' concepts of war by over-estimating the lack of political motivation of wars in 'vast areas beyond the Occidental world' and by counterposing 'civilization' to 'state' as the frame of reference in the analysis of the contemporary war. It also seems premature to conclude that the 'Occidental' state has eroded as the fundamental, shared norm of political organisation and consequently as a reliable mechanism for realistic differentiation among types of war and a reliable indicator or measure of both international and internal war.

[50] In some Soviet typologies a fifth type of war is presented, including wars between 'young national states' in the Third World (cf. J. Lider, On the Nature of War, Ch.11, esp. p.218).

[51] Filosofskoe nasledie, p.14.

[52] Cf. note 1 to Chap. 2.

[53] One of the main themes in Timofeev, 1976. Cf. studies on the world correlation of forces, the number of which constantly increases. See note 17 to Appendix.

[54] Popov, 1964, p.68; Grudinin, 1971, p.22.

Appendix
Criticism of Western approaches to the causal relationships of war

The aim of this Appendix is to complement the analysis of the direct exposition by Soviet scholars of the concept and system of laws of war by referring to the criticism of certain Western approaches and theories.

I believe that review of such a criticism, even if brief, can contribute to the purposes of this study, since in Soviet theory criticism of other opinions is viewed as a means of developing and presenting one's own. Soviet ideology requires that each theory in social science develops through the criticism of so-called bourgeois views and thereby, at the same time, contributes to the ideological struggle.

There is no theory of laws of war in contemporary Western thought that pretends to the explanatory scope of the Soviet doctrine, and it would hardly be claimed that there exist any systematic concept and exposition of such laws. As mentioned above in Chapter 1, some researchers are reluctant to accept the concept of a 'law' which, in their view, suggests a type of determination too strong for the explanation of social behaviour; and they find it even less acceptable with regard to war, which is a particularly complex socio-political phenomenon subject to change and unexpected shifts. This may partly explain why the problem of laws of war is touched on often only indirectly in Western science, and why there is a wide range of views concerning both the kind of relationships of war (i.e. laws or simply links, causal or non-causal, etc.) which should be sought, and factors which are more or less directly relevant to them.

This results in a wide range of critical differentiation in any assessment of Western views. On the other hand, the Soviet assessments are dispersed in many studies and made from various angles.[1]

A selection may be made from these problems which Soviet scholars consider as complements to their views, and I would suggest the following four: (1) the philosophical premises of the Western concepts of causal relationships of war, of which the criticism - as 'subjectivistic' and 'idealistic' - serves to clarify the Soviet approach to the objectivity of laws of war; (2) the 'non-political' approaches as contrasted with the concept of war as a political act; (3) the Western 'political' approaches, of which the criticism for the distortion of the class character of politics and war allows emphasis on the Soviet view of the class nature of war; finally (4) the methods used in the Western search for the causal relationships of war which according to criticism distort the nature of war and lead nowhere in the search for its causal relationships; again an assessment of them may serve to explain the Soviet method.

The philosophical premises

Soviet criticism of the underlying philosophical premises of certain prevalent Western ideas on the causal relationships of war is focused on the problem of (1) the existence and cognisability of social laws and, concomitantly, (2) the problem of laws of history and war.[2]

The premises

The main idea which is said to permeate many Western writings on causation in society, and to be directly relevant to the approach to war, is that social laws either do not exist or cannot be cognised. The former is often disguised by the latter. Critics say that, since the objective ties between phenomena in nature and society cannot be cognised, nothing can be asserted about laws.

Even if the cognisability of objective ties between phenomena is admitted, the critics continue, their causal character is either questionable or uncognisable. In one philosophy, causation is replaced by the more general notion of interrelations between phenomena, interpreted as functional dependence: events which according to causal principle are results of other events, here constitute the function. In another approach, the tangle of ties and relationships between phenomena excludes the possibility of discovering the determining cause, or of disentangling one condition as the cause. The category of causation is here one of many categories of interaction, or a particular case of the interaction (or interdependence) category. All these variants of approaches to the existence of causal ties in society are regarded as erroneous, and tantamount to the negation of any possibility of cognising social laws. This is reflected, in particular, in an erroneous approach to the laws of history and war.

The consequences: negation of laws

As with social laws in general, the two errors in the approach to the laws of history and war are that either their existence is denied[3] or they are interpreted in a non-dialectical and non-materialistic way.

The Marxist-Leninist approach assumes that social events are rooted in the development of the material basis and they have their determined and definite place in this development. Links between them reflect the laws of dialectics: they necessarily recur as the conditions recur and can be cognised, and the knowledge of them can be utilised.

The criticised approaches are said to be based on the contrary assumptions. In particular, historical events, including wars, are regarded as single, individual happenings, non-repetitive, and not explicable in terms of any laws of social development.

Wars are regarded as full of fortuitous circumstances and not subsumed to laws. The prevailing Western appcoaches are said to negate the determination of the character of war, its main development and final outcome by reference to the political aims, to the underlying socio-economic system and to such international factors as the socio-political structure of the world and the dynamic correlation of world forces. Factors influencing war - policy, economy, the moral condition - are deprived of their class content i.e. of their law-like influence, and consequently their impact is superficial; it does not concern the essence of war. Policy, for instance, is regarded as influencing only the external form of war - its scope, intensity and strategy - but not its socio-political class character, just or unjust, and its role in social development, progressive or reactionary.

The consequences can be assessed only as harmful to science, Soviet scholars say. History, including military history, becomes a chaotic process, consisting of accidental events and can be interpreted and presented wilfully and variously, depending on the views and wishes of each researcher. Consequently, no objective view of the history of war, and of individual wars, thus of the nature of war, and its causal relationships, is possible. Indeed, any possibility of a science of war is here denied. Therefore there is no possibility of discovering laws of the genesis of war, of its prevention and of its elimination in the future.

This brings us to the motives for taking such a position, say the critics. 'No laws of history, no laws of war' means that no laws should be advanced which state or imply that the present capitalistic - socio-economic formation must disappear in the course of lawful social development and that only then will war disappear.

(To turn the argument around, this also points to the motives of the criticism itself. History is presented as prejudging the victory of socialism; laws of war as derived from laws of social development, must serve the same aims, scientific and ideological; they point out that wars for which imperialism is responsible will disappear together with class society. In this sense also the criticism of Western views of laws of war complements the direct exposition of the Soviet concept of these laws).

Other consequences: the mystification of laws

Objections of the second kind are levelled against attitudes which although accepting the existence of the laws of social change, do not consider them springing from the material basis of society. This also leads to the distortion of the nature of war. The bourgeois views criticised have many variants, but common to them all is that the material and objective laws have been substituted for various kinds of non-material ones.

In one of the main currents of this philosophical stream, called by the Soviets objective idealistic, which is said to spring from the Hegelian tradition, history is regarded as the manifestation and expression of the self-development of the 'world spirit'. The laws and regularities of social development, which we detect, are but a reflection and expression of the laws of development of this world spirit. This means, say the critics, that material reality has no movement of its own. The process of thinking, of the development of ideas, the tendency of the world spirit towards self-perfection and the acquisition of full 'consciousness' are the creators of reality, which follows the laws imposed by the spirit, thought, or mind. The development of material reality is an external manifestation and reflection of the mind's development.

According to another view, called by the Soviet critics subjective-idealistic, human intellect is the 'creator'. Its development underlies social development, the latter depends on the development of human knowledge. The main motive forces of history are great individuals, since knowledge develops through their intellectual efforts.

In a variant of this, the psychological development is said to underlie social development as a whole. Critics consider that since the development of the social (i.e. collective) psyche is in the criticised approach regarded as a projection of the individual psyche, and the latter is governed by its own laws, the motive force of social development is here reduced once again to the individual psyche.

In the argument against both of these currents, Soviet scholars repeat the main assumptions of historical materialism which underlie the criticism of all non-Soviet philosophy, sociology, economics and other social sciences: that the lawful development of the system of production (with its basic law of the correspondence of productive relations to the means of production) determines the lawful development of the whole political, ideological, legal and moral superstructure i.e. the whole material and spiritual life of society. Therefore, the laws of the material development are the primary ones, they determine the course of history, including the history of wars; and laws of war must be sought in this conceptual framework.

In both approaches, what is secondary in real social life becomes primary and vice versa; what is, in fact, only superstructure becomes the motivating force, and the real motivating force - the economic basis - is presented as following laws invented and imposed by the spiritual superstructure. In both approaches, war loses its anchorage in the material conditions of social life, and thus the existence of law-like regularities in the outbreak and waging of it is, in fact, negated.

Non-political approaches

According to the Soviet assessment, the erroneous philosophical positions in the question of the very existence and nature of the laws of social development, history and war have been reflected in serious shortcomings in all Western approaches to the causal relationships of war, and especially to the causes of its origin and the relationships of politics and warfare. Although the main emphasis in contemporary Western studies of war is on the investigation of war as an instrument of policy, and on the search for regularities in its occurrence and conduct, very little attention is given to the problem of laws, as it is seen by Soviet researchers.

Before considering this criticism I shall briefly recall the main points of the

Soviet criticism of the *non-political* approaches to the study of war.[4] As the Soviet critics emphasise, to see war in a wrong perspective, to be mistaken concerning the dimension which determines its characteristics, precludes any possibility of discovering not only the laws but even the particular links and relationships between its nature and the complex of material and spiritual social factors. This is said to be the case with many Western approaches.

The non-political approaches to the nature of war,[5] and to laws governing its genesis and course may be divided, primarily, into those oriented towards discovering the causes of war in extra-societal forces and those asserting that war is rooted in the very nature of social life.

Theories which imply that war, like all other human activities, is steered by forces beyond society and history, and is the manifestation of mystical laws, or an expression of the will of God, are categorically rejected by Soviet scholars not only as anti-scientific,[6] but also anti-human. Man would be defenceless against the occurrence of wars that are believed to be a form of punishment for the sins of mankind, or an expression of laws of nature which imply that wars are as eternal as nature itself. Both the alleged absence of laws, if wars are ordered by God, and the opposite idea of the alleged rule of laws of nature, which would in a fatalistic way prejudge the course of human history, deprive man's conscious actions of any value.

As regards the search for the explanation of the genesis and nature of wars in the peculiarities of social life with its concentration on the non-political dimensions of fighting, the list of theories that have been assessed and condemned by Soviet scholars is very long. Only a few items have been chosen for the sake of illustration.

The so-called biological approach which attributes war to the aggressive nature of man, is presented as implying that war is the reflection of the natural law of the survival of the fittest and therefore is a natural and necessary part of the life-cycle of nations. This is rejected on the grounds that it replaces the genuine social laws of the genesis and nature of wars by alleged relationships based on a false picture of human nature.

Interrelated is the psychological approach which attempts to explain wars as the outcome of psychological processes, as a product of frustration, or learned aggressive behaviour, and the like, and treats them as autonomous processes. In fact, however, social psychology, as one of several factors influencing the outbreak of wars, is rooted in, and dependent on, the material conditions of social life and the contradictions and conflicts generated by these conditions. Thus such theories also substitute real social dependencies, and ties, for the alleged ones.[7]

Next come theories connecting war with the human struggle for better conditions of existence. The ecological approach, in its 'pure' form, regards war as a manifestation of the struggle for better environmental conditions and/or as an instrument in this struggle; the geopolitical approach, which may be regarded as its variant (and predecessor), sees in war the manifestation and instrument of the struggle for more space, more secure boundaries, or an improved geographical situation. Interrelated are the views that war is the result of demographic developments, e.g. of overpopulation pressure; these are presented as considering war to be a sui generis instrument of redressing the balance between the number of people and the limited means of subsistence i.e. bringing the size of the population into accord with the environment; Soviet scholars call them 'neo-Malthusian theories'.[8] The critics consider that all such theories treat the problem of the environment and geographical location separately from the factors which really determine the development of social life i.e. from the character of the socio-economic and political system. It is the latter, they say, which really decides in what way and in what degree society utilises the environment, controls it, and transforms it. Dependences and ties of an ecological or geopolitical nature are at best secondary; at worst, they falsify the picture of social reality.

Theories which hold that war is the product of cultural evolution, and at the same time its instrument, are criticised mainly for presenting a very general and unclear picture of cultural development instead of the genuine development of the socio-economic formations and political systems; instead of uncovering the role of war in the basic mechanism of social development, i.e. in class struggle, and consequently, in the socio-economic and political progress, they seek its role in cultural development, which is secondary to the former. Even more unscientific are approaches to war as a means of perfecting man or society, or - in the most anti-human variant - of perfecting the human race. It goes without saying that such approaches cannot serve as an instrument for analysing the causal relationships of wars.

In summary, the non-political approaches to the causation of wars have been criticised as follows:

1 They ignore the main characteristics of war as a socio-political phenomenon.

2 They are based on the subjective-voluntaristic philosophy which asserts the primacy of the moral and spiritual nature of man as the motivating force in history; man is free to act according to his nature, and he is influenced by society only to the extent that he may or may not respect the restrictions it imposes. Although it is accepted even in this philosophy that the way to war may lead through politics, war is said to be, in the final analysis, the indirect product of the inherent biological and psychological characteristics of the individual personality.

3 Viewed in another perspective, these theories fail to see the class society as based on a system of production characterised by internal contradictions and class struggle, and consisting of antagonistic classes. They fail to see class struggle reflected in political struggle as the motivating force of social development; therefore they fail to see war as a social phenomenon closely related to other social phenomena and dependent on the material conditions of social life.

4 Since, as a result of their faulty philosophical outlook and methodology,

the authors of these theories either deny the existence of laws of social development, or cannot discover them, they deny or cannot discover the laws of war and, in particular, of the genesis of war.[9] The search for the principal causal relationships of war is replaced by the preoccupation with secondary ties and dependences.

5 The failures mentioned are not accidental, they have their ideological and political roots; and they serve specific ideological and political interests.[10] In spite of the diversity of views and explanations they have much in common: they divert attention from the real nature of war and its roots in the class system, and nowadays, in the imperialist system, from the lawful dependences of the occurrence of wars on this system. Thereby they justify the wars generated by imperialism as natural and inevitable.

The implications of these theories are independent of whether their authors intend them or not, and of whether they are aware of them or not. The manner in which the socio-economic and political system affects the views and position of the scholar is very complex, but its determining influence is indisputable.

Socio-political approaches

The Soviet criticism of Western socio-political theories relevant to the concept of causal relationships of war,[11] is here presented in accordance with the ideas regarded by Soviet scholars as basic for their interpretation of war and its causal relationships i.e. according to certain selected Western attitudes to the subject.

For instance, the criticism of power theories which is the most frequent topic in Soviet assessments of Western theories, seems to complement the critics' views of the roots and social function of wars; their objections to Western models of distribution of power give them an opportunity to present their own model of the international system. The assessment of system theories serves Soviet scholars as a framework for presenting their views on the applicability of this theory and of the relationship between the international system and the causes of wars. Finally, the criticism of the general theory of conflict as the basis for the explanation of wars reveals much better than the rare direct statements of this problem the differences between the Soviet approach and various theories of evolution, equilibrium and conflict which, in different combinations, underlie the Western attitudes to war.

Power theories

It may be appropriate first to review Soviet criticism of approaches which seek the causal relationships of war with other social phenomena in the interpretation of the international system as based on the alignment of power and struggle for power.[12]

In the main, such approaches stem from the so-called political realist view of

223

international relations.[13] Here only some of the main points of this political philosophy related to the problem of the causal relationships of war will be taken up.

Political realism is criticised for two connected ideas on which it is said to be based: (1) the treatment of violence as the primary force of social development, rooted in the nature of man, and (2) the extension of this principle to explain international relations and war. International relations are presented as based on the search for power i.e. on the struggle by states to accumulate power in order to fight for their interests and on the use of power to satisfy these interests. According to critics, the search for power, and in particular for military power, is considered in the political realist approach to be the motive force of international relations.

However, Soviet scholars say, violence is not the primary force of social development inherent in human nature, but a product of socio-political, and ultimately, economic forces; and its use therefore depends on historical circumstances. The same can be said of military power, of which the acquisition and use has never been an autonomous process but a product of economic and social relations and an instrument of policy.

The political realist assumption that the search for power reflects the search for dominance which characterises individual man is countered by the proposition that the feelings, emotions and views of the individual (like the views and actions of the leaders of states) are a social and class product; both depend on class interests and only a class-political analysis can explain them. Neither a collective nor an individual 'search for power' can explain the occurrence of conflicts and wars.[14]

The 'search for power' theories for the explanation of the genesis of wars have one consequence that is particularly criticised: they imply that the existence of independent states which compete with each other for power is the main cause of international wars.[15] Western scholars are quoted as saying that 'war ultimately arises from the existence of national sovereignty'.[16] This, according to the critics, may be regarded as a proposition concerning the main cause of wars. A corollary assertion would be that wars have always aimed at strengthening sovereignty.

This view is countered by the comment that although most wars are waged by sovereign states this cannot be regarded as the evidence of any *causal* relationships. It should be pointed out that the national state is a later product of social historical development than war; and, on the other hand, in future the number of wars will decrease as the number of socialist states increases. As to the corollary assertion, the critics stress that war usually means a violation and not a defence of national sovereignty, and of a nation's right to manage its own affairs.

Thus far the criticism of some initial assumptions of power theories. The most frequent object of critical assessment, however, is the application to the mechanism of international relations of this philosophy which implies that regularities connected with the incidence of conflicts and wars should be sought in the first

224

place in the power structure of the international system.[17]

1 One tendency in Western research is to focus on the various conceivable kinds of distribution of power in the world. In the Soviet assessment the underlying idea is that the occurrence of conflicts and wars depends very much on the kind of power distribution that prevails.

2 An interrelated tendency in research concerns the impact of one or other correlation of forces between the two superpowers on the occurrence of conflicts and wars.

3 Other, less frequent, subjects of criticism include the attempts to find correlative relationships between the incidence of wars and the so-called alliance aggregation.

The criticism consists of pointing our errors in the Western picture of international relations, criticising particular concepts and setting Soviet ideas against the Western concepts.

In all the theories criticised, the struggle of the two principal antagonists, of the two opposing socio-economic and political systems, ideologies and policies, which is the main feature of the contemporary international system, has been replaced by various artificial models of balance of power.[18]

In this distorted picture, the significance of military power as the determinant of the global power of states and groups of states, and the role of military power as the motive force of international relations, have been overestimated.

Interrelated with these errors, the role of war has been approached from the wrong angle. On the one hand, according to power theories, the principal purpose of the balance of power, whatever its structure, is the creation of conditions for social development and the stablility of the international system. On the other hand, such theories assume war to be a natural means of maintaining the balance of power, and this necessarily increases the danger of its outbreak and the frequency of its occurrence.

As regards the assessment of particular theories, no model of the balance of power has been tested against its actual influence on the incidence of conflicts and wars - indeed, this would not be possible. It does not make sense to consider what kind of distribution of power, bipolarity, multipolarity, or combination of both (called by certain scholars the bi-multipolar system) is better or worse, since this does not decide the outbreak of wars or decisively influence their character, scope, duration and so on. No evidence can be provided - for instance, in the past three decades - either for a major change in the distribution of power between states or groups of states, or for a change in the frequency of wars allegedly connected with the distribution of power.[19] All hitherto discovered or hypothesised regularities are highly abstract and do not correspond to actual developments. The main error is that they replace the correlation of forces between two antagonistic camps by constructions lacking any real socio-political content i.e. actual motive forces of the international development by the alleged ones. Another objection is that, even if one accepts the very idea of a balance of power influencing the course of world events, all models based on the classification of states (or groups of states) according to their military power appear unrealistic when confronted with the actual condition of world affairs. No even distribution of power between a number of states exists; and no great power enjoys the strategic advantage of acting as a central balancing mechanism; no constant adjustment of the balance of power by armed violence is possible since war is too dangerous; finally, military power has ceased to be a universal means that can be directly translated into a political instrument.

The same criticism is levelled against attempts to seek regularities in the occurrence of conflicts and wars in models of the relationships between superpowers. The very concept of superpower as used in the West is considered an artificial construction which tries to encompass different phenomena. The United States and the Soviet Union have contrary socio-political contents, contrary policies and contrary impacts on world events. The Soviet Union plays a progressive and peace-making role, the United States a reactionary and war-mongering one. The use of the idea of the superpowers in statements about regularities, correlates and the like only makes them more unscientific.[20]

The same can be asserted concerning the impact of the so-called alliance aggregation on the occurrence of conflicts and wars.[21] Any conjectures as to whether more or less alliance aggregation results in more or fewer wars, must be based on artificial terminological constructions.

Particular alliances differ so much in content that their influence on the incidence of conflicts and wars cannot be treated as one variable. They have no common features or regularities. To the critics the strength of the socialist coalition, for instance, not only excludes any conflict within it, but favours peace outside it, since the united power of peaceful states helps to prevent war. At the same time, the imperialist coalition not only is not immune from internal conflicts but its existence greatly endangers the world peace. Consequently, changes in the different kinds of alliance aggregation cannot influence the incidence of wars in the same way i.e. regardless of which alliance is used as the variable. It can only confirm the general assumption that one cannot discover and derive regularities (not to mention laws) concerning the incidence of wars from any model based on the number, size and power of alliances.

As always in such a criticism, the erroneous content of the theories is said to be deeply anchored in an erroneous philosophy and its role in the ideological competition. Power theories, in all versions and with all corollary concepts, are said to justify the bellicose policy of imperialist states, by disguising the actual causation of wars, and diverting attention to non-existent or secondary links and to the dependence of war on the structure of the international system.

In the Soviet concept, the very fact of the existence of world competition and confrontation, as well as its course and predicted outcome are presented as following the laws of social history i.e. serving the purposes of progressive change. Imperialism, on the contrary, is presented as resisting the world revolutionary process by force, by unleashing wars, which is also in accordance with laws,

226

since imperialism must resist progressive changes and defend the status quo. To the Soviet scholars, it is no wonder that such attempts fail and that imperialist doctrines mention no laws that would reveal the nature and destiny of imperialism.

Concomitantly, in the balance of power theories, there seems to be no place for laws of war and, in particular, laws of the genesis of war. The occurrence of wars depends on assessments by individual states, or groups of states, of whether or not the balance of power is endangered, and - as more often happens - whether or not war can serve their individual or group interests. Obviously, such assessments are not set in a broader framework governed by laws.

Concerning one of the main aims of this Appendix, it seems that the criticism of Western views may complement the direct exposition of Soviet views which to some observers appears not to differ greatly from political-realist ideas. In the Soviet theory of international relations, and even more in Soviet military theory, military power is one of the main factors affecting the development of world affairs; and the so-called correlation of world forces, with its main component, the world correlation of military power, is regarded as significantly affecting certain aspects of the situation with regard to wars i.e. the origin or the prevention of them. Thus, the Soviet approach apparently resembles the Western power theories.

Here an attempt may be made to clarify the main points of disagreement between the Soviet and the political-realist viewpoints. Power theories which assume that no radical change in the existing structure of the international system is either predictable or desirable, are concerned with the problem of its stability, with the search for the most stable type of this system and for regularities in the dependence of wars on its form.

Soviet theorists, on the other hand, while holding that interstate wars are undesirable as a means of changing the international structure, assume that the international system will and should be transformed and that it must sooner or later be replaced by the system of socialist states. Instead of the more or less stable balance of power envisaged in the political realist version, they see a dynamic correlation of forces between the two antagonistic camps, which constantly changes in favour of the so-called socialist and progressive forces. The concept of the correlation of world forces is class-oriented: instead of referring the balance to states, it considers the balance between the world working-class and the world bourgeoisie; instead of treating the elements in question as homogeneous, it emphasises the principal value-differences under various socio-political systems: the quality of the economic potential, the solidity of the economic structure of society, the scope of cooperation between its different classes and strata, the amount of popular support for the government, the political and ideological strength, efficiency of state power and so on. The Soviet concept emphasises the importance of non-military components of the correlation of forces, such as the alignment of class forces and the moral-political awareness of popular masses.

Consequently, laws of the genesis and conduct of war, as well as the conditions governing its prevention, have to be sought in this picture of a dynamic and changing world, in the essence of the world-wide struggle between the two antagonistic camps, in the nature of imperialism which uses armed violence to preserve its existence and spheres of influence, and in the activities of the progressive and anti-war forces. In other words, while power theorists assess causal relationships of war from the angle of the balance of power, the Soviets consider that they are to be found in the dynamic picture of the changing world and the changing correlation of forces, which is the factor that significantly influences this change.

Soviet scholars present laws of war - especially laws of its origin - on the assumption that they must reflect the socio-economic and political antagonisms as primary. Such laws do not concern homogeneous states (and consequently homogeneous state power, state interests, military power and the like), as it is implied, they contend, in the theories of political realism. On the contrary, laws are related to states with quite different socio-economic and political contents and structures.

Power theorists sometimes assume that their scientific efforts should be devoted to the discovery of laws and frequently assert that their aim is the discovery of regularities concerning war. In practice, however, they abandon this aim in the course of research and seek particular ties and dependences. Soviet scholars emphasise that they are not interested in secondary ties and dependences and that the theory of war, and of laws of war (its core), must indicate the nature of war, its main roots and the main laws and conditions governing its occurrence.[22]

Systems theories

Systems theories are regarded by Soviet scholars as attempts to derive the explanation of the mechanism of international relations and events, including conflicts and wars, from the characteristics of the community of states as a system. Within the international system, considered as a coherent whole consisting of interdependent parts, all events are said to be determined by its structure, by relationships between these parts as components of this structure, and concomitantly by patterns of behaviour proper to the system.

In principle, such an idea would not be rejected by Soviet theory, which regards the procedure of the systemic structural analysis of the social processes as the basic one:[23] all internal and international social processes and all laws and regularities of their occurrence and course are said to be rooted in the internal structure of the class society. Such an approach also includes the characteristics of the international system as an important factor influencing all international events. Wars are rooted in the nature of the class system of society and in the nature of the international system that includes class societies. Soviet scholars, however, criticise various Western system theories for the following characteristics:[24]

1 Systems theorists try to apply to the analysis of international relations and, in particular, to the genesis of conflicts and wars, the concept of a homogeneous stable system, characterised by a structure and regularities designed to preserve and maintain its stable identity. This implies that the present international system will preserve its form for ever, which is obviously erroneous.

2 Systems theorists see the international system not only as a timeless but also a classless construction. The variables proposed by particular scholars are deprived of any concrete socio-political content.[25]

3 The models of the international systems presented are highly abstract, and artificial; they bear very little resemblance to the systems which have existed in some periods of history, and even less to the present system.[26]

4 Consequently, no analysis of international relations, and particularly of conflicts and wars, the regularities of their occurrence and their nature and role in social development, can be based on such abstract and artificial models, and their hypothesised attributes, regularities and impact on war.[27]

5 By disguising the true nature of the international system, these theories justify policies for preserving the unjust socio-economic and political status quo both in the international system itself and in particular class societies.

Such a criticism complements the systemic analysis of international relations made by Soviet researchers themselves. Soviet scholars insistently contend that the actual international system is a unique phenomenon. Unlike all previous systems, it is heterogeneous; it is based on the competition of two antagonistic socio-economic and political groupings. Its radical transformation in future is desirable and inevitable. No essential features of this actual system can be derived from abstract and artificial models, and no phenomena and processes in it can be explained by the structure of such models. Causes of war and factors influencing war in our times cannot be explained by systems theories as attempted in some studies, since they are not proper to all systems but only to this unique one. All laws and regularities concerning war develop together with the changes in this concrete system and they will disappear together with its radical transformation into a socialist world system.

Power theorists apply in their world vision certain ideas similar to those of systems theories, and systems theorists accept the crucial role of power in the structure of system models and patterns of behaviour characteristic of them. The application to the analysis of the real and actual world situation of the conceptual framework used by these two types of theorists often results in models of the contemporary, or future, or desirable, international system based on the distribution of power. When Soviet scholars criticise either of these approaches they implicitly criticise also the other one.

Systems theory is also criticised in a somewhat different perspective for certain underlying sociological premises, so-called structural functionalism. Such ideas assume that all systems, including class society and the international system, possess structures designed to satisfy standard functional requirements.[28] These functions are the determining characteristics of the systems, they maintain them in a stable shape. The constant patterns of action followed in the fulfilment of these functions are necessary for the continued existence of the system.

In this approach, the critics say, the erroneous idea that both class society and the international system, as classified with the category of systems, possess stability, is combined with the further erroneous assumption that such stablility is connected with certain inherent functions of the system. This approach is rooted in the philosophy of society as a harmonious organism, the elements of which serve its preservation; such a philosophy is naturally rejected by Soviet scholars.

It is not surprising, they say, that no pattens of internal as well as international behaviour and no regularities of the causation of conflicts and wars can be discovered by a comparison of the actual class society or international system with some model system built on the alleged patterns of behaviour, links, dependences and factors which are regarded as common to all systems, or at least to a group of them.

Consider, for instance, the concept presented by George Modelski.[29] He proposes four basic functions which he considers to be common to all international systems: resource allocation, authority, solidarity and culture. In this structural-functionalist perspective, Modelskie proposes a spectrum of models of international relations with two models at each end of it: Agraria and Industria. The former, which poorly fulfils its basic functions, is regarded as generating wars, while in Industria, which is viewed as much more homogeneous, integrated and politically conscious i.e. much better as a functioning system, the resort to war is generally regarded as undesirable. All really-existing systems should be studied and assessed in relation to these extremes.

This concept is criticised not only for its structural-functionalist philosophy but also for its (above-mentioned) application. Imperialist powers, which are highly industrial and fit the model of Industria, are presented as peaceful, while agrarian states and all under-developed countries fall into the Agraria category and are accused of causing conflicts and wars. The veritable division of the world is obviously quite different from this concept, as also is the role played by particular groups of countries. Causes and laws of war are rather disguised than discovered by associating them with the level of economic development.[30]

While the criticism of the above-mentioned concrete models of international systems is quite understandable from the Soviet angle of approach, the motives for criticism of the main ideas of the theory of structural functionalism deserve a brief comment.

The Soviet theory of war does not, in principle, reject the idea (which is obviously true) that class society and the international system are during many periods, sometimes long ones, relatively stable, that in these periods they have relatively durable structures, that in the international system all the component states contribute to its functioning on the basis of some - tacit or open - consensus. Obviously, the very fact that the international system is a system, assumes some repetitive functions which characterise the relations between its members. This is in full accordance with the above-mentioned Soviet view that society is a system since it consists of classes each of which performs functions indispensable for the existence of society. Without the interaction of the antagonistic classes the class society would lose its identity.

Thus the criticism is levelled not against the idea of the stability of the system, which in some sense, and within certain limits, is also accepted in Soviet theory, but against the equation of the stability of both the class society and the international system with their ability to survive regardless of conditions intrinsic to the system. The latter springs from the assumption that the system is maintained in stable shape by the function which its structure fulfils.

Soviet scholars emphasise that the stability is only relative and temporary. It is based not on harmonious cooperation but on a relative balance between members having conflicting interests, which is unlike a balance between homogeneous members. It is a dynamic correlation of forces between opposing social and political forces, pregnant with revolutions and wars, and sooner or later their conflict often leading to wars must lead to a replacement of the given system by another one.

Thus if in the structural-functional concept both internal and international wars are normal if they help to maintain the stability, and abnormal if they endanger it, in the Soviet concept they are always natural in the sense that they are rooted in the very essence of the class society and of the international system with its interaction of conflicting class and national interests.

Once more, the criticism reveals how deeply the Soviet concept of the nature of war and its laws is anchored in a philosophy of society presented as unique in the history of science and politics, and its intolerance of any ideas that would not fit the determination of social events by class struggle and their development, through the use of violence, towards a classless society.

The general theory of conflict and the causes of war

War is an armed conflict; it belongs to the class of conflicts. Can laws governing the outbreak and conduct of war be considered as an application of more general laws governing all conflicts? Can they be derived from them? And can a general theory of conflict explain essential features of war, especially its incidence, and thereby help in the search for the laws of war?[31]

Soviet scholars answer in the negative. Their position has been revealed in the frequent criticism of particular theories and of any attempt to construct a general theory of conflict. The main objections may be summarised as follows:

1 Conflicts differ in many essential respects: the field of human activity (political, economic, cultural, psychological, ideological, etc.); the social level (interstate, interclass, interpersonal, intrapersonal); the method of re-

solution (peaceful or by armed violence); and the social setting (capitalistic or socialistic). So various, indeed, are the kinds of conflict that no regularities common to all can be found.

2 A general theory of conflict tends to obscure not only the qualitative distinctions between various kinds of conflict but also between their causation and role in social life. Different conflicts'have different causes, and different correlates, links and dependences with other phenomena. Laws of war must indicate what is primary and what secondary, which causal relationships are essential to the origin and the character of war, and which affect only to some degree its outbreak, course and outcome. This is impossible in the framework of the general theory of conflicts, which aims at building a model encompassing not only all kinds of conflict but also all kinds of causal and correlative relationships.

3 Two consequences may be distinguished as the most harmful. The lumping together of all conflicts without due differentiation obscures the fact that the economic class struggle is the mainspring of all social and political conflicts and wars, and that imperialism is the main source of wars in our epoch. And such lumping together diverts attention from identifying the characteristics of the main types of conflict that may now lead to war and thus makes it more difficult to investigate the causation of particular types of war.

The criticism by Soviet scholars of all attempts to explain the causation of wars by a general theory of conflicts (or at least to put it in such a framework) may seem strange to those who classify Marxist-Leninist theory with conflict theories of society (or social change).[32] However, the main Soviet objections, outlined above, seem to indicate significant differences between the Soviet concept of social conflict and ideas implied in any other theory of conflict, at least as the Soviets see them.[33]

These differences can, perhaps, be attributed to the role which conflict plays in the various concepts of society; there are differences not only between Marxist-Leninist and other theories of conflict but also between the former and evolutionary and equilibrium theories.

Marxism-Leninism shares with the *evolutionary* theories the view that society develops in the direction of increasing complexity; instead of seeing progress as proceeding through smooth, cumulative changes, however, it posits the mechanism of leap-like revolutionary jumps which radically change the whole social structure.

Marxism-Leninism shares with the *equilibrium* theories, and with their structural-functional premises, the view that conflicts may produce a better adaptability to the environment; but instead of believing that conflicts do not affect the foundations of the equilibrium and stability of the social system (and that if serious disturbances occur, social mechanisms always restore equilibrium) it regards conflicts as leading to a revolutionary transformation of the temporarily equilibrated society.

And finally, Marxism-Leninism differs from theories of *conflict* which assert the ubiquity of conflict. These theories state that each element in society is subjected at every moment to change, but do not point out which conflict is the basic one and how to resolve it. Such an assumption means that society is constantly experiencing a multitude of conflicts that are different in form, degree of intensity, and extent of the resultant changes, and this obscures the principal question: how do radical structural changes occur?[34]

This question is the primary concern of Soviet research, and it concerns one of the determining characteristics of the Soviet concept. Society develops by means of jumps i.e. revolutionary structural changes effected by violence in the form of social revolutions. These radical changes in the whole socio-economic and political structure are seen as milestones in social development. Such changes can occur only as a result of an aggravation of the basic class conflict which underlies all others, a fact which should not be allowed to become obscured or drowned in the multitude of ubiqiutous lesser conflicts.

All the above differences in the conceptual setting in which conflicts are placed by Marxism-Leninism and other theories can only increase with regard to war as a kind of conflict. In any theorising about the relationships between war and conflict, one cannot disregard the fact that although war is conflict, it is also policy and armed struggle. Its nature as a conflict is only one component of its more complex nature. Thus it is impossible to include it in a single class of social phenomena, since it also belongs to the others, and in each of them it is included only partially. It is a phenomenon that cuts across social classes. Consequently, laws of war cannot simply be an application of laws of conflicts, laws of policy or laws of armed struggle; they constitute a unique combination of all of them and also of laws of psychological, ideological, ethical and other conflicts.

First of all, however, war is an instrument of policy. Since the role played by war depends on the class character of the policy concerned i.e. which class formulates it, wars differ not only as regards their individual causes, but also their concrete social functions and role in social development. To subsume war to any law or regularity encompassing all conflicts can only add to the difficulties.

Summing up, in such a conceptual framework, any attempt to establish certain alleged laws or regularities is tantamount to an attempt to disguise the class character of war in general and of individual wars.

The methods

Up to now I have reviewed the Soviet criticism of the Western philosophical and sociological premises in the study of causal relationships in war and of particular approaches to war: as an aim and means in power policy, as a pattern of behaviour springing from the characteristics of the international system and society as systems, and as a kind of conflict, whose characteristics and causal relationships may be sought in the framework of the general theory of conflict. The criticism of both the premises and particular approaches has always been connected with criticism of the methodology which is an inherent part of philosophy, and underlying the particular approaches: with the so-called idealist, non-dialectical and classless analysis. Such a methodology, attributed to Western scientists by the Soviets, has been said to involve erroneous methods. One of these was the presentation of the struggle for power as the alleged motive force of policy instead of the internal and international class struggle with its deep economic sources. Another error was the investigation of the properties of the system in general, or conflict in general, in order to discover causal relationships of war.[35]

There is however one complex of methods, or rather techniques of analysis, which has received special attention from Soviet criticism and which cannot be attributed only to this or that approach to war, for instance for the so-called scientist one; this is the broad spectrum of quantitative-empirical techniques, used in varying degrees in all approaches.

The 'scientists' appeared on the scene with the claim of making the study of international and domestic relations a science by freeing traditional research not only from fruitless speculative methods but also from the ideological ballast. However, the political realists also soon began to use the new methods, and the scientists began to work from the political-realist version of the balance of power paradigm.

Soviet criticism implies that empirical-quantitative methods are always deeply ideological. For instance, the abstract models have ideological content just because they are abstract. This seems to be a paradox, but is not. If a model, or scheme, or paradigm can be presented as deprived of any socio-political content then it implies that such content is irrelevant. Since the opposite is true and since no concept within the social sciences exists beyond its concrete socio-political framework, to suggest the opposite means to hide - as the critics contend - the truth which is uncomfortable for the reactionary forces. For instance, to present a model in which conflict or war is dealt with as a phenomenon beyond the class-political struggle means to assert that it is not connected with this struggle and to conceal its social roots i.e. imperialism.

Without going into details of the criticism of empirical-quantitative studies, the following main objections can here be briefly pointed out.

1 The quantitative techniques of empirical research aim at reducing all social phenomena to the individual ones, ignoring the specificity and different quality of the former. It contradicts the aims of any *social* research.

2 This method aims at measuring social phenomena by mathematical units of measurement. Social life, however, is governed by social or socio-political laws, not by mathematical or physical ones, and cannot be expressed in mathematical formulae. Quantitative research reduces the required data to a minimum of variable indicators which can be measured by mathematics and statistics (GNP, sources of energy, size of population, age, education, sex, etc.).

These cannot, however, characterise the essence of war as a social phenomenon, its determining features, the internal dynamics of the processes of war and their interaction with other complex social factors. Quantitative research would place economics, culture, development, science, including military science, in a diagram with axes of coordinata, and build mathematical models deprived of concrete socio-political content to characterise social phenomena, including war.[36] Game theory operates with abstract actors, not representing concrete social forces.

3 The most important variables which can serve for socio-political analysis (namely, the objective socio-political contradictions and the ideology of classes which reflect these contradictions) are absent from the variables used to build the models and factors influencing games. No model or game without these variables and factors can be used to analyse important socio-political problems, such as social conflicts and social violence - and war as their extreme form.

4 The meagreness of the hitherto achieved findings of the quantitative-empirical and mathematical-logical research into great social problems testifies to the small scientific value of the method.

5 Such distortions are not accidental. The quantitative method needs large laboratories - men and money - since it uses means involving great masses of people and other costly techniques of research. Only big institutions, and especially military establishments, are in a position to cover the costs, impose the subjects of research, and thereby, to a considerable degree, predetermine the findings.

6 Last but not least, the method in question tends to play a reactionary role as regards science and policy. It often focuses attention on secondary and partial problems, diverts it away from urgent and primary problems, thus it helps to freeze the status quo. Then, by focusing on quantitative analysis of the social development and (as usual in this connection) working out a purely quantitative theory of social development, it diverts attention from the necessity and possibility of qualitative changes in the entire socio-political system.

As we see, these critical comments concern the use of the empirical-quantitative methods of discovering causal relationships of war as a socio-political phenomenon. These methods borrowed from the natural sciences would be at variance with the nature of war as an action governed by specific social laws.

However, the critics do not reject all the above-mentioned methods as such because of some inherent deficiencies. Soviet scholars often stress that they can be useful and are used successfully by Soviet science on condition that they complement the basic qualitative analysis.

The Soviet position is that the search for laws and regularities of war must be based primarily on the qualitative analysis which leads to the discovery and interpretation of the nature of war, its determining features, structure, function and its relationships with other social phenomena. Such an analysis can be made only by using the propositions of philosophical materialism and dialectics and applying them in the form of the laws and propositions of historical materialism (see Chap. 7).

The quantitative analysis may only complement the qualitative one. It aims at discovering and measuring the external, quantitative definiteness of things and processes, their size, number, intensity, duration, etc. It can help to explain their action. It is indispensable to the more precise assessment of the manifestation of the essence of the phenomena, and their quality, and it may help to explain the mechanism of their development and its tendencies. However, it can do so only if it is subordinated to the qualitative analysis and accomplished in the general framework of the latter i.e. by application of the general ideas of the Marxist-Leninist methodology. For instance, the treatment of the international system as a macro-model, which has not only qualitative characteristics but perhaps also quantitative variables i.e. indicators which are interconnected and vary during the functioning of the system can contribute to understanding the mechanism of international relations by providing initial material for predicting the development trends in such relations. However, since only the Marxist-Leninist world outlook enables us adequately to reflect the objective reality, only Soviet scholars can make proper use of systems analysis to place this reality in a correct socio-political framework.

Armed struggle, which may also be treated and analysed as a system e.g. consisting of components such as the activities of armed forces, military techniques and enemy activities, can be better explained if armed forces, armament, and conditions of fighting are given quantitative assessments. But this matter cannot be separated from the qualitative characteristics.

Similarly, the models of conflict situations, with quantitative indices, established by mathematical methods, can be of some use in predicting the alternatives of the development of conflict, especially its escalation, and they can help to provide a typology of conflicts. They might to a limited extent contribute to the analysis of the real objective and subjective factors leading to conflict and determining the mode of conflict, such as the techno-material basis, the socio-economic system, the political organisation of the conflicting parties and their policy, social consciousness, the positions of particular classes and so on. One quotation may perhaps illustrate this view of limited applicability: '. . . the formalisation cannot be separated from the qualitative analysis. The mathematical calculation of the possibilities and resources cannot be separated from the socio-political, economic, military, ideological and socio-psychological analyses, and cannot ignore the qualitative opposition of the external policy of the socialistic and capitalistic countries'.[37] Similar applicability - with the same reservations - is asserted concerning the game theory.[38]

Up to now, however, Soviet scholars have not convincingly demonstrated how to apply successfully models, game theory and quantitative methods as a whole to the analysis of the genesis of wars, their character, course and outcome i.e. to the problem of conceptualisation of the general laws of war. Also the attempts to apply systems theory and the other above-mentioned methods to the analysis of armed struggle as a whole, considered as a system, do not seem to be successful.[39]

Quite a different picture can be observed in the Soviet approach to the use of quantitative, and in particular, mathematical and modelling, techniques in developing the most effective methods of preparing for and waging military operations. Here the requirement that the qualitative and quantitative analysis shall be interrelated seems to be fulfilled to a much higher degree that in the search for the general laws of war. It is accepted that some generalisation concerning the effectiveness of armed struggle must be based on quantitative indicators of armament, equipment resources, temporal and spatial characteristics of military operations and so on. Thus here the quantitative conceptual and technical apparatus has been introduced and is being used to a constantly increasing extent. Modelling is used to analyse the effectiveness of fighting in alternative situations. Mathematical methods are applied to assess the expected effectiveness of weapons and equipment and thereby the most rational use for them. These methods are also used in the management of troops, etc. Apart from modelling, the following other methods are applied: statistics, probability theory, mathematical programming, queueing theory, search theory and solution-seeking theory. Nonclassified studies have been published, emphasising the importance of quantitative methods in the everyday preparation of armed forces for a future war.

Researchers are attempting, apparently, to combine the philosophical-dialectical materialistic-basis of military theory with the increasing role of the quantitative technique in the preparation of troops for war. The qualitative approach, they say, should be applied to the search for laws, to analysis of their essence and determination of the principles for their utilisation. The quantitative methods are useful for the application of the laws in everyday practice, and perhaps in some generalisations filling out the laws, or even leading to some modifications in their formulae. The Marxist-Leninist philosophy and methodology must also in such cases underlie the assessment of the situation and choice of the course of action.

A quite different problem is that the emphasis on the need to preserve the leading role of the dialectical materialistic philosophy and methodology may also be connected with both the conviction that only such an approach serves the scientific character of any theory and the value of its practical application, and use of it as an argument for the superiority of Soviet military theory to any non-Marxist science (see Ch.8).

In this criticism it seems to be implied that if a particular researcher does not share with the critics the Marxist-Leninist view of the essence in being, the possibility of its cognition, the interpretation of society and the laws of its development, his position *eo ipso* is erroneous. The neglect of class struggle as the motivating force in history, and of class contradictions as the root of all conflicts and wars, is often the main charge. The researcher might be criticised for the opposite views if these are not based on the right philosophy and methodology: either for overestimating, or underestimating the generic role of politics in war; either for emphasising or neglecting the role of the ideological division of the world in the causation of war; either for believing that the development of science and technology inevitably leads to wars or that, on the contrary, it eliminates the risk of war; either for disregarding the conflicts in society and the international system or for asserting their ubiquity; either for the view that war is impossible, or that it is inevitable. All approaches to the causal relationships of war are considered erroneous which do not set them in the framework of the historical materialist concept of society, and whatever the methods, they lead nowhere if they are not a component part of the materialist dialectical methodology.[40]

Such criticism, instead of showing how Soviet scholars really assess their adversaries, at times indirectly reveals what they wish to emphasise and what they wish to reject; the arguments which they use in these connections complement the direct exposition of their doctrine.

Notes

[1] Some items of the abundant bibliography: Sotsiologiya segodnya. Problemy i perspektivy. Amerikanskaya burzhuaznaya sotsiologiya serediny XX veka, Moscow 1965; Problems of War and Peace. A Critical Analysis of Bourgeois Theories, Progress Publishers, Moscow 1972; Sovremennye burzhuaznye teorii mezhdunarodnykh otnoshenii, Izd. 'Nauka', Moscow 1976; D.G. Tomashevskii, Leninskie idei i sovremennye mezdhunarodnye otnosheniya, Izdatelstvo Politicheskoi Literatury, Moscow 1971; E.A. Pozdnyakov, Sistemnyi podkhod i mezhdunarodnye otnosheniya, Moscow 1976; Sotsiologicheskie problemy mezhdunarodnykh otnoshenii, Izd. 'Nauka', Moscow 1970; S.A. Tyushkevich, Filosofiya i voennaya teoriya, Izd. 'Nauka', Moscow 1975; 'Sovremennye burzhuaznye teorii voiny' in Sovetskaya Voennaya Entsiklopediya, v.1, Moscow 1976, pp.283-84; I.I. Lebedev, N.M. Nikolskii, eds., Vneshnyaya politika Sovetskogo Soyuza. Aktualnye problemy, Izd. 'Mezhdunarodnye Otnosheniya', Moscow 1976, esp. 'Kritika sovremennykh burzhuaznykh kontseptsii mezhdunarodnykh otnoshenii', pp.278-96; V.F. Petrovskii, Amerikanskaya vneshnepoliticheskaya mysl'. Kriticheskii obzor organizatsii, metodov i soderzhaniya burzhuaznykh issledovanii v SShA po voprosu mezhdunarodnykh otnoshenii i vneshnei politiki, Izd. 'Mezhdunarodnye Otnosheniya', Moscow 1976; G.A. Trofimenko, SShA. Politika, Voina, Ideologiya, Izdatelstvo 'Mysl', Moscow 1976. O sovetskoi voennoi nauke, 1964; Milshtein, Slobodenko, 1961; cf. Günter Rau et al., Gerechte und ungerechte Kriege, Deutscher Militärverlag, Berlin 1970; Politik in unserer Zeit, ditto, 1969.

[2] Adam Schaff, Narodziny i rozwoj filozofii marksistowskiej, Książka i Wiedza, Warsaw 1950; his: Obiektywny charackter praw historii, P.W.N., Warsaw 1955; Osnovy marksistskoi filosofii, 1959, Ch.XIX; Metodologicheskie problemy, Ch.1; Tuyshkevich, 1975; Milshtein, Slobodenko, 1958, 1961, Part II.1; Cackowski, 1970; Kondratkov, 1975; Volkogonov, 1976; Chelyshev, 1977;

Migolat'yev, 1978.

[3] A class for itself constitute theories which present the development of society as repetitive cycles, or sets, or phases. For instance, Giambattista Vico sees this development as going through phases of gods, heroes and men, Arnold Toynbee as periods of the origin, development and collapse of civilisations. These theories are not theories of social development *sensu stricto*, however.

[4] Cf. J. Lider, on the Nature of War, Ch.13.

[5] Agressivnaya ideologiya i politika amerikanskogo imperializma, Moscow 1950; Ideologi imperialisticheskoi burzhuazii — propovedniki agressii i voiny, Akademia Nauk SSSR, Institut Filosofii, Moscow 1952; Problems of War and Peace, 1972; N. Ponomarev, 'Krizis burzhuaznkh teorii voiny i mira'. *Kommunist Vooruzhennykh Sil*, 1964:16; Nikolskii, 1964 Ch. 'Nekotorye burzhuaznye teorii proiskhozhdeniya voin'; Marxism-Leninism on War and Army, 1972, Ch.I.5, 'Modern Bourgeois Theories About the Causes, Essence and Role of Wars in History'; O sovetskoi voennoi nauke, 1964, Ch.III; Rybkin, 1973a, Ch.III.

[6] The critics assume that any theory of war based on belief in God or other supernatural forces is *eo ipso* unscientific and there is no need to produce any specific argument against it. But they often make brief comments to the effect that history knows societies without wars (primitive society) and without any need for a war (socialistic society).

[7] Modrzinskaya, 1970, regards behaviourism as the main variant of the psycho-sociological approach (pp.9 ff.). The search for the causes of international conflicts and wars in human nature and their reduction to individual psychology are characteristic of contemporary bourgeois sociological studies and 'the reduction of the social to the individual is the main fault (porok) of the methodology of idealistic social psychology' (E.A. Bagramov, 'Burzhuaznaya sotsiologiya ob istochnikakh mezhdunarodnykh konfliktov', in: Sotsiologicheskie problemy mezhdunarodnykh otnoshenii, pp.140, 151). The analysis of the role of particular social groups, political parties and personalities i.e. of the concrete role of the subjective factor in international politics, may be useful, but it cannot be separated from a general sociological theory which would mean an over-estimation of the role of personalities (E.D. Modrzinskaya, V. Semenov, 'Marksistskaya i burzhuaznaya sotsiologiya i problemy mezhdunarodnykh otnoshenii', in: Sotsiologicheskie problemy, p.58). Cf. Sotsiologiya segodnya, 1975.

'The projection of political processes by bourgeois futurology is based on a voluntarist view of politics. Consequently, politics is reduced to decision and other expressions of will by politicians and statesmen, or at best, to the relations and interaction between government administrative agencies, or to relations between various states and their governments' (A. Sergiyev, 'Bourgeois Pseudo-Science about the Future', *International Affairs* (M.), 1972; p.82).

[8] Volkogonov, 1976; Kondratkov, 1975; Migolat'yev, 1978; Cf. Kiessling, 1976. For a sharp criticism of the French 'polemologists', in particular of Georges Bouthol, for 'demographic' (in fact 'neo-Malthusian') theories, see Che-

lyshev, 1977.

[9] 'There is much in the objective laws and objective conditions which bourgeois military science cannot cognise, and even if cognising, cannot utilise (O sovetskoi voennoi nauke, 1964, p.77); cf. Marxism-Leninism on War and Army, Ch.I.5; Kondratkov, 1976; Volkogonov, 1976; Migolat'yev, 1978.

[10] Bourgeois theories and views of the alleged causes and essence of wars are 'inimical to the vital interests and progressive strivings of all of mankind. The false, pseudo-scientific theories about the nature and sources of wars are ideological weapons that have enabled the imperialists to draw peoples into the two sanguinary wars which have exacted a heavy toll from mankind. The imperialist bourgeoisie continues to preach these immoral theories in order again to deceive the proples and to draw them into new military adventures' (Marxism-Leninism on War and Army, p.61). In pursuit of class interests, various social, technocratic, naturalistic, religious and irrational concepts of war advanced by the apologists of the bourgeoisie distort the truth on the problems of the origin, essence, social character and types of wars of the contemporary epoch. Thereby they disguise the militaristic and aggressive nature of the imperialism ('Voina', in: Sovetskaya Voennaya Entsiklopediya, vol.2, p.310).

[11] Cf. J. Lider, On the Nature of War, Chs.13 and 14.

[12] Karenin, 1971; Kulakov, 1970; Voennaya sila i mezhdunarodnye otnosheniya, 1972; Problems of War and Peace, Ch.X; Marxism-Leninism on War and Army, Ch. One; A. Kunina, 'A Critique of Bourgeois Theories of the Development of International Relations', *International Affairs*, Moscow, 1973:2, Filosofskoe nasledie, 1972; Filyov, 1974.

[13] J. Lider, On the Nature of War, Ch.1, and Part I.

[14] Bagramov, op. cit.; Modrzinskaya, op. cit.

[15] Problems of War and Peace, Ch.VII, 'National Sovereignty and War', pp.130-45; E.A. Bagramov, 'Burzhuaznaya sotsiologiya ob istochnikakh mezhdunarodnykh konfliktov', in: Sotsiologicheskie problemy, pp.138-57; E.D. Modrzinskaya, Sotsiologicheskie aspekty natsionalnogo suvereniteta, ibid., pp.188-219; Mezhdunarodnye konflikty, 1972.

[16] Problems of War and Peace, p.130.

[17] Cf. J. Lider, On the Nature of War, Ch.13, pp.274 ff. S. Tyushkevich 'Sootnoshenie sil v mire i faktory predotvrashcheniya voiny', *Kommunist Vooruzhennykh Sil*, 1974:10; S. Shaknazarov, 'O sootnoshenii sil v mire', *Kommunist*, 1974:3; Michael Voslensky, 'The Correlation of Forces, The Soviet View', Paper prepared for Peace Science Society, Conference in Zurich, 1975; G. Shaknazarov, 'Deistvennye faktory mezhdunarodnykh otnoshenii', *Mezhdunarodnaya Zhizn*', 1977:1; V. Zhurkin, 'Detente and International Conflicts', *International Affairs*, Moscow, 1974:7; V. Kelin, 'Dangerous Concepts', *Izvestiya*, 24.02.1975, after Izv-APN, 25.02.1975; A. Sergiyev, 'Leninism on the Correlation of Forces as a Factor of International Relations', *International Affairs*, Moscow, 1975:5.

Cf. Karenin, 1971; Voennaya Sila i Mezhdunarodnye Otnosheniya, 1972;

Marxism-Leninism on War and Army; Karenin, 'Teoriya 'Balansa Sil'', *Voprosy Istorii*, 1975:2; V. Kortunov, 'New Factors in International Relations and Bourgeois Politology', *International Affairs* (M.), 1977:9.

[18] For instance, 'triangles' (the United States, the Soviet Union, and China) 'pentagons' (the previously mentioned three powers plus the Western Europe and Japan); a combination of two triangles (of competition - the United States, the Soviet Union, and China - with that of cooperation - the United States, the Western Europe, and Japan); a combination of a 'Western triangle' (United States, Western Europe, and Soviet Union) with an 'eastern quadrangle' (United States, Soviet Union, China, Japan),

Petrovskii, 1976, lists the following 'politico-geometrical combinations of power centres': one (USA), two (USA-USSR), three (USA-USSR-China), five (USA-USSR-China-EEC-Japan). These models are said to be rooted in the traditional geopolitical ideas which attempted to explain and justify the foreign policy of great powers by their geopolitical location. Cf. Topornin, 1970, pp.3 ff.; Karenin, 1971; Karenin, 1975, (note 17), contends that geopolitical considerations directly led to the concept of balance of power, since American theorists and politicians contended that the heartland position of the Soviet Union must be balanced by alliances dominated by the United States and by a net of military bases.

[19] Filyov, 1974.

[20] Tyulin, 1977, p.121. It seems, however, that Soviet scholars do not reject the concept of superpower. They accept that differences in state power involve differences in influence on the course of world affairs. Tomashevskii mentions 'great powers', 'middle' and 'small' countries (1971, p.62); in a collective book on the theory of international affairs all countries are divided into the following groups: two most powerful world powers, the developed states, the developing states (Voennaya sila i mezhdunarodnye otnosheniya, 1972, pp.36 ff.). But accepting the fact of the extraordinary influence of superpowers on the course of world affairs, Soviet scholars distinguish between the character of this influence: while the United States acts on behalf of war and suppression, the Soviet Union promotes peace and the independence of nations. Thus no common concept can be applied in the search for regularities.

[21] Deutsch and Singer supposed that the greater the number of states that were members of alliances the greater the probability of war with states outside the alliances. Singer and Small tested this hypothesis and came to the conclusion that, while in the XIXth century an even distribution of power and more alliance aggregation resulted in fewer and less intensive wars, in our century, characterised by the growth of superiority in power by some states over others and increase in alliance aggregation, the latter co-varies with the incidence of wars. In other words, the incidence of war was in a quite contrary correlative relationship with the alliance aggregation in these two centuries, and no common regularity, valid for the whole time, can be asserted.

[22] The research carried out by a group of scholars led by J. David Singer

provides an example. While, in principle, Singer accepts that peace research should be mainly concerned with the causes of wars, and that the effort to gather what he calls 'descriptive and existential knowledge' should be followed by 'correlational' knowledge, and finally by 'explanatory' or 'causal' knowledge, the point of departure for his 'Correlations of War Project' is that 'the notion of causality may be inappropriate in the social sciences'. To discover causal regularities is regarded as an even less attainable aim. Among his writings, see 'An Assessment of Peace Research', *International Security*, Summer 1976; Preface to: Jürgen Dedring, Recent Advances in Peace and Conflict Research, SAGE, London 1976; 'The Correlates of War Project': Continuity, Diversity and Convergence, in: Francis W. Hoole, Dina A. Zinnes, eds, Quantitative International Politics, An Appraisal, Praeger, New York 1976.

[23] Soviet scholars do not deny the importance of the general systems theory (or the general theory of systems theory) and accept that it would be appropriate to develop it; they point out, however, that it has not so far received a uniform interpretation (cf. V.N. Sadovskii, 'Obshchaya teoriya sistem kak metateoriya', *Voprosy Filosofii*, 1972:4).

[24] Cf. Sovremennye burzhuaznye teorii, Ch.III.1.a) 'Teoriya mezhdunarodnykh sistem', Mortona Kaplana, pp.216-31.

[25] For instance, in the Kaplan's concept, the state of the system at any point of time is determined by the values of five sets of variables: the essential rules, the transformation rules, the actor classification variables, the capability variables, and the information variables. These are presented as deprived of a concrete socio-political content; however, such variables as 'the actor classification variables' i.e. the military and political potentials are obviously dependent on the type of the socio-political systems (Sovremennye burzhuaznye teorii, ibid.).

[26] Kaplan presents six such models, of which only two (the balance of power system, and the loose bipolar system) resemble some real systems which existed in the past (ibid.).

[27] One cannot separate the analysis of a given system from its concrete content; form and content constitute one whole, and it would be erroneous to 'apply' the former to the latter (E.A. Pozdnyakov, Sistemnyi podkhod i mezhdunarodnye otnosheniya, Moscow 1976, p.14). Raymond Aron's concept of the international system is criticised from this angle by Tyulin, 1977, pp.116 ff.

[28] Structural functionalism is regarded as one of two main sociological approaches to the study of international relations in Western science, the other being the so-called psycho-sociological approach (E.D. Modrzinskaya, O teoreticheskikh problemakh sovremennykh mezhdunarodnykh otnoshenii, in: Sotsiologicheskie problemy mezhdunarodnykh otnoshenii, 1970, pp.5-14). 'By the use of the structural-functional analysis bourgeois sociology attempts to consider society as a single comprehensive and stable system, in which stability of the system is equated with its capacity for survival' (Sovremenny burzhuaznye teorii, 1976, p.41); 'Considering the social functions from the standpoint of "stabilisation" and "equilibrium" it (structural functionalism) fully corresponds to

the reactionary bourgeois ideology of conservatism and social stagnation' (Modrzinskaya, op.cit., p.13).

[29] Cf. Sovremennye burzhuaznye teorii, Ch.III.1.g) 'Strukturno-funktsion-alnyi podkhod Dzordza Modelskogo', pp.242-5.

[30] The presentation and assessment of the concept advanced by Charles A. McClelland, another kind of systemic approach, may serve as an example of the diversity of the Soviet criticism. McClelland is criticised for the interpretation of international relations as an expanded version of two interacting states, which takes the form of a behaviourist demand-response interaction: initial action - response from another state - response by the state which initiated the interaction. To put it in the perspective of the international system, the activity of any state takes the form of taking from and giving to the international environment. 'All the giving and taking, when considered together - and for all the national actors - is called the international system'.

The critics charge McClelland with reducing all the complexity of international relations to a single behaviourist model deprived of any socio-political content and to the above-mentioned two-way activity of taking from and giving to the international system. It is contended that McClelland, in a mechanically simplified way, combines the structural-functional method with the behaviourist approach, which only increased the deficiencies of both. (Cf. Sovremennye burzhuaznye teorii, Ch.III.1. 'Model sistemy vzaimodeistvuyushchikh gosudarstv Charlsa Maklellanda', pp.239-42.)

[31] Cf., J. Lider, On the Nature of War, Ch.17.

[32] For instance, Richard P. Appelbaum, Theories of Social Change, Markham Publ. Co, Chicago, 1971.

[33] The criticism of the attempts to create a general theory of conflict is however accompanied by many studies on particular kinds of conflict. Some items of the abundant bibliography are: Sotsiologicheskie problemy mezhdunarodnykh otnoshenii, 1969; Mezhdunarodnye konflikty, 1972; Smolyan, 1968. The latter contends that theory of conflict can be regarded as a special discipline of science subordinated to historical materialism, but not as a 'philosophical methodology'.

[34] Even Dahrendorf's model of a constant conflict within each 'imperatively coordinated group' between interest groups with opposing interests concerning the change or preservation of the status quo, which leads to changing the dominance relations and restructuring the group, does not satisfy Soviet critics. It is too abstract and it does not directly point to revolutionary structural change in society. Cf. Ralph Dahrendorf, Soziale Klassen und Klassenkonflikt in der industriellen Gesellschaft, Stuttgart 1957; his Essays in the Theory of Society, Stanford University Press, Stanford 1968.

[35] Marksistskaya i burzhuaznaya sotsiologiya segodnya, Izd. 'Nauka', Moscow 1964 (F.V. Konstantinov, G.V. Osipov, V.S. Semenev, V.V. Kolbanovsky, 'Bor'ba marksistskikh i burzhuaznykh uchonykh po voprosu sotsiologicheskikh teorii', pp.287-97; L.A. Cypnik, 'Sovremennaya burzhua-

znaya sotsiologiya i ee kritika Wrightom Millsom, pp.386-99; M.T. Iovchuk, G.V. Osipov, O nekotorykh teoreticheskikh printsipakh, problemakh i metodakh sotsiologicheskikh issledovanii, pp.306-20); I. Golubnicky, 'The Games Theory and International Relations'. *International Affairs*, 1973:1; Metodologicheskie problemy, 1969; Gennadi Gerasimov, 'War and Peace Problems as Viewed from the Angle of the Game Theory', *Coexistence*, vol. 1971:2; Krupnov, 1963 ('O matematicheskikh metodakh issledovaniya v voennoi nauke', pp.119-26); A. Volkov, 'Matematika i upravlenie voiskami', *Krasnaya Zvezda*, 9.08.1973; Milovidov, 1973; I. Anureyev, A. Tatarchenko, Primenene matematicheskikh metodov v voine, Voenizdat, Moscow 1967; N. Smirnov, N. Bazanov, 'Mathematical Methods in Warfare', *Soviet Military Review*, 1968:8.

[36] The principal objections are levelled against the statistical methods. In the assessment of the research into 'correlates of war' (Singer and others), the main criticism holds that the quantitative changes in the distribution and alignment of the military potentials do not, and cannot, reflect changes in the incidence of wars, especially since the variety and diversity of the types and cases of wars is by no means a direct reflection of the above-mentioned alignment of military potentials. The main deficiency of the empirical-quantitative approach - ignorance of the social causes of war - is evident here.

[37] Milovidov, 1973. He states: 'The application of these methods, however, can give desired result only if the researcher takes as the basis the general dialectical-materialistic methodology' (op. cit). In the opinion of a reviewer, one of the main conclusions to the book by Petrovskii, 1976, about American ideas on international politics, may be stated thus: 'Because bourgeois theoreticians disregard class and social factors and because they resist, often subconsciously, the historically irreversible process of social change, they cannot explain correctly the substance of the matter or investigate the basic laws of world politics'. (V. Kelin, 'Evolution of U.S. Foreign Policy Doctrines', *International Affairs*, Moscow, 1977:4, p.127).

[38] Gerasimov warns: 'Neglect of the specifity of the background leads to errors. Especially, one of the dangers of game-theoretical analysis lies in the tendency to neglect the genesis of phenomena, their historical background. Another danger is that of neglecting the class aspect in politics. Quantitative evaluation of qualitative data is always a matter of considerable difficulties' (op.cit.) 'But in the opinion of specialists, this is no insuperable barrier'. Golubnicky contends: '. . . it is not the games theory that is defective as such, but the unscientific methodology of bourgeois scientists who use the theory to study of international relations'. (op.cit.).

[39] Consider, for example, the analysis made by Tyushkevich, who devoted a considerable part of his comprehensive study on the interrelation between philosophy and military theory to the problem of armed struggle as a system.

In its first part, this analysis is reduced to the repetition of traditional general statements on theory of war, military art and armed forces, to the effect that armed struggle is engaged to hurt the enemy, that the use of modern techniques has not made human action superfluous, that there must be a correct proportion between the quantity and quality of military technology and the number of troops, that the quantity and quality of military technology is the determining indicator of combat power and the organisation of troops also depends on it. The only change is the use of the term 'system' with reference to armed struggle; but there is no theory of laws and regularities stemming from the properties and internal structure of this system, from the interrelation between military technology, human activity, and actions of the enemy, which are said to be the main components of armed struggle as a system.

Only the second part of the analysis resembles systemic investigation. However, it concerns only one sub-system i.e. armed forces; correlational and functional ties between its organisation, deployment and methods of action are analysed. (Tyushkevish, 1975, Ch.III, 'Sistemnyi analiz voennoi praktiki' pp.166-215).

The last part of this 'systemic' analysis is devoted to apparently different problems - namely, to some aspects of the transition of war from one state to another and, in particular, to the criticism of Western ideas on the indeterminism in predicting such a transition.

[40] Two examples of such a criticism. 'Contemporary bourgeois military ideologists elaborate theories of war and military science from the standpoint of anti-Communism, substantiations of and justifications for aggressive wars against the USSR and the world system of socialism, against socialist and national liberation revolutions. The class interest of the monopolist bourgeoisie today not only is consolidating the antiscientific methodology of bourgeois military theory but is predetermining it.

Deliberate deception and falsification of facts in the interests of the exploiter classes are thus a principal component part of the methodology of bourgeois military history and theory of military science' (Filosofskoe nasledie, p.152).

'When a bourgeois military theorist analyses the relationship of military-technical and military-economic resources and capabilities of opposing sides, he can, from the positions of elemental materialism, more or less correctly take into account the role and significance of industrial potential, weapons, combat equipment, the relationship between change in forms and methods of conducting military operations on the one hand and changes in weapons, combat equipment, means of transportation, troop control, etc. on the other. These elementary-materialistic concepts are formed in him primarily as empirical knowledge, as a reflection of multiple-repeating experience'. However, it is added, that elemental materialism is not a scientific methodology since, in addition to a correct reflection of reality, it may contain elements of metaphysics and open up a loophole for vulgar materialism or idealism (p.153).

In another study: '. . . this does not mean that the bourgeois military theoreticians have abandoned the creation and development of military theory or are not concerned with the problem of modern warfare. They do this, in carrying out the instructions of the imperialist bourgeoisie, and have achieved *certain suc-*

cesses in the area concerning the *military-technical* aspects of modern war. As for the *social* aspects of a war, here they encounter *insurmountable difficulties*, since the creation of a truly scientific theory is impossible from the position of a reactionary class' (Nauchno-tekhnicheskii progress, 1973, p.238). (*italics* added).

Select bibliography

Books

Ajdukiewicz, Kazimierz, *Zagadnienia i kierunki filozofii*, Czytelnik, Warsaw 1949

Anureev, I.U., A.Y. Tatarchenko, *Primenenie matematicheskikh metodov v voennom dele*, Voenizdat, Moscow 1967

Azovtsev, N.N., *V.I. Lenin i sovetskaya voennaya nauka*, Izd. 'Nauka', Moscow 1971

Babin, A.I., F. Engels — *Vydayushchiisya Voennyi Teoretik Rabochego Klassa* Voenizdat, Moscow 1970 (a)

Bochkarev, K.S., I.P. Prusanov, A.A. Babakov, *Programma KPSS o zashchite Sotsialisticheskogo otechestva*, Voenizdat, Moscow 1965

Bokarev, V.A., *Kibernetika i voennoe delo*, Voenizdat, Moscow 1969

Bunkina, M.K., *Centry mirovogo imperializma: itogi razvitiyi i rasstanovka sil*, Izd. 'Mysl', Moscow 1970

Cackowski, Zdzislaw, *Glówne zagadnienia i kierunki filozofii*, KiW, Warsaw, 4 ed. 1970

Danto, Arthur, C., *Analytical Philosophy of History*, Cambridge Univ. Press, Cambridge 1968

Dray, William, *Laws and Explanation in History*, Oxford Univ. Press, Oxford 1957

Druzhinin, V.V., D.J. Kontorov, *Idea, Algoritm, Reshenie*, Voenizdat, Moscow 1972

Dvizhushchie sily vneshnei politiki SShA, Akademiya Nauk SSSR, Izd. 'Nauka', Moscow 1965

Efremov, A.Y., *Za shirmoi 'ogranichennykh' voin*, Voenizdat, Moscow 1960

Fridrikh Engels i voennaya istoriya, Voenizdat, Moscow 1972.

Faramazyan, R.A., SShA: *Militarizm i ekonomika*, Izd. 'Mysl'', Moscow 1970

Filosofskoe nasledie V.I. Lenina i problemy sovremennoi voiny, A.S. Milovidov, V.E. Kozlov, eds, Voenizdat, Moscow 1972

Filozofia i pokój, Instytut Filozofii i Socjologii PAN, P.W.N. Warsaw 1971

Gorbatenko, D.D., *Faktor vremeni v sovremennom boyu* Voenizdat, Moscow 1972

Gorshkov, Sergei, G., *Red Star Rising at Sea*, ed. by Herbert Reston, US Naval Institute, 1974

Grechko, A.A., *Na Strazhe Mira i Stroitelstva Kommunizma*, Voenizdat, Moscow 1971

Grechko, A.A., *Voouruzhennye Sily SSSR*, Voenizdat, Moscow, 1st ed. 1974,

2nd ed. 1975 (changed title: *Vooruzhennye Sily Sovetskogo Gosudarstva*)

Grechko, A.A. (ed.), *Liberation Mission of the Soviet Armed Forces in the Second World War*, Progress Publishers, Moscow 1975

Grigorenko, P.G., et al., *Metodika voenno-nauchnogo issledovaniya*, Voenizdat, Moscow 1959

Grigor'ev, V.G., *Ekonomicheskii i moralnyi potentsialy v sovremennoi voine*, Voenizdat, Moscow 1970

Grudinin, I.A., *Voprosy dialektiki v voennom dele*, Voenizdat, Moscow 1960

Grudinin, I.A. *Dialektika i voennoe delo*, Voenizdat, Moscow 1971

Gurov, A., *Tekhnicheskii progress i militarizm*, Voenizdat, Moscow 1963

Hempel, Carl G., *Aspects of Scientific Explanation And Other Essays in the Philosophy of Science*, The Free Press, New York 1968

Ideino — politicheskaya sushchnost' maoizma, Izd. 'Nauka'; Moscow 1977

Ideologi imperialisticheskoi burzhuazii — propovedniki agressii i voiny, Akademia Nauk SSSR, Institut Filosofii Moscow 1952

Il'in, S.K., *Moralnyi faktor v sovremennoi voine*, Voenizdat, Moscow, 2nd ed. 1969

Istoricheskaya nauka i nekotorye problemy sovremennosti Akademiya Nauk SSSR. Izd. 'Nauka', Moscow 1969

Istoricheskii materializm i sotsialnaya filosofiya sovremnnoi burzhuazii Akademiya Nauk SSSR, Institut Filosofii, Izd. Sotsialno-Ekonomicheskoi Literatury, Moscow 1960

Istoriya voennogo iskusstva, A.A. Strokov, ed., Voenizdat, Moscow 1966

Istoriya voin i voennogo iskusstva, Voenizdat, Moscow 1970

Ivanov, D.A., V.P. Savel'ev, V.P. Shemanskii, *Osnovy Upravleniya Voiskami*, Voenizdat, Moscow 1971

Ivanov, S.P., *O nauchnykh osnovakh upravleniya voiskami*, Voenizdat, Moscow 1975

Ivanova, I.M., *Mirnoe sosushchestvovanie i krizis vneshnepoliticheskoi ideologii imperializma SShA*, Izd. 'Mezhdunarodnye Otnosheniya', Moscow 1965

Kadishev, A.B., ed., *Voprosy strategii i operativnogo iskusstva v Sovetskikh voennykh trudakh, 1917-1940* Voenizdat, Moscow 1965

Karenin, A., *Filosofiya politicheskogo nasiliya*, Izd. 'Mezhdunarodnye Otnosheniya', Moscow 1971

Kende, Istvan, *Local Wars in Asia, Africa, and Latin America 1945-1969*, Center for Afro-Asian Research of the Hungarian Academy of Science, Budapest 1972

Kirillov, A.A., *Predotvrashchenie voiny — vazhneishaya problema sovremennosti*, Socekgiz, Moscow 1962

Kornienko, A.A., *K kritike sovremennykh teorii militarizatsii ekonomiki*, Voenizdat, Moscow 1960

Korotkov, G.I., *Amerikanskii militarizm v voinakh*, Voenizdat, Moscow 1973

Kovalev, A.M., ed., *Sovremennaya epokha i mirovoi revolutsionnyi protsess*, Izd. Moskovskogo Universiteta, Moscow 1970

Kozlov, S.N., M.B. Smirnov, I.S. Baz', P.A. Sidorov, *O sovetskoi voennoi nauke*, Voenizdat, Moscow, 1st ed., 1960, 2nd ed. 1964

Kozlov, S.N., *Spravochnik ofitsera*, Voenizdat, Moscow 1971

KPSS o vooruzhennykh silakh Sovetskogo Soyuza, K.U. Chernenko, N.I. Savinkin, eds., Voenizdat, Moscow 1969

Kritika sovremennoi burzhuaznoi politekonomii, Akademiya Nauk SSSR, Institut Mirovoi Ekonomiki i Mezhd. Otnosh. Izd. 'Nauka', Moscow 1977

Krupnov, S.I., *Dialektika i voennaya nauka*, Voenizdat, Moscow 1963

Kulakov, V.M., *Ideologiya agressii*, Voenizdat, Moscow 1970

Kurochkin, P.A., ed., *Osnovy metodiki voenno-nauchnogo issledovaniya*, Voenizdat, Moscow 1968

Kuz'min, E., *Mirovoe gos udarstvo: ilyuzii ili realnost'?*, Izd. 'Mezhdunarodnye Otnosheniya', Moscow 1969

Kuz'min, N.F., *V.I. Lenin vo glave oborony Sovetskoi strany (1918-1920 gg.)*. Voenizdat, Moscow 1958

Lagovskii, A.N., *Strategiya i ekonomika*, Voenizdat, Moscow 1961

V.I. Lenin o zashchite sotsialisticheskogo otechestva, Voenizdat, Moscow 1968

Lenin i problemy obronnosci Wyd. M.O.N., Warsaw 1970

Leshchinskii, L., *Bankrotstvo voennoi ideologii germanskikh imperialistov*, Voenizdat, Moscow 1952

50 let vooruzhennykh sil SSSR, Voenizdat, Moscow 1968

Lider, Julian, *Pogadanki o dialektyce i materializmie*, P.I.W., Warsaw, 5th ed. 1951

Lider, Julian, *On the Nature of War*, Saxon House, London 1977

Lomov, N.A., *Nauchno-Tekhnicheskii Progress i Razvitie Voennogo Dela*, Izd. 'Nauka', Moscow 1970

Lototskiy, V.K., *The Soviet Army*, Progress Publishers, Moscow 1971

Makharov, V.S., A.V. Veshentsev, eds., *Voina, Istoriya, Ideologiya*, Izd. Politicheskoi Literatury, Moscow 1974

Marksistsko-leninskaya metodologiya voennoi istorii, P.A. Zhilin, ed., Izd. 'Nauka', Moscow 1st ed. 1973, 2nd ed. 1976

Marksizm-Leninizm o voine i armii (Sbornik statei), Voenizdat, Moscow 1956

Marksizm-Leninizm o voine i armii, Voenizdat, Moscow 1st ed., 1957, 2nd ed. 1961, 3rd ed. 1962, 4th ed. 1965, 5th ed. 1968

Marxism-Leninism on War and Army, Progress Publishers, Moscow 1972

Maryganov, I.V., *Peredovoi kharakter sovetskoi voennoi nauki*, Voenizdat, Moscow 1963

Metodologicheskie problemy voennoi teorii i praktiki, A.S. Zheltov, T.P. Kondratkov, Y.A. Khomenko, eds. Voenizdat, Moscow 2nd ed. 1969

Metodologiya voenno-nauchnogo poznaniya, I.E. Shavrov, M.I. Galkin, eds., Voenizdat, Moscow 1977

Mezhdunarodnye konflikty, V.V. Zhurkin, Y.M. Primakov, eds. Izd. Mezhdunarodnye Otnosheniya, Moscow 1972

Militarizm v ideologii i praktitke maoizma, Y.L. Ivanov, ed., Voenizdat, Moscow 1976

Milshtein, M.A., Slobodenko A.K., *O burzhuaznoi voennoi nauke,* Voenizdat, Moscow 1961

Mirskii, G.I., *Armiya i politika v stranakh Azii i Afriki,* Izd. 'Nauka', Moscow 1970

Mirskii, G.I., *'Tretii mir': obshchestvo, vlast', armiya,* Izd. 'Nauka', Moscow 1976

Mochalov, V., *Bolshaya lozh o malykh voinakh,* Voenizdat, Moscow 1965

Moralno-politicheskii faktor v sovremennoi voine, Voenizdat, Moscow 1958

Moskvichov, L.N., *The End of Ideology Theory: Illusions and Reality,* Progress Publishers, Moscow 1974

Nauchno-Tekhnicheskii Progress i Revolutsiya v Voennom Dele, Voenizdat, Moscow 1973

Nikolskii, N.M., *Osnovnoi Vopros Sovremennosti,* Izd. 'Mezhdunarodnye Otnosheniya', Moscow 1964

Nikolskii, N.M., *Nauchno-Tekhnicheskaya Revolutsiya:Mirovaya Ekonomika, Politika, Naselenie,* Izd. 'Mezhdunarodnye Otnosheniya', Moscow 1970

Osnovy marksistskoi filozofii, F.W. Konstantinov, chief ed., Gospolitizdat, Moscow 1959

Partiya i armiya, A.A. Yepishev, ed., Politizdat, Moscow 1977

Pokrovskii, G., *Nauka i tekhnika v sovremennykh voinakh,* Voenizdat, Moscow 1956

Popov, M.V., *Filosofskie osnovy issledovaniya zakonomernosti vooruzhennoi bor'by,* Moscow 1958

Popov, M.V., *Sushchnost' zakonov vooruzhennoi bor'by,* Voenizdat, Moscow 1965

Problems of war and peace, Progress Publishers, Moscow 1972

Problemy revolutsii v voennom dele (sbornik statei) Voenizdat, Moscow 1965

Problemy voiny i mira, Izd. 'Mysl'', Moscow 1967

Prokop'ev, N.P., *O voine i armii,* Voenizdat, Moscow 1965

Pryadyshev, B.D., *Voenno-promyshlennyi kompleks SShA,* Voenizdat, Moscow 1974

Pukhovskii, N.V., *O mire i voine,* Voenizdat, Moscow 1965

Rybkin, Y.I., *Voina i politika,* Voenizdat, Moscow 1959

Rybkin, Y.I., *Voina i politika v sovremennuyu epokhu,* Voenizdat, Moscow 1973 (a)

Savkin, V.Y., *Osnovnye printsipy operativnogo iskusstva i taktiki,* Voenizdat, Moscow 1972

Schaff, Adam, *Narodziny i rozwój filozofii marksistowskiej,* KiW, Warsaw 1950

Schaff, Adam, *Wstęp do teorii marksizmu,* KiW, Warsaw 1950

Schaff, Adam, *Obiektywny charakter praw historii,* P.W.N., Warsaw 1955

Schaff, Adam, *Główne zagadnienia i kierunki filozofii, vol. 1. Teoria poznania* P.W.N., Warsaw 1965

Sekistov, V.A., *Voina i politika*, Voenizdat, Moscow 1970

Seleznev, I.A., *Voina i ideologicheskaya bor'ba*, Voenizdat, Moscow, 1st ed. 1964, 2nd ed. 1974

Sidorenko, A.A., *Nastuplenie*, Voenizdat, Moscow 1970

Skirdo, M.P., *Narod, armiya, polkovodets*, Voenizdat, Moscow 1970

Slovar' osnovnykh voennykh terminov, Voenizdat, Moscow 1965

Sokolovskii, V.D., ed., *Voennaya strategiya*, Voenizdat, Moscow, 1st ed. 1962, 2nd ed. 1963, 3rd ed. 1968

Sotsiologicheskie problemy mezhdunarodnykh otnoshenii, Izd. 'Nauka', Moscow 1970

Sovetskaya Voennaya Entsiklopediya, vol. vol.1-4, Voenizdat, Moscow 1976-1977

Sovremennaya epokha i mirovoi revolutsionnyi protsess, A.M. Kovalev, ed., Izd. Moskovskogo Universiteta, Moscow 1970

Sredin, G.V., *Na Strazhe Rodiny*, Voenizdat, Moscow 1974

Strokov, A.A., *Istoriya voennogo iskusstva. Kapitalisticheskoe obschchestvo od francuzskoi burzhuaznoi revolutsii do perioda imperializma*, Voenizdat, Moscow 1965

Strokov, A.A., ed., *Istoriya voennogo iskusstva*, Voenizdat, Moscow 1966 (a)

Strokov, A.A., *Lenin o voine i voennom iskusstve*, Izd. 'Nauka', 1971

Strokov, A.A., *Vooruzhennye sily i voennoe iskusstvo v pervoi mirovoi voine* Voenizdat, Moscow 1974

Sulimov, Y.F., V.V. Shelyag, *Voprosy Nauchnogo Rukovodstva v Sovetskikh Vooruzhennykh Silakh*, Voenizdat, Moscow 1973

Sushko, N.J., J.F. Sulimov, J.A. Khomenko, eds., *Filosofskie problemy sovremennoi voiny i sovetskoix voennoi teorii*, Voenizdat, Moscow 1962

Sushko, N., *Marksistsko-Leninskaya filosofiya — metodologicheskaya osnova sovetskoi voennoi teorii i praktiki* (na pravakh rukopisi) (Moscow 1963)

Shabad, B., *Imperializm i burzhuaznaya sotsialno-politicheskaya mysl'*, Izd. 'Mezhdunarodnye Otnosheniya', Moscow 1969

Shabad, B., *Politicheskaya filosofiya sovremennogo imperializma*, Izd. 'Mezhdunarodnye Othosheniya', Moscow, 1st ed. 1963, 2nd ed. 1966

Sheinin, Y.M., *Nauka i militarizm v SShA*, Izd. Akademii Nauk SSSR, Moscow 1963

Shramchenko, A.F., *Voprosy psikhologii v upravlenii voiskami*, Voenizdat, Moscow 1973

Taranchuk, M.V., *O Postoyanno deistviyushchikh faktorakh reshayushchikh sud'bu Voiny*, Voenizdat, Moscow 1952

Tomashevskii, D.G., *Leninskie idei i sovremennye mezhdunarodnye otnosheniya*, Izd. Politicheskoi Literatury, Moscow 1971

Trifonenkov, P.I., *Ob osnovnykh zakonakh khoda i iskhoda voiny*, Voenizdat, Moscow 1962

Trofimenko, G.A., *Strategiya globalnoi voiny*, Izd. Mezhdunarodykh Otnoshenii, Moscow 1968

Trofimenko, G.A., *SShA:politika, voina, ideologiya*, Izd. 'Mysl'', Moscow 1976

Tsvetkov, V.G., ed., *O voenno-teoreticheskom nasledii V.I. Lenina*, Voenizdat, Moscow 1964

Tsvetkov, V.G., *V.I. Lenin i Sovetskie Vooruzhennye Sily*, Voenizdat, Moscow, 1st ed. 1967, 2nd ed. 1969

Tyagunenko, V.L., *Voiny i kolonii*, Voenizdat, Moscow 1957

Tyushkevich, S.A., *Neobkhodimost' i sluchainost' v voine*, Voenizdat, Moscow 1962

Tyushkevich, S.A., *Filosofiya i voennaya teoriya*, Izd. 'Nauka', Moscow 1975 (a)

Usenko, I., *Prichiny imperialisticheskikh voin*, Gospolitizdat, Moscow 1953

Vazhentsev, A.I., *K. Marks i voennaya istoriya*, Voenizdat, Moscow 1969

Velikaya Otechestvennaya Voina 1941-1945, P.A. Zhilin, ed. Izd. Politicheskoi Literatury, Moscow 1970

Vlasov, I.I., *V.I. Lenin i stroitelstvo Sovetskoi Armii*, Voenizdat, Moscow 1958

Voennaya sila i mezhudunarodnye otnosheniya, Izd. Mezhdunarodnye Otnosheniya, Moscow 1972

Voennaya Strategiya, see: Sokolovskii 1962

Voina, Istoriya, Ideologiya, see: Makharov, Veshentsev, 1974

Volkogonov, D., Milovidov, A., Tyushkevichc, *Voina i armiya*, Voenizdat, Moscow 1977

Vorontsov, G.F., *Voennye koalitsii i koalitsionnye voiny*, Voenizdat, Moscow 1976

Vakhrushev Vasily, *Neocolonialism: methods and manoeuvres*, Progress Publishers, Moscow 1973

Wiatr, Jerzy J., Marksistowska teoria rozwoju spolecznego, KiW, Warsaw, 1973

Wright, George Henrik von, *Explanation and Understanding*, Routledge and Kegan Paul, London 1971

Yakovlev, Aleksander, *Ideologiya amerikanskoi 'imperii'*, Moscow 1967

Yakovlev, Aleksander, *Pax Amerikana*, Izd. 'Molodaya Gwardiya', Moscow 1969

Yakubovskii, I.I., *Za prochnyi mir na zemle*, Voenizdat, Moscow 1975

Yegorov, P.T., I.A. Shlyakov, N.I. Alabin, *Grazhdanskaya Oborona*, Izd. 'Vysshaya Shkola', 2nd ed. Moscow 1970

Yepishev, A.A., *Ideologicheskaya Bor'ba po Voennym Vpprosam*, Voenizdat, Moscow 1974

Yepishev, A.A., ed., *Partiya i Armiya*, Politizdat, Moscow 1977

Zakharov, M.V., *O nauchnom podkhode k rukovodstvu voiskami*, Voenizdat 1967

Zakharov, M.V. *V.I. Lenin i Voennaya Istoriya*, Voenizdat, Moscow 1970

Zamkovoi, V.I., *Kritika burzhuaznykh teorii neizbezhnosti novoi mirovoi voiny*, Izd. 'Mysl'', Moscow 1965

Zheltov, A.S., T.P. Kondratkov, Y.A. Khomenko, eds., *Metodologhcheskie problemy y voennoi teorii i praktiki*, Voenizdat, Moscow 2nd ed. 1969

Zhilin, P.A., *Problemy voennoi istorii*, Voenizdat, Moscow 1975 (a)

Zhilin, P.A., ed., *Marksistsko-leninskaya metodologiya voennoi istorii*, Izd. 'Nauka'; Moscow, 1st ed 1973, 2nd ed. 1976

Articles

Abbr. of periodicals
J.P.R. — *Journal of Peace Research*
K.V.S. — *Kommunist Vooruzhennykh Sil*
S.M.R. — *Soviet Military Review*
V.I.Zh. — *Voenno—Istoricheskii Zhurnal*

Azovtsev, N.N., 'V.I. Lenin — osnovopolozhnik sovetskoi voennoi nauki', *K.V.S.*, 1968:18

Babin, A., 'Frederick Engels'. Outstanding Military Theoretician', *S.M.R.*, 1970:11 (b)

Barsegow, Yuri, Rustem Khairow; A Study of the Problems of Peace', *J.P.R.*, 1973:1-2

Baskakov, V., 'O sootnoshenii voiny kak obshchestvennogo yavleniya i vooruzhennoi bor'by', *K.V.S.*, 1971:1

Baz', I., 'Sovetskaya voennaya nauka o kharaktere sovremennoi voiny', *Voennyi Vestnik*, 1958:6

Belyi, P., 'V tipakh neprimirimykh protivorechii', *K.V.S.*, 1977:13

Bochkarev, K.S., 'O kharaktere i tipakh voin sovremmennoi epokhi', *K.V.S.*, June 1965

Bochkaryov, K., 'Lenin on Just and Unjust Wars', *S.M.R.*, 1971:4

Bochkarayov, K., 'Wars: Their Sources and Causes', *S.M.R.*, 1972:5

Boltin, E., 'The Triumph of the Soviet Art of War', *S.M.R.*, 1967:2, 6, 10, 11

Bondarenko, I.M., 'Nauchno-tekhnicheskii progress i upravlenie voiskami', *K.V.S.*, 1973:10

Bondarenko, V., 'Sovetskaya nauka i ukreplenie oborony strany', *K.V.S.*, 1974:18

Chelyshev, I., 'Za fasadom 'novoi nauki' o voine,' *Krasnaya Zvezda*, 7.12.1977

Cherednichenko, M.I., 'Ob osobennostyakh razvitiya voennogo iskusstva v poslevoennyi period, *V.I.Zh.*, 1970:6

Cherednichenko, M.I., 'Sovremennaya voina i ekonomika', *K.V.S.*, 1971:18

Derevyanko, P., 'Soviet Military Science', *S.M.R.*, 1966:10

Derevyanko, P., 'Revolution in Military Affairs and the Soviet Armed Forces' *S.M.R.*, 1967:11

Derevyanko, P., 'Progress in Science and Technology and Military Development' *S.M.R.*, 1972:8

Dmitriev, A., 'Marksistsko-leninskoe uchenie o voine i armii — vazhneishii aspekt nauchnogo mirovozzreniya voennykh kadrov', *K.V.S.*, 1975:13

Dolgopolov, Y., 'Just Wars by Oppressed Peoples', *S.M.R.*, 1965:1

Dolgopolov, Y., ' National Liberation and Armed Struggle', *S.M.R.*, 1968:9

Dshordshadse, I., 'Militarpolitische Aspekte der allgemeinen Krise des Kapitalismus', *Militärwesen*, 1976:11

Filyov, A., 'In the labyrinth of numbers' *International Affairs* (M.), 1974:7

Galkin, M., 'Besonderheiten, Arten und schöpferischer Charakter der militarwissenschaftlicher Forschung,' *Militärwesen*, 1975:6

Gareyev, M., 'Military Science as an Important Factor of Defence Potential', *S.M.R.*, 1976:12

Garejew, M., 'Das System wissenschaftlicher Kentnisse uber Krieg und Streitkräfte', *Militärwesen*, 1977:5, 6

Golikov, S.G., 'Marksizm-Leninizm o voinakh spravedlivykh i nespravedlivykh *Propagandist i Agitator*, 1949:1

Gorshkov, S.G., 'Opyt istorii i sovremennost', *Voprosy filosofii*, 1975:5

Gorynin, V., 'Marksizm-Leninizm o voine i armii', *Propagandist i Agitator*, 1954:1

Grechko, A.A., 'Na strazhe mira i komunizma', *Kommunist*, 1973:7

Grechko, A.A., 'Nauka i iskusstvo pobezhdat'', *Pravda*, 19.02.1975

Grudinin, I., 'Sub'ektivnyi faktor i sluchainost' v voine', *V.I.Zh.*, 1965:6

Grudinin, I.A., 'K voprosu o sushchestve voiny', *Krasnaya Zvezda*, 12.07. 1966

Hempel, Carl G., 'The Function of General Laws in History', *Journal of Philosophy*, 39, 1942

'Istoricheskii i logicheskii metody', in : *Sovestskaya Voennaya Entskilopediya*, vol. 3, pp.623-4

Ivanov, S., 'V.I. Lenin i sovetskaya voennaya strategiya', *K.V.S.*, 1970:8

Izmailov, V., 'Kharakter i osobennosti sovremennykh voin', *K.V.S.*, 1975:6

Kára, Karel, 'On the Marxist Theory of War and Peace', Journal of Peace Research, 1968:1

Karenin, A.A., 'Teoriya "balansa sil"', *Voprosy Istorii*, 1975:2

Kazakov, D., 'Sources and Causes of Wars', *S.M.R.*, 1975:12

Khalipov, V., 'Sovremennyi mirovoi revolutsionnyi protsess: kharakter i osobennosti', *K.V.S.*, 1974:3

Khalipov, V., 'Sovremennaya epokha i ee osnovnoe protivorechie', *K.V.S.*, 1975:9

Khmara, N., 'Nekotorye osobennosti grazhdanskikh voin v sovremennuyu epokhu' *K.V.S.*, 1974:16

Khmara, N., 'Interventsionizm — politika pozora i provalov', *K.V.S.*, 1975:10

Khomenko, E., 'Wars, Their Character and Type,' *S.M.R.*, 1965:9

Khrustov, F., 'Marksizm-Leninizm o voine i armii', *Propagandist i Agitator*, 1950:6

Kiech, W., 'Die marxistisch-leninistische Philosophie als Grundlage für die Klassifikation der Militarwissenschaft', *Militärwesen*, 1976:4

Kiessling, G., 'Zur Verfälschung der Ursachen der Kriege der Gegenwart durch burgerliche Ideologen', Militärwesen 1976:2

Kiryan, M.M., 'Prevoskhodstvo sovetskoi voennoi organizatsii,' *Krasnaya Zvezda*, 4.04.1975

Kondratkov, T., 'The Substance of War', *S.M.R.*, 1968:6

Kondratkov, *T.*, 'War and Politics', *S.M.R.*, 1971:10

Kondratkov, T., 'Sotsialnyi kharakter sovremennoi voiny', *K.V.S.*, 1972:21

Kondratkov, T., 'War as a Continuation of Policy', *S.M.R.*, 1974:2

Kondratkov, T., 'Problema klassifikatsii voin i ee otrazhenie v ideologicheskoi bor'be', *K.V.S.*, 1974:11

Kondratkov, T., 'Das Wesen des Krieges und seine Wiederspiegelung im ideologischen Kampf', *Militärwesen*, 1975:12

Kondratkov, T., 'XXV s'ezd KPSS i problema mira i voiny', *V.I.Zh.*, 1976:7

Konovalev, V., 'Leninskie idei zashchity sotsializma v deistvii', *K.V.S.*, 1975:21

Kornienko, A., 'Ekonomicheskie osnovy voennoi moshchi gosudarstv', *Voennaya Mysl'*, 1968:8

Korotkov, I., 'O partiinosti voenno-istoricheskoi nauki', *V.I.Zh.*, 1965:10

Kozlov, S.N., 'Tvorcheskii kharakter sovetskoi voennoi nauki', *K.V.S.*, 1961:11

Kozlov, S.N., 'K voprosu o razvitii sovetskoi voennoi nauki posle vtoroi mirovoi voiny', *Voennaya Mysl'*, 1964:3

Kozlov, S.N., 'Voennaya doktrina i voennaya nauka', *K.V.S.*, 1964:5

Kozlov, S.N., 'O nekotorykh voprosakh sovetskoi voennoi nauki', *K.V.S.*, 1967:2

Kozlov, V., 'Kharakter i osobennosti sovremennoi voiny', *K.V.S.*, 1969:19

Koslow, Swjatoslav, 'Militärwissenschaft, Kriegskunst und Strategie', *Österreichische Militärische Zeitschrift*, 1973:2

Krasin, Yu., 'Detente and the Class Struggle' *Pra-APN* 29.09.1976 (*Pravda*, 24.09.1976)

Krupnov, S.I., 'Po zakonam dialektiki', *Krasnaya Zvezda*, 7.01.1966

Kulikov, N., 'The popular masses — decisive force in war', *S.M.R.*, 1978:3

Kulikov, V., 'Sovetskie Vooruzhennye Sily i voennaya nauka', *Kommunist*, 1973:3

Kulikov, V.G., 'Mozg armii', *Pravda*, 13.11.1974

Kulikov, V., 'Sovetskaya voennaya nauka segodnya', *Kommunist*, 1976: May

Kunina, A., 'A Critique of Bourgeois Theories of the Development of International Relations', *International Affairs*, Moscow 1973:2

Larionov, V.I., 'Vzaimosvyaz' voennoi nauki i voennoi doktriny', *Voennaya Mysl'*, 1964:12

Larionov, V., 'Strategiya bezopasnosti i izobraziteli antisovetskikh mifov *Krasnaya Zvezda*, 31.03.1978

Lototskii, S., 'Klassiki marksizma-leninizma o zakonomernostyakh razvitiya voennogo iskusstva', *V.I.Zh.*, 1973:9

Malinovskii, G., 'Lokalnye voiny v zone natsionalno-osvoboditelnogo dvizheniya', *V.I.Zh.*, 1974:5

Malinovskii, G., 'Teorii neokolonializma — oruzhie reaktsii', *Krasnaya Zvezda*, 20.04.1978

Migolatyev, A., 'Reaktsionnyi kharakter sovremennykh burzhuaznykh teorii voiny i mira', *K.V.S.*, 1978:6

Milovidov, A., 'Filosofskii analiz voennoi mysli', *Krasnaya Zvezda*, 17.05.1973

Milovidov, A., 'Marksizm-Leninizm — teoreticheskaya osnova Sovitskoi voennoi nauki', *K.V.S.*, 1974:19

Milshtein, M., A. Slobodenko, 'Problema sootnosheniya politiki i voiny v sovremennoi imperialisticheskoi ideologii', *Mirovaya Ekonomika i Mezhdunarodnye Otnosheniya*, 1958:9

Milshtein, A., Semeiko, L.S., 'Problems of the Inadmissability of Nuclear Conflict', *International Studies Quarterly*, 1976:1

Morozov, V., 'The Laws of War and Military Art,' *S.M.R.*, 1974:11

Morozov, V., 'Politics and War' *S.M.R.*, 1975:11

Morozov, V., S. Tyushkevich, 'O sisteme zakonov voennoi nauki i printsipov voennogo iskusstva', *Voennaya Mysl'*, 1967:3

Müller, D., 'Zum System von Kentnisse über Krieg und Streitkräfte', *Militärwesen*, 1977:10

Ogarkov, N., 'Zashchita Sotsialisticheskogo Otechestva — delo vsego naroda', *Krasnaya Zvezda*, 27.10.1977

Ogarkov, N., 'Voennaya nauka i zashchita sotsialisticheskogo Otechestva', *Kommunist*, 1978:7

Palevich, D., 'Kharakter i osobennosti sovremennoi voiny', *K.V.S.*, 1962:21

Pilipenko, H.P., 'Vzaimosvyaz' prichinnosti, neobkhodimosti i sluchainosti', *Voprosy filosofii*, 1973:9

Ponomarev, N., 'Krizis burzhuaznykh teorii voiny i mire', *K.V.S.*, 1964:16

Popov, M.V., 'The Principles of Military Art and the Laws of Armed Struggle' *S.M.R.*, 1966:3 (a)

Popov, M., 'Sootnoshenie ob'ektivnogo i sub'ektivnogo v boevykh deistviyakh voisk', *Voennaya Mysl'*, 1966:5 (b)

Popov, M., 'Neprimirimost' k sub'ektivizmu kak trebovanie nauchnogo rukovodstva voiskami', *K.V.S.*, 1968:16

Popov, M.V., 'Problema osnovnogo zakona voiny', *Voennaya Mysl'*, 1969:11

Radzievsky, A., 'Military Science and Armed Struggle', *S.M.R.*, 1971:7

Rodin, V., 'Nekotorye problemy proiskhozhdeniya i razvitiya voennykh soyuzov *V.I.Zh.*, 1975:2

Ruban, M., 'Moralnyi faktor v sovremennoi voine', *K.V.S.*, 1972:24

Rybkin, Y., 'O sushchestve mirovoi yaderno-raketnoi voiny', *K.V.S.*, 1965:

Rybkin, Y., 'Voiny sovremennoi epokhi i ikh vliyanie na sotsialnye protsessy' *K.V.S.*, 1970:11

Rybkin, Y., 'V poiskakh vykhoda iz typika (Kritika popytok 'modernizatsii' imperialisticheskikh kontseptsii voiny', *K.V.S.*, 1973:1 (b)

Rybkin, Y., 'Sotsiologicheskii analiz istorii voin:osnovnye kategorii' *Voprosy Istorii KPSS*, 1973:1 (c)

Rybkin, Y., 'Leninskaya kontseptsiya voiny i sovremennost', *K.V.S.*, 1973:20 (d)

Rybkin, Y., 'Just and Unjust Wars', *S.M.R.*, 1974:4

Rybkin, Y., 'Dialectics of War', *S.M.R.*, 1975:8

Rybkin, Y., C. Tyushkevich, 'Marksizm-Leninizm o vzaimosvyazi voennoi istorii i sotsiologii, *V.I.Zh.*, 1975:11

Ryzhenko, F., 'Detente and Class Struggle', *Pravda*, 22.08.1973

Safronov, B., 'Laws of Materialist Dialectics in Warfare', *S.M.R.*, 1977:6-7

Sanakoyev, Sh., 'Vneshnyaya politika sotsializma:istoki i teoriya', *Mezhdunarodnaya Zhizn*', 1975:4

Sbytov, N.A., 'Revolutsiya v voennom dele i ee rezultaty', *Krasnaya Zvezda*, 15.02.1963

Seleznev, K.L., 'Gegen die Verfälschungen des militärtheoretischen Erbes von Marx and Engels', (I-III), *Militärwesen*, 1975:1-3

Sidelnikov, I., 'Zashchita zavoevanii sotsializma - ebshchaya zakonomernost' sotsialisticheskogo i kommunisticheskogo stroitelstva', *K.V.S.*, 1973:23

Shabrov, I., 'Lokalnye voiny i ikh mesto v globalnoi strategii imperializma' *V.I.Zh.*, 1975:3-4

Shelyag, V., 'Dva mirovozzreniya — dva vzglyada na voinu', *Krasnaya Zvezda*, 7.02.1974

Shelyag, V., T. Kondrakov, 'Leninskii analiz sushchnosti voiny i nesostoyatelnost' ego kritiki', *K.V.S.*, 1970:12

Skrylnik, A., 'Ideology and War', *S.M.R.*, 1976:7

Smolyan, G.L., 'Printsipy issledovaniya konflikta', *Voprosy Filosofii*, 1968:8

Sokolovsky, V., 'On the Soviet Military Doctrine', *S.M.R.*, 1965:4

Sredin, G.V., 'Marxist-Leninist Doctrine on War and Army', *S.M.R.*, 1978:1

Strokov, A., I Maryganov, 'Ob osnovakh sovetskoi voennoi nauki', *Propagandist i Agitator*, 1954:2

Strokov, A., 'Engels as a Military Theoretician', *S.M.R.*, 1966:11 (b)

Sumbatyan, Y., 'Razryadka napryazhennosti i natsionalno-osvoboditelnoe dvizhenie', *K.V.S.*, 1975:24

Sumbatyan, Y., 'Mirovoi revolutsionnyi protsess, ego cherty i dvizhushchie sily', *K.V.S.*, 1976:21

Sushko, N., 'Metod vseobshchii, revolutsionnyi' *Krasnaya Zvezda*, 31.01.1964 (a)

Sushko, N., 'Sushchnost' voiny', *Krasnaya Zvezda*, 4.01.1964 (b)

Sushko, N., 'Zakony opredelyayushchie khod i iskhod voiny', *Krasnaya Zvezda*, 7.01.1964 (c)

Sushko, N., 'The Essence of War', *S.M.R.*, 1965:7

Tabunov, N., 'Novoe oruzhie i moralnyi faktor', *K.V.S.*, 1969:2

Talenskii, N., 'K voprosu o kharaktere zakonov voennoi nauki', *Voennaya Mysl'*, 1953:9

Timofeev, T.T., 'Realizatsiya programmy mira i nekotorye voprosy ideologicheskoi bor'by', *Voprosy Filosofii*, 1976:1

Topornin, A., 'The Balance of Power Doctrine and Washington, *SShA: Ekonomika, Politika, Ideologiya*, 1970:11

Trofimenko, Henry, 'The 'Theology' of Strategy', *Orbis*, Fall 1977

Trushin, B., Lipkin, R., 'Imperializm — istochnik voennoi opasnosti', *Voennyi Vestnik*, 1975:11

Tyulin, I., 'Ob odnoi iz burzhiaznykh "teorii" mezhdunarodnykh otnoshenii', *Mirovaya Ekonomika i Mezhdunarodnye Otnosheniya*, 1977:8

Tyushkevich, S., 'Science and Military Affairs', *S.M.R.*, 1966:5

Tyushkevich, S., 'Balance of Forces in Armed Struggle', *S.M.R.*, 1968:4

Tyushkevich, S., 'Politicheskie tseli i kharakter voiny', *K.V.S.*, 1969:7

Tyushkevich, S., 'Problemy metodologii sovetskoi voennoi historii', *V.I.Zh.*, 1974:2

Tyushkevich, S., 'Razvitie ucheniya o voine i armii na opyte Velikoi Otechestvennoi voiny', *K.V.S.*, 1975:22

Tyushkevich, S., 'Vooruzhennye Sily Obshchenarodnogo gosudarstva', *K.V.S.*, 1978:4

Yasyukov, M., 'Obshchestvennyi progress i voennoe nasilie', *K.V.S.*, 1973:12

Yuriev, N., 'Imperialism, The Source of Wars and Violence', *S.M.R.*, 1970:7

Vlasevich, Y., 'Na sluzhbe militarizma. Analiz sovremennykh burzhuaznykh voenno-ekonomicheskikh kontseptsii', *K.V.S.*, 1976:11

Volkogonov, A., 'Mirnoe sosushchestvovanie — alternativa voiny', *K.V.S.*, 1973:19

Volkogonov, D.A., 'Militarizm i vneshnyaya politika imperializma', *Voprosy Filosofii*, 1974:10

Volkogonov, D., 'Nesostoyatelnost' burzhuaznykh kontseptsii prichin voin', *Voennyi Vestnik*, 1976:3

Volkov, A., 'Nauchnye osnovy upravlencheskoi deyatelnosti voennykh kadrov', *K.V.S.*, 1976:15

Zakharov, M.V., 'Leninizm i sovetskaya voennaya nauka', *Krasnaya Zvezda*, 5.04.1970

Zamorsky, V., 'Laws of Battle', *S.M.R.*, 1975:3

Zavizion, G., Y.Kirshin, 'Sovetskaya Voennaya Nauka:sotsialnaya rol' i funksii', *K.V.S.*, 1972:17

Zavizion, G., 'O predmete sovetskoi voennoi nauki' *K.V.S.*, 1973:12

Zavylov, I.G., 'O sovetskoi voennoi doktrine', *Krasnaya Zvezda*, 30-31.03.1967

Zavyalov, I.G., 'Novoe oruzhie i voennoe iskusstvo', *Krasnaya Zvezda*, 30.10.1970

Zavyalov, I.G., 'Weapons and Military Art' *S.M.R.*, 1971:8

Zavyalov, I.G., 'Nauchnoe predvidenie v voennom iskusstve', *Krasnaya Zvezda*, 3.08.1972

Zavyalov, I.G., 'Tvorcheskii kharakter sovetskoi voennoi doktriny', *Krasnaya Zvezda*, 19.04.1973

Zavyalov, I.G., 'Die Dialektik des Krieges und die Militardoktrin', *Militärwesen*, 1976:1

Zemskov, V.V., 'Nekotorye voprosy rukovodstva voinoi', *K.V.S.*, 1972:22

Zhilin, P., 'Military History and Modern Times', *S.M.R.*, 1966:10

Zhilin, P., 'Voennaya istoriya i sovremennost', *V.I.Zh.*, 1975:5 (b)

Zhilin, P., 'Karl Marx and Military History', *S.M.R.*, 1978:5

Zubarev, V., 'Lenin i voennaya nauka', *Propagandist i Agitator*, 1955:13

Zubarev, V., 'Die Entwicklung der Theorie der Verteidigung des Sozialismus', *Militärwesen.*, 1976:9

Name Index

Subject Index